D0846832

R A D I O H E A D
WELCOME TO THE MACHINE

WITHDRAWN
FROM THE RECORDS OF THE
MID-CONTINENT PUBLIC LIBRARY

782.421660922 F739
Footman, Tim.
Radiohead : welcome to the
 machine

MID-CONTINENT PUBLIC LIBRARY
South Independence Branch
13700 E. 35th Street
Independence, MO 64055   **SI**

Radiohead - Welcome To The Machine
OK Computer And The Death Of The Classic Album
by Tim Footman

A CHROME DREAMS PUBLICATION
First Edition 2007

Published by Chrome Dreams
PO BOX 230, New Malden, Surrey,
KT3 6YY, UK
books@chromedreams.co.uk
WWW.CHROMEDREAMS.CO.UK

ISBN 1 84240 388 5
978 184240 388 4

Copyright © 2007 by Chrome Dreams

Editorial Assistant   Jake Kennedy
Cover Design   Sylwia Grzeszczuk
Layout Design   Marek Niedziewicz

Photographs courtesy of Retna, LFI, Rex, Paul Joseph.

All rights reserved. No part of this book may be reproduced without
the written permission of the publishers.

A catalogue record for this book is available from the British Library.

Printed and bound in Great Britain by William Clowes Ltd, Beccles, Suffolk

R A D I O H E A D

WELCOME TO THE MACHINE

OK COMPUTER

AND THE DEATH OF THE CLASSIC ALBUM

Tim Footman

MID-CONTINENT PUBLIC LIBRARY
South Independence Branch
13700 E. 35th Street
Independence, MO 64055

SI

MID-CONTINENT PUBLIC LIBRARY

3 0000 10359499 4

INTRODUCTION

THIS IS WHAT YOU GET

I want a perfect body.
I want a perfect soul.
—Radiohead, 'Creep'

1993. I think it was a Sunday, about lunchtime. I was in my flat in Streatham, south London, staggering into some semblance of life after a heavy-duty night at the Fridge club. The phone rang.

"Look at the telly." It was G.

"What am I looking at?" I asked, still not entirely awake. There was a band on, playing a tune I thought I'd probably heard on the radio over the previous few weeks. American, I presumed.

"It's Thom," said G, excitedly.

"Thom who?"

"Thom Thingy," she said. "He was at Exeter about the same time as us. You remember. With the funny eye. He's on telly with his band."

"Bloody hell," I said, or something pretty close. They weren't American. And I did remember the little bloke with the funny eye, just about.

"Thom Thingy's a pop star. Like he said he'd be," said G.

No kidding. I'd seen the booklet produced for the final-year art show. Each student was allocated a page. Thom had declared his ambition: "TO BE A POP STAR." And now he was.

G and I listened and watched, united in contemplation from opposite sides of the Thames. I remembered his other band, the one in Exeter. The drummer used to live next door to me.

As it faded out, G said: "Even I didn't shag Thom." G, as I'm sure she wouldn't mind me saying, had an eventful love life when she was at Exeter University in the late 1980s. But she hadn't shagged Thom Thingy.

The song was 'Creep'. 'Creep', as you may be aware, is a song about what is known in some circles as low self-esteem. Indeed, it could be read as an anthem for the sort of people that even G wouldn't shag.

'Creep' wasn't quite Radiohead's first record, but if anybody says they'd heard of Radiohead earlier, they're probably lying.

I hadn't heard of them. I'd heard of Thom Yorke, though; I'd seen him; even to the extent of wary, nodded acknowledgements in the Ram Bar. He was in a band called Headless Chickens then. In fact, I'd sort of, kind of, shared a stage with them, I think, at some charity show or another. I recited some bloody awful poetry[1]; Thom played some pretty good guitar and occasionally sang. The Headless Chickens covered 'Raspberry Beret' by Prince and 'All I Have To Do Is Dream' by the Everly Brothers. I think G shagged the bass player, but not Thom.

'Creep' made the British Top 10, and also did well in the States. It cemented Thom's image, fairly or unfairly, as a spokesman for the damaged, the confused, the angry and unloved. His short stature and droopy eye only provided part of the equation. If you sing about being a creep and a weirdo, you don't get sympathy sex. You get the reputation of being a creep and a weirdo. People are literal like that.

But at the same time, Thom Yorke was, indeed, a pop star. His band, Radiohead, were [2] signed to the legendary Parlophone label, which had sprung The Beatles on an unsuspecting planet 30 years before. They were on *Top Of The Pops*. They were on *Arsenio* and *Conan*. They were on MTV, in front of half-naked teenagers, looking uncomfortable. It was all terribly exciting.

And they released an album, called *Pablo Honey*, and a few more singles, and it was still quite exciting, but people wanted them to produce more songs like 'Creep', with that guitar bit that went "*DUH-DUH, DUH-DUH, DWAAAANNNNNGGGG*", but they didn't. And, a bit later on, they released another album, called *The Bends*, which was absolutely chock full of songs that weren't 'Creep'. By this time, other pop stars were singing music hall songs at dog tracks, and appearing under Union Jack duvets on the cover of *Vanity Fair*. It was all quite different. In fact, it looked rather as if that was what being a pop star was all about. Those that didn't do this tended to kill themselves, or disappear. Thom was in the wrong game. If only someone would change the rules...

"What is this shit?" was the notorious and justified response of *Rolling Stone* critic Greil Marcus to Bob Dylan's 1970 double album *Self Portrait*. Maybe it's something that writers and musicians – in fact, anybody doing anything that requires time or effort – should ask themselves a little more often. It's certainly a question that potential consumers – that's you, probably – are entitled to ask.

This, then, is a book about *OK Computer*, the third album by the British band Radiohead. There's some biographical and contextual background about the band (chapters 1 and 2); then a track-by-track analysis of the album itself, and related activities (chapters 3-18). Chapter 19 deals with the critical response, while the next chapter is on the creative response by other musicians, in the form of many and various cover versions of the 12 original tracks. Chapters 21 and 22 take the Radiohead story up to the time of writing. There are three conclusions: the first considers one of the key themes of *OK Computer*, the relationship between people and their environment; then the album's place within the genre into which Radiohead, however grudgingly, fall (indie/alternative rock) is examined; and finally, there's a chapter about its standing in the wider continuum of The Classic Rock Album (maaaan).

So that's the shit, in basic terms. But it doesn't quite explain why the book came about; why it's about this album and not another album; why there are so many footnotes. So…

OK Computer is a record that seemed to encapsulate its time (1997), and yet still seems as resonant and relevant today. Radiohead are rare in that they have balanced critical and commercial success for many years, and their most famous offering exemplifies that achievement, enduring analysis at the fingertips of academics even as it exists as background music in coffee bars. It's a rock record in the sense that there are guitars and drums in there, but it also rubs its back against dance music and electronica, jazz, modern classical forms and that old devil called prog. Its lyrics cover politics, economics, alienation, transportation, paranoia, science fiction, suicide, microwaves and the occasional pig. Despite persistent rumours, Stephen Hawking isn't on it, but maybe he should be. Its cover is, in many ways, more unnerving than its contents.

The real answer to Marcus's question, then, comes in the form of a further barrage of questions. How did a bunch of middle-class men in their mid-to-late 20s, in love with popular music, but deeply mistrustful of all its traps and trappings, craft something that defines our age in the same way that Beethoven's Ninth Symphony and Eliot's *Waste Land* and Warhol's Marilyns define theirs? Where did it come from? What were the influences, conscious and unconscious? What effect did it have, on the band, on their fellow musicians, and on culture as a whole? And a final, potentially self-defeating conundrum: what's it all about? I may not answer all of these (almost certainly not that last one) but I aim to have fun trying. That, then, is the shit.

As far as I know, the only other book solely about *OK Computer* is a volume in the excellent Continuum $33^1/_3$ series, by Dai Griffiths. It's a superb book, and I fully agree with Dr Griffiths' starting point, that "Radiohead is already interviewed to death"[3] and that there are already numerous examples of straightforward chronological biographies of the band. However, he is Head of the Music Department at Oxford Brookes University (Jonny Greenwood's alma mater, trivia fans) and he loses patience with those who lack his technical abilities:

> There's still every need to learn how to read music [he declares]: not being able to do so is another indication of the lazy, slobby aspect of computer- and tv-centred life, which plays straight into the hands of scummy, dumbing-down capitalists.[4]

Well, I'll admit that I can't read music.[5] In fact, I realise I'm probably already on Dr Griffiths' enemies list, when he attacks much writing about pop music as being "overly contextual, overly sociological".[6] In other words, this book is about *OK Computer*, but it also suggests that there's life beyond a single record. I've attempted to put *OK Computer* in some sort of context, considering it as a product of its time and its culture, as well as the work of five (sorry, Nigel, six) blokes in a recording studio. So there may be references to other music, to literature, film, art, politics, history, even philosophy, religion and science. And maybe a bit of sociology. But not much. If *OK Computer* is as important as its status in all those 'best of' lists suggests (and how can all those critics and fans be wrong?), I'd hazard the suggestion that it must be down to something more than the simple noises that come out of the speakers, the ones and zeroes that make up its digital DNA. Pop music does not exist in a vacuum, even if some of it really should, for all our sakes. In any case, even if we consider Radiohead as the collective identity of five musicians, only one of them has studied music at university level, and he dropped out. The others followed courses in either literature or politics, which (unless they picked their college careers with a pin) has surely had some bearing on the finished product; the experience of meeting the band members en masse has been described as "kind of like getting high with a bunch of librarians".[7] Thom Yorke has claimed that his literary training "sometimes… really hampers me because I'll start analyzing what I've written or I'll worry about the meter".[8] It's a problem for the artist, but not necessarily for the critic.

One result of this approach is that a few traditional rules of rock criticism might get a little bit twisted. For example, some of what follows edges into the realms of post-structuralism, by arguing that the 'author' (Radiohead) of a 'text' (*OK Computer*) is not the definitive authority on what that text means. As a result, when I'm talking about possible influences on the album, I don't necessarily suggest that the band read or watched or listened to them. The fact that a subsequent listener to the album has experienced both is enough.

Phew. For a minute there... Is this the sort of thing Dr Griffiths meant? OK, here's an example. Martin Clarke, in his biography of the band, makes the following comment when discussing critical responses to the album immediately after its release:

11

The online magazine *Addicted To Noise* claimed, wrongly, that it was inspired by Philip K. Dick's monumental book *Valis*, even though Thom stated he had never read it.[9]

Now, one response to the above might be that it's irrelevant whether or not Thom Yorke had read it. The reviewer, presumably, had. He or she found some link between the two texts; so the reviewer's response was affected by the Dick novel. *OK Computer*, once it's been released into the public domain by its creators, is potentially influenced by any other cultural manifestation, before or since. Shakespeare can be subject to Marxist readings, feminist readings and readings that involve Radiohead songs over the end titles (despite the fact that Shakespeare had never heard of Marxism or feminism or Radiohead); so *OK Computer* can legitimately be compared with things that happened before, during or after its release. As Yorke said, during the interminable touring that followed the album's release (and seemed liable to destroy the band on several occasions):

> We have a direct experience of our music only briefly. Like Patti Smith said, when she writes a song, she's proud of it for about the length of time it takes to finish it. Then it's never hers again. It's always other people's. They'll give it back to you in responses, but essentially [the experience] is over [for the musician].[10]

In other words, *OK Computer* is up for grabs, and the opinions of Yorke and his bandmates are no more or less valid than yours or mine. And you thought 'Fitter Happier' gave you a headache.

Although I disagree with some of what Dai Griffiths says, his book has given me much to chew over, as have a number of other Radiohead-related volumes. I'm particularly indebted to the insights of the various authors (including Griffiths) whose thoughts are collated in Joseph Tate's collection *The Music and Art of Radiohead* (Ashgate, 2005); in particular, Tate's own essay, '*Hail To The Thief:* A Rhizomatic Map in Fragments', has influenced the way

I've looked at the individual tracks on *OK Computer*, although I'd started writing these chapters well before I read his piece.[11] Back to Philip K. Dick. The DVD *OK Computer: A Classic Album Under Review* (Sexy Intellectual, 2006) offers a similar collection of opinions to Tate's book, this time concentrating on music journalists rather than academics; although Dai Griffiths even manages to get in here as well. Of the many Radiohead biographies, Mac Randall's *Exit Music* (Omnibus, 2004) is probably the most thorough. References to other books are, of course, noted as appropriate.

Beyond Radiohead, five books in particular have influenced me. It was *Lipstick Traces* (Harvard UP, 1989), by that man Greil Marcus again, that first demonstrated to me how popular music fits into a wider social, political and artistic landscape, even if its physical creators aren't always aware of the fact. Paul Morley's *Words And Music* (Bloomsbury, 2003) elaborated on this theme, and also gave me a few tips on how to have fun with footnotes. And then, for reasons which may become clearer, there are two volumes about The Beatles. Everyone goes on about *Revolution In The Head*, by the late Ian MacDonald (Pimlico, 1995), but it's true; he makes you hear new things in a piece of music that you think you've heard a thousand times. David Quantick's *Revolution: The Making Of The Beatles' White Album* (Unanimous, 2002), while acknowledging its debt to MacDonald's work, proved that you can love a record, and still take the piss out of the rubbish bits. We'll get to 'Electioneering' in due course. Finally, way beyond the realm of popular music, Martin Gardner's *The Annotated Alice* (1960) is an eye-opener for anyone who thinks that Lewis Carroll just wrote a fairy story. I hope I've picked up a few of Gardner's tips on joining the literary dots; rhizomatics before its time.

Since we seem to be in award-ceremony mode, now seems as good a time as any to thank a few others: Rob Johnstone and Jake Kennedy at Chrome Dreams for faith and patience; Alistair Fitchett, Barney Hoskyns and Everett True for giving me room to roam across the years; the many and various visitors to Cultural Snow; and Melanie Andres, Michael Ascot, Essi Berelian, Noel Boivin,

Tew Bunnag, James Burke, Andrew Collins, Jerramy Fine, Brian J Ford, Annette Hull, Richard Lloyd Parry, Campbell MacKay (R.I.P.), Nicholas Pegg, Simon Reynolds and Joseph Tate, for assistance, encouragement, inspiration and/or provocation, even if some of them didn't know it at the time.

Thanks, of course, to Radiohead for making music rich and dense and infuriating enough to allow me to write a book of this length, yet still be aware that I'm only tapping away uncertainly at the surface; and to Aretha Franklin, Haruki Murakami and Dr Gregory House,[12] for those times when I couldn't listen to any more bloody Radiohead. General Sonthi Boonyaratglin of the Royal Thai Army was considerate enough to stage a military coup and declare martial law just as I was finishing Chapter 24, which provided an unusual backdrop to the writing process, to say the least. Praise unto the Flying Spaghetti Monster, without whom none of this would be possible; and Bertie B, may you forever dream of chasing crows in your smart blue jumper. Love and thanks to my parents and the Powell gang, for plausible expressions of pride and support at appropriate moments.

And to Small Boo, thanks for most of the above and more.

Tim Footman, Bangkok, 2006

Notes:

[1] Thanks to the likes of John Cooper Clarke, Attila the Stockbroker, Steven Wells and others, stand-up poetry was then an acceptable form of artistic expression for people who couldn't sing.

[2] Note to North American readers: I've retained the (technically un-grammatical) British habit of referring to bands in the plural, even if they have a singular, collective name. So, "Radiohead are…" rather than "Radiohead is…" Sorry if this grates a little. We do the same with sports teams. Awful, isn't it?

[3] Dai Griffiths, *OK Computer* (New York/London: Continuum, 2004), p. ix. Radiohead do give good quote, but quotes don't tell the whole story.

[4] Griffiths, *OK Computer*, p. 102.

[5] As the rentaquote conductor Thomas Beecham is alleged to have quipped: "The English may not like music, but they love the sound it makes."

[6] Griffiths, *OK Computer*, p. 103.

[7] Chuck Klosterman, 'No More Knives', *Spin*, July 2003. Kloster-man acknowledges the inherent risk in spending too much time over-analysing Radiohead's lyrics: "Sometimes you can't find the meaning behind the metaphor because *there is no metaphor*."

[8] Krishna Rau, interview, *Shift*, June 1996.

[9] Martin Clarke, *Radiohead: Hysterical and Useless* (London: Plex-us, 2003), p. 122.

[10] Mary Gaitskill, 'Radiohead: Alarms and Surprises', *Alternative Press*, April, 1998. If this sort of thing really floats your boat, take a look at Roland Barthes's essay 'The Death Of The Author' in *Image-Music-Text* (tr. Stephen Heath, New York: Hill and Wang, 1977), pp. 142-148.

[11] Tate's critical technique owes a great (acknowledged) debt to the works of Gilles Deleuze and Félix Guattari, none of which I've read, but somehow this doesn't seem to matter. It also seems to sug-gest at the "garbled version" method of music-making that Jonny Greenwood describes (see Chapter 5).

[12] One of whom, at least, is a self-confessed Radiohead fan.

CHAPTER 1

I DON'T WANT TO GO TO SEATTLE –
1980S-1993

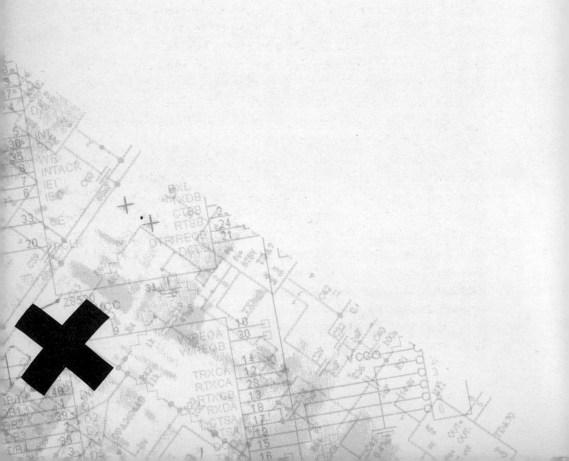

Misericordas domini in aeternum cantabo
—Abingdon School motto (*"I will forever sing praises to the Lord"*)

I'm just aggressive and sick.
—Thom Yorke, 1991

Radiohead announced that they weren't a normal band before any of them had picked up a guitar in anger. Credible, influential rock bands, you see, don't tend to spring from the loins of the comfortable affluent middle classes; and if they do, they keep quiet about the fact.

But even in a postmodern world where 'facts' are simply raw chunks of data to be processed and manipulated by the machinery of media conglomerates, a fact (sometimes) is a fact. And the fact remains that Thomas Edward Yorke was born on October 7, 1968 in Wellingborough, Northamptonshire, a small town with a smaller rock 'n' roll tradition.[1] His father's work took the family around the country; Thom's early life was also disrupted by numerous spells in hospital for treatment on his partially closed left eye.

An unusual face and small stature (he wouldn't grow to more than five and a half feet, or 170 centimetres) would have created difficulties for any child. To be thrown into the philistine, conformist, oppressively masculine environment of the British independent school system must have been horrific.

Thom found a degree of solace with an acoustic guitar he'd received for his eighth birthday; an occasion that came just a few weeks after the Sex Pistols' legendary appearance at the 100 Club punk festival. With numbing inevitability, the young Yorke began devoting himself to the creative pursuit of horrible noise. At the age of 10, he formed a duo with a school friend that coupled his own rudimentary guitar technique with the sound of exploding televisions, and shortly afterwards wrote his first song, the nuclear-themed 'Mushroom Cloud'.

However, such experimental self-expression was not particularly welcome at Abingdon School, a 13th Century institution that exists to mould the young gentlemen of Oxfordshire into upstanding members of the establishment. Thom inevitably found himself at odds with the school's focus on apparently meaningless rules and traditions, and the muddy misery of compulsory team sports. He maintained a particular loathing for the headmaster, one Michael St John Parker, whose predilection for dressing up as a Victorian clergyman would later be commemorated on the Radiohead song 'Bishop's Robes', released in 1996 as an extra track on the 'Street Spirit' single.[2]

However, Yorke, T.E., does not appear to have troubled the school's disciplinary system too much. He found refuge in the music department, which was headed by Terence Gilmore-James, a teacher of whom he has fond memories. "I was a sort of leper at the time," he recalled in 2001, "and he was the only one who was nice to me… [it] was bearable for me because the music department was separate from the rest of the school."[3]

As well as hiding away in the piano booths, Yorke also vented his frustrations on his guitar, at first as the lead singer for a short-lived punk group called TNT. After a few months, a combination of creative differences and boredom led Yorke to jump ship, accompanied by the bass guitarist, a devoted Joy Division fan called Colin Greenwood, who resembled both Oscar Wilde and Christopher Walken at the same time. On the lookout for potential collaborators, they seized upon the lanky, sporty son of an osteopath, Edward O'Brien; although the initial attraction was not his basic guitar skills, but the fact that he rather resembled Morrissey, then the fey frontman of The Smiths, and thus a spokesman for everything Abingdon wasn't.

The three formed a band of sorts, taking advantage of Abingdon's excellent music rehearsal facilities. A number of drummers and horn players moved in and out of the band, which operated under various abysmal names, including Shindig, Dearest and Gravitate.[4] Unhappy experiments with a drum machine prompted them to poach the drummer from a band called Jungle Telegraph, an older Abingdonian called Philip Selway. The acquisition of an analogue percussionist also coincided with another name change. They were now known as On A Friday, a reference to the only mutual window they could find for rehearsals.

Colin's younger brother attended a number of these rehearsals. Thirteen-year-old Jonny evidently had more raw musical talent than the four members of On A Friday combined, having already become proficient on guitar, piano, viola, banjo, recorder and harmonica. But an age difference of three or four years is a gaping chasm to teenagers, and Greenwood minor spent a lot of time just watching the others perform, desperate to be invited to join in, but not wanting to push his luck.

So what did On A Friday sound like at the time? Those privileged enough to be among the small audiences at those early gigs report a taste for experimentalism, and noise for its own sake. The song 'Rattlesnake', for example, was based on a looped drumbeat, over a decade before the band used a similar technique on 'Airbag'; 'What Is That You Say?' was an explosion of feedback that may have owed something to the Jesus and Mary Chain (see Chapter 7).[5] Overall, the band's influences represented a healthy selection of post-punk and indie greats: Joy Division; Magazine; The Smiths; Talking Heads; Elvis Costello. Whether the inspiration of these acts meant that On A Friday actually sounded like them is another matter, and a retrospective comment by Colin Greenwood suggests that the spirit and attitude of the music was more important than technical quality. "We all wore black and played very loud," he recalled, "because that's what you had to do."[6]

Somebody must have enjoyed the noises they were making, because by 1987, On A Friday had even begun to play the occasional proper gig, often at a venue called the Jericho Tavern, which served as the hub of Oxford's small and somewhat incestuous music scene. Jonny began to ease his way into the line-up, at first on harmonica and keyboard, before becoming the band's third and most proficient guitarist; the five-piece was also augmented by a number of female saxophonists.

By this stage, however, the band existed in a fragmented state, with only Thom and Jonny still living in Oxford. The others had begun their higher education: Phil studying English and history at Liverpool Polytechnic (now John Moores University), and playing drums for a number of musical theatre productions; Ed getting to grips with economics in Manchester, then experiencing the early rumblings of the so-called Madchester scene that would dominate the British music press at the turn of the decade, which inspired the guitarist to apodt a particularly floppy haircut; and Colin reading English literature at Peterhouse, the oldest college at Cambridge University, Oxford's eternal rival for academic top-dog status. Jonny still had time to serve at Abingdon; Thom, who had elected to take a year out before starting college, embarked on a number of part-time jobs. The fact that the various members were loyal and disciplined enough to return to Oxford for rehearsals and performances boded well for the future. Colin, who was entertainments secretary of his college, exercised some benevolent nepotism by booking his own band for functions.

Thom Yorke's gap year employment included work in a gentlemen's outfitters and a mental hospital (the latter providing part of the inspiration for 'Climbing Up The Walls'). He was also involved in a serious car accident, which encouraged his mistrust of mechanical transport (see Chapter 3). He finally began his degree course in October 1988, shortly before his 20th birthday, studying English Literature and Art at Exeter University, in the South-West of England. It was an institution that had a not entirely undeserved reputation as a laid-back finishing school for posh kids who weren't quite clever enough to make it to Oxford or Cambridge.[7]

Thom was disappointed to discover that Exeter's music scene was even less thrilling than Oxford's, a situation not helped by a frosty relationship between students and locals, and a council that insisted on shutting all nightclubs at 1am. He made the most of what was there, though, forming a DJing team with Felix Buxton (later one half of Basement Jaxx) and playing guitar in a band called Headless Chickens.

The latter outfit was fronted by Simon 'Shack' Shackleton (later of Lunatic Calm and Elite Force), and has the distinction of providing the first commercially available recording by a future member of Radiohead. Their song 'I Don't Want To Go To Woodstock' appeared on a four-track EP called *Hometown Atrocities*, copies of which would later change hands for £100. A cheery sneer at wannabe hippies (for one performance it mutated into 'I Don't Want To Go To Glastonbury'), it was distinguished from the other tracks on the record by the interesting deployment of a two-person violin section. Headless Chickens later mutated into a techno-influenced outfit called Flickernoise, to which Thom contributed a little guitar, but it was clear where his priorities lie.

Although Thom was clearly happier at Exeter than he had been at Abingdon, some of his later comments seem to suggest that he saw a continuity between the two environments, not least because of the wealthy, elitist, sheltered nature of the students at both institutions. He recoiled from the more 'Hooray Henry' antics of his contemporaries (which seemed to revolve around stealing traffic cones and vomiting in the streets) and has described his own education as "very privileged... very expensive".[8] Yet his key musical collaborators at Exeter, Shack (Shrewsbury) and Felix Buxton (Loughborough Grammar) came from similar, privately educated backgrounds. At least his social scene was less restricted than that available to Colin at Peterhouse, which has a reputation for upper-class fustiness, even by the standards of Cambridge: Thom later alleged, presumably with his tongue slightly to one side, that his colleague and friend "loves to go to all those dinners and wear bow ties... In fact, his favourite thing is to have these dinners where everyone starts speaking in Latin and throwing food at each other. He loves all that."[9]

Thom always seemed slightly baffled as to how he'd ended up as an art student, declaring that he couldn't paint or draw. His academic bacon was saved, however, by the department's acquisition of some high-end Apple Macs, which he used to scan and re-colour Michelangelo's Sistine Chapel ceiling, an act of creative terrorism that he presented as part of his final portfolio.

On A Friday squeezed in a number of gigs while its members were dispersed around the country, but by the summer of 1991 they were again all based in Oxford. The fact that the band had survived their enforced separation indicated that there was something worth fighting for, and they invested in a proper, three-song demo tape, recorded at a 16-track studio on the edge of Oxford; it included a new song called 'Stop Whispering'. They also took the Monkees-like step of renting a house together.

The band's musical influences had shifted since the Abingdon days. Thom's interest in techno and other forms of dance music was resisted by some of his colleagues, although the work of acts such as Happy Mondays and Primal Scream suggested ways in which dance beats might be integrated with guitar music. Another influence, closer to hand, was a strain of indie rock heavily influenced by the dense, wall-of-guitar soundscapes deployed by My Bloody Valentine. 'Shoegazing', as it was dubbed by the music press, provoked an unlikely shift of media attention from Manchester to Oxford and the Thames Valley, where bands such as Ride, Slowdive and Chapterhouse played entire gigs without making eye contact with the audience.

On A Friday moved in the same circles as these bands, but their sound was more aggressive and confrontational. Their major influences at the time were a crop of American bands that had poked their noses over the media parapet in the late 80s and early 90s: specifically, REM, The Pixies, Dinosaur Jr and Nirvana. The latter, in particular, fronted by the beautiful, damaged Kurt Cobain, were on the verge of dragging post-punk guitar rock out of its self-imposed ghetto and into the mainstream.

The Oxford quintet were thus pressing all the right, *NME/Melody Maker*-approved buttons; but they still sounded rather different from the maudlin, self-absorbed bands that surrounded them. Their return to their hometown meant that gig bookings were more frequent, although they were still playing tiny venues. The resulting buzz was enough to attract the attention of Chris Hufford, who operated a recording studio in Sutton Courtenay, a village to the south of Oxford. He went to see the band play at the Jericho Tavern, and immediately offered to produce their next demos. He and his business partner, Bryce Edge, were so impressed by the resulting tape (entitled *Manic Hedgehog*, after an Oxford record shop) that they offered to manage the band, a relationship that survives to the present.

The most memorable response to that tape came in an anonymous letter sent to Thom Yorke, saying: "Your lyrics are crap.

They're too honest, too personal, too direct and there's nothing left to the imagination."[10] But this opinion wasn't unanimous, by any means. Colin Greenwood, who was working in a record shop, passed a copy of *Manic Hedgehog* to a former sales rep called Keith Wozencroft, who was about to start work for the A&R department of Parlophone Records, once home to The Beatles. The next thing the band knew, a couple of dozen A&R men were in the audience at one of their gigs, and before the end of 1991, they had signed a deal with Parlophone. As a result, Jonny Greenwood, who had finally escaped the clutches of Abingdon School, walked away from his music and psychology studies at Oxford Polytechnic after a few weeks.

Wozencroft was deeply committed to the band, with one key exception; he loathed the name. Matters came to a head when an otherwise positive review in *Melody Maker* described their collective title as being "apt for beer-gutted pub rockers".[11] Several alternatives, including Jude and The Music, were considered and spiked without too much ceremony. The precise path by which the Radiohead butterfly emerged from the chrysalis of On A Friday is unclear, although the fact that 'Radio Head' was a (not terribly good) song by one of the band's early influences, Talking Heads, may have swayed it. In any case, by the time Parlophone's new signing released their first material, the *Drill* EP, it was under their new name. 'Prove Yourself', with its quasi-Morrissey moan about being "better off dead", was the lead track; 'You' and 'Thinking About You' were re-runs from *Manic Hedgehog*; and 'Stupid Car' was the first hint of the singer's fraught relationship with the internal combustion engine.

Problems at the pressing plant delayed the release of the EP, and the only mainstream media support came in the unlikely form of the defiantly mainstream Radio One DJ Gary Davies, who played 'Prove Yourself' a few times. *Drill* failed to reach the UK Top 100; EMI thought the homespun production might be at fault, asking the Boston-based duo of Sean Slade and Paul Q Kolderie to work on Radiohead's next recordings.

Slade and Kolderie had liked several of Radiohead's early songs, and thought that with a different production approach (specifically, highlighting the unique qualities of Thom Yorke's voice, which had previously been buried in a quintessentially early-90s guitar sludge) they could be more successful. However, they were disappointed by the quality of the songs that Parlophone had earmarked as potential singles, and it was only when the band played them a new piece that they thought they might have a potential hit. 'Creep' showed Thom's anguished, angelic pipes to their best effect, and contained a lyric of unrequited adoration and unabashed self-loathing, redeemed from potential self-parody by the occasional swear word and titanic explosions of feedback from Jonny Greenwood.[12] Yorke referred to it obliquely as "our Scott Walker cover", and Slade and Kolderie needed some persuading that the song was an original.

'Creep' quickly replaced 'Inside My Head' as the band's next single, and received an unprecedented level of support from Parlophone: not only a promo video, but a radio-friendly edit that replaced the 'fucking's with 'very's. This level of commitment and investment was to no avail, however. Released in September, 1992, it improved on *Drill*'s chart performance by just 23 places, stalling at number 78 in the UK charts.

Radiohead ploughed grimly through a UK tour of colleges and medium-sized venues, attempting to provoke a degree of anticipation for their forthcoming album, due for release in early 1993. But even as they did so, a chain of events was beginning that would change their fortunes irrevocably. 'Creep' had become a big radio hit in, of all places, Israel. Enthusiasm for the track subsequently spread as far afield as Spain and New Zealand, before reaching a number of alternative radio stations in California, including KROQ in Los Angeles. American audiences, it appeared, had heard something in the song that the Brits had missed. Its mixture of soft strumming and savage guitar abuse echoed The Pixies' paradigm (usually reduced by music critics to 'quiet bit-LOUD BIT') which had been picked up a few years later by Nirvana and the other bands that created the 'Seattle sound'. In fact, more than one journalist took the lazy option of labelling Radiohead as a British grunge act; the band disliked this pigeonhole, but it's easy to see the superficial connections with Nirvana, who were about to release *In Utero*, the follow-up to their global smash *Nevermind*.

This international success boosted the band's morale just as their debut album hit the shops. *Pablo Honey* (a title taken from a routine by the New York telephone pranksters the Jerky Boys) was an uneven collection. The strongest tracks had already seen the light of day in various forms: 'Creep', of course; the punkish, chaotic 'Anyone Can Play Guitar', the single release of which had trailed the album and earned Radiohead their first Top 40 placing in the UK singles charts; and the epic, quietly angry 'Stop Whispering', a highlight of the first On A Friday demo tape. However, there was quite a bit of filler as well, such as the lumpen 'Ripcord', and 'I Can't', the grinding, studenty self-pity of which ("gutted like I've never been before") makes it sound like a second-rate 'Creep' parody. Overall, the album remains a competent selection of noisy indie rock that might not be grunge, but certainly shares a few predecessors in common (most clearly, The Pixies).

Pablo Honey received respectable reviews and sales figures, entering the UK charts at number 25. However, rather than building on this, the band's next single was the adolescent anti-musicbiz diatribe 'Pop Is Dead', which hadn't appeared on the album. It failed to make the UK Top 40, although at this point, the band's attentions were elsewhere. The performance of 'Creep' in the States had exceeded all expectations, and Radiohead prepared for their first North American dates.

By this stage, the single had broken out of the college-rock ghetto of West Coast alternative stations, and had even been name-checked by MTV's own cultural arbiters, Beavis and Butt-head. It was clear that the band's Stateside promoters were keen to squeeze every last drop of exposure from the single's success, even getting them a birth on MTV's *Beach Party* show, an experience memorably summed up by Jonny Greenwood as "all these gorgeous, bikinied girls shaking their mammary glands, and we're playing 'Creep' and looking terrible."[13]

With the song in heavy rotation on hundreds of radio stations across North America, it seemed as if the band had stumbled backwards into the Zeitgeist. 'Creep' joined Nirvana's 'Smells Like Teen

Spirit' as an anthem for a youth demographic variously described as 'slackers' or 'Generation X'[14]; mostly white, middle-class teens and 20-somethings who found themselves in dead-end, unfulfilling jobs during an era of unprecedented material prosperity.

It was a startling turnaround for a band whose progress back home had been fitful, but this sort of fame was potentially problematic. For one thing, all the focus seemed to be on 'Creep', rather than on the band; in any case, the mixed reaction to *Pablo Honey* and 'Pop Is Dead' suggested that the band didn't have major reserves of material to satisfy fans lured by the promise of that breakout single. Live appearances were characterised by a fan frenzy during 'that song', and polite interest for everything else.

Also, Radiohead faced a problem peculiar to British bands. The UK music press, and by extension many of its readers, has a particular, perverse loathing for home-grown acts that become big in the United States before they've earned their dues in their homeland. If Radiohead were going to become Britain's answer to Nirvana with such indecent haste, they may as well have renounced their citizenship.[15]

This last obstacle was remedied in September, 1993, when 'Creep' was reissued in the UK and became the band's first Top 10 hit. If Radiohead now wanted to make it big across the Atlantic, they were permitted to do so.

By this stage, however, they were more concerned with the immediate problem of being identified as one-hit wonders. If they were to benefit from their initial, unexpected burst of acclaim, they had work to do.

Notes:

[1] Although, to be fair, Peter Murphy, voice of proto-Goth quartet Bauhaus and cadaverous face of Maxell tapes, grew up there.

[2] James Doheny, *Radiohead: Karma Police; Stories Behind Every Song* (London: Carlton, 2002), p. 134.

[3] Alex Ross, 'The Searchers: Radiohead's unquiet revolution', *The New Yorker*, August 20-27, 2001.

[4] Mac Randall, *Exit Music: The Radiohead Story* (London: Omnibus, 2000), p. 23.

[5] Clarke, p. 17.

[6] Randall, p. 25.

[7] Thom: "Colin Greenwood's the one who got the degree in English from Cambridge, for which I'll be eternally jealous because he got in and I didn't." Krishna Rau, interview, *Shift*, June 1996.

[8] Sylvia Patterson, 'Let's Try And Set The Record Straight', *NME*, May 19, 2001. Dai Griffiths offers an interesting perspective on the class influences on Radiohead in 'Public Schoolboy Music: Debating Radiohead', in Joseph Tate (ed.), *The Music and Art of Radiohead* (Aldershot: Ashgate, 2005).

[9] Krishna Rau, interview, *Shift*, June 1996.

[10] Phil Sutcliffe, 'Death Is All Around', *Q*, October, 1997.

[11] John Harris, live review, *Melody Maker*, February 22, 1992.

[12] The origins of Greenwood's six-string meltdown are lost in the mists of legend. Some have said it was an accident; another theory is that it was a conscious act of sabotage on a song that the guitarist disliked.

[13] JD Considine, 'Harmony In My Head', *Spin*, July, 1996.

[14] These tendencies were commemorated by Richard Linklater's film *Slacker*, and Douglas Coupland's novel *Generation X*, both released in 1991 (the same year as *Nevermind*).

[15] Britain's eventual answer to Nirvana was, of course, the band Bush, whose success in the States was greeted with incomprehension and derision in the UK, mainly because they were utterly atrocious.

CHAPTER 2

A HOUSE IN THE COUNTRY –
1994-1997

They're the ones who'll hate you
When you think you've got the world all sussed out.
—Radiohead, 'High And Dry'

*It's strange how quickly you forget details like what instru-
ment is playing the melody, where you got that sound or where
the melody is coming from... We don't ruminate over which
combination of amplifier, cabinet or guitar is going to make
the best sounds. You lose interest if you worry about sounds
or tones so much. We just work blind, in a kind of panic. It's
all done in a bit of a fury, really.*
—Jonny Greenwood, 1997

Before long, 'Creep' took on a life beyond the control of its
creators. It seemed to be the background music of choice for any TV
producer or film-maker who wanted to express alienation, outsiderdom, mental anguish. It was used on an American documentary
about travelling freak shows, and a British film about Bret Easton
Ellis, the author of *American Psycho*. It turned into a variety of
audio shorthand. Physically disfigured? Psychologically damaged?
Like to cut hookers up with chainsaws? This song's for you![1]

The unexpected success of this one song had presented Radiohead with a number of pressures and dilemmas; but the actual
recording of *Pablo Honey* had been a relatively straightforward,
business-like process. The birth of the second album, begun in early
1994, would not turn out to be such a routine delivery.

The new producer was John Leckie, an industry veteran
whose credits ranged from engineering work on early John Lennon
and Pink Floyd albums, to producing major post-punk acts including XTC, Magazine and The Fall. He had also manned the consoles
for The Stone Roses' self-titled debut and, less happily, for some of
the tracks on their follow-up, *The Second Coming*. His sympathy
for the contemporary alt-rock scene was demonstrated by his supervision of recent albums by Ride and The Verve.

29

Here, then, was a man whose musical scope extended beyond a narrow notion of 'indie rock', and who was open-minded to new ideas. Significantly, he hadn't much cared for *Pablo Honey*, but was impressed by some demos of newer Radiohead songs that Keith Wozencroft had sent him.[2] Unfortunately, any potential for creative harmony was torpedoed by the various record executives. Parlophone wanted to get a new album out by the end of 1994; Capitol, the US label, had an option to release the second album but (not unreasonably) wouldn't exercise it until they had heard some vaguely releasable material.

If this level of pressure was intended to spur the band on to knock out a string of million-sellers, it failed dismally. Radiohead were caught in a paradox. They were expected to come up with a follow-up to 'Creep'; but it was the success of 'Creep' that was causing them to re-evaluate what they wanted from their sudden fame and fortune, and pushing them to do something as different as possible from their biggest hit so far. It seemed that forces outside the tight-knit band were moving in a direction that was diametrically opposed to where the musicians themselves wanted to go. The atmosphere in the studio became rancorous, with Thom Yorke in particular feeling the pain. Matters were soothed only when John Leckie told Thom to play him all the new songs on an acoustic guitar, having sent the others home for a few days.[3]

The enforced change of pace calmed a few frayed nerves, and helped to restore camaraderie and morale within the band. However, by this stage, Radiohead were committed to a two-month tour, covering Europe, Asia and Australasia, with a slot at the Glastonbury Festival at the end of June. With other festival dates scheduled for July and August, it seemed pretty clear that Parlophone's wishes for an autumn album would come to nothing.

The gigs were eventful. In Manchester at the end of May, Thom sustained a hairline fracture of his left ankle; later, Jonny Greenwood began to experience pains in his arm that would be diagnosed as repetitive strain injury, a problem that forced him to wear the brace that has become his onstage trademark.

Two days after the Manchester escapade, Radiohead played the Astoria in London. The gig would provide the raw material for their first official concert video, and the band's rendition of a new song 'My Iron Lung', became the basis for the next single, released in October. Only Thom's vocal was re-recorded.

'My Iron Lung' seemed an odd choice as a single, but by this stage the EMI executives were glad to have squeezed anything out of their truculent charges. Its guitar sound gave more than a nod to Nirvana, whose tormented leader Kurt Cobain had finally succumbed to his demons, in April. But, possibly thanks to the influence of John Leckie, the band's frame of reference was widening. Various listeners to 'My Iron Lung' have pinpointed the influences of Jimi Hendrix, Queen, early Pink Floyd (in particular the 1970 album *Meddle*, on which Leckie had worked as a studio engineer)[4] and The Beatles' 'White Album', especially the song 'Dear Prudence'.[5]

It was pretty clear that Radiohead were desperate to break away from the general perception that they were gloomy post-punks trying to frame a British response to grunge. If anybody missed the newfound sophistication of the music, the lyrics were obviously a pointed reproach to the label bosses who wanted 'Creep #2'; "This is our new song," sneered Thom, "just like the last one, a total waste of time."[6] The title was apparently inspired by the singer's discovery of a picture of a child in an iron lung, a fearsome-looking medical device for people who have lost their respiratory function; but the 'iron lung' was clearly a metaphor for 'Creep'. The breakthrough single had raised the band's profile across the world, and had been a nice little earner for them as well; but it was also a massive encumbrance against which all their subsequent music would be measured. The band had grown to hate it, and they played it live with visible and audible resentment.

'My Iron Lung' did respectable but not spectacular business in the UK, entering the chart at number 24 and going no further. In the United States it disappeared without trace. The Capitol executives were disappointed, but the material selected for the second album, due in March 1995, had persuaded them to exercise their option anyway.

The album took its title from a song called 'The Bends', which in turn referred to the condition, caused by nitrogen bubbles in the bloodstream, that affects divers who ascend too quickly. The metaphor was obvious: Radiohead had achieved fame too quickly, and had suffered as a result. As with 'My Iron Lung', the track suggested that Thom's lyrical interests had progressed beyond hopeless love and self-loathing, although he wasn't about to write any cheery Britpop anthems just yet. 'Black Star' cast a cool eye over the traumas of a superficially stable relationship; 'Sulk' took as its bleak inspiration the Hungerford Massacre of 1987, in which a young man murdered 13 people in his home town.

However, the real progress came with the hugely expanded instrumental palette with which the musicians were working. Radiohead were pushing hard against the amped-up Pixies/Nirvana sound, exploring new textures and dynamics. The looped drums in 'Planet Telex' and the multi-tempo guitar fest that was 'Just' demonstrated that someone (almost certainly John Leckie) had been encouraging the band to look for influences beyond their own record collections. The repressed tension audible in the grooves of 'Street Spirit (Fade Out)' pointed forward to the damaged souls that would populate *OK Computer*, although the lyrics verged on hippy-dippy mantra-speak.

The clearest example of the change, though, is the trio of acoustic-based songs that dominates the first half. 'High And Dry' had originally been written for The Headless Chickens, Thom's Exeter band. His fellow ex-Chicken John Matthias played violin and viola on the next track, 'Fake Plastic Trees', which was influenced by seeing the doomed singer songwriter Jeff Buckley play one of his earliest London gigs, in 1994. Meanwhile, the superficial prettiness of '[Nice Dream]' masked a surreal and somewhat disturbing lyric, and hints a little towards 'Subterranean Homesick Alien' on *OK Computer* (see Chapter 5). By forgoing volume and aggression, without ever becoming narcotically easy on the ear, Radiohead seemed to be taking a few hints from REM, whose *Automatic*

For The People had become a massive commercial success without quite sacrificing the band's weirdness. Thom Yorke and REM's Michael Stipe would soon form a mutual appreciation society that led to Radiohead supporting the Athens, Georgia quartet on their Monster tour, later in 1995 (see Chapter 12).

Although Radiohead had sidestepped their label bosses' demands for another killer radio hit, EMI insisted on squeezing four more singles from the album, only one of which (oddly, the final one, 'Street Spirit') made the UK Top 10. The album reached number 6 in the British charts, but languished at 88 in the States. This time round, at least, they weren't going to suffer the inverted snobbery of the British music press over their transatlantic success.

The critics were almost unanimous in their acclaim for *The Bends*, and the band seemed at last to have escaped the clammy embrace of their earlier hit. "I was surprised to see what the music meant to people," said Yorke, later. "We went from being a novelty band to being the band that everyone quoted in the *NME* and *Melody Maker* 'Musicians wanted' columns."[7]

Radiohead were also becoming a massive draw on the live circuit, especially in North America (despite the relatively poor sales for the album there). The pressure began to tell on the band members; Jonny Greenwood developed a serious ear infection, and Thom's throat was beginning to suffer. Morale wasn't exactly boosted when, in Denver at the beginning of October, the band's equipment was stolen. The mental and physical pressures finally took their toll in Munich in November, when Thom collapsed on stage (an occurrence inevitably dismissed as a bout of rock star histrionics by the cynical British music press).

The band took a break in January, 1996. Thom and Ed O'Brien went travelling; Colin Greenwood, with characteristic studiousness, took a few bass lessons. They knew exactly what confronted them, and they knew their response had to be something different from what they had done before. As Thom told the *NME*:

The big thing for me is that we could really fall back on just doing another miserable, morbid and negative record lyrically, but I really don't want to, at all. And I'm deliberately just writing down all the positive things that I hear or see. I'm not able to put them into music yet and I don't want to just force it.[8]

In February, Radiohead began planning their "positive" next album. After two albums, the band felt rather more at home in a studio environment, and a number of big-name producers, including Scott Litt (famed for his work with REM), turned down the chance to work with them, declaring that they didn't need any supervision.[9] They elected to bring in Nigel Godrich, who had engineered *The Bends*, as well as producing 'Black Star', 'Talk Show Host' and a number of b-sides. His first task was to fit out Canned Applause, their Oxfordshire studio space, with recording equipment.

Entire books have been written about the role of the rock record producer, and it's fair to say that there's no standard job description. At one end are the legends of the 1960s, such as Joe Meek, Phil Spector, Brian Wilson and the various Motown producers, who used the whole studio as an instrument, imposing their idiosyncratic sounds on the often anonymous performers. At the other is the glorified engineer or tape operator, who pretty much does what the performer asks. Innovative figures such as dub pioneer Lee 'Scratch' Perry began to fill the roles of performer, producer and engineer at the same time; by the 1990s, with the development of dance music, sampling and digital recording, any distinction was blurred out of existence.

Rock bands, however, still tended to follow a more traditional structure. At this stage, Godrich had yet to receive a production credit for a whole album, and it seems likely that the original intention was to have someone manning the console and checking the levels, while the band got on with the music. As time went on, however, his importance increased, and he took on the role that George Martin had occupied for The Beatles from around 1965; someone who could use his technical and musical knowledge to translate their ideas into reality. Just as Martin has the best claim to the accolade of 'the fifth Beatle', Godrich is often described as 'the sixth member of Radiohead'. The eccentric credits on the *OK Computer* sleeve (see Chapter 15) don't actually identify a producer as such. Instead, we get "committed to tape by nigel godrich with radiohead. / audio levels balanced nigel godrich.", which pretty much amounts to Godrich being identified as co-producer and engineer, a role he would occupy for all their subsequent albums.

After a few weeks' work in Canned Applause, their Oxfordshire studio space, the band had to take a break during March and April, for yet another North American tour; in August they were booked for a further trip, in the unlikely company of the earnest Canadian singer-songwriter Alanis Morisette. In between, they realised that the sessions at Canned Applause weren't working out, partly because they all lived nearby, and found it too easy to slink off home rather than work. The lack of a toilet didn't help much, either. At the same time, none of them liked recording in purpose-built studios. Despite these frustrations, they had all but finished four songs that would appear on the album: 'Electioneering'; 'No Surprises'; 'Subterranean Homesick Alien'; and 'The Tourist'.[10]

The solution came in the shape of St Catherine's Court, a 15th-century mansion near Bath, in England's West Country. It was owned by Jane Seymour, an actress best known for playing the medium Solitaire in *Live And Let Die*, the best James Bond film of all time; and, more recently, as the eponymous medic in the TV drama *Dr Quinn, Medicine Woman*. The lovely Ms Seymour wasn't at home – in fact, the band never met her – but she did leave a nice note asking them to make sure the cats were fed.[11]

St Catherine's Court fulfilled the band's key criteria. Above all, it wasn't a studio, although acts as diverse as Johnny Cash and The Cure had recorded there; and the architecture provided a number of fascinating variations in acoustics, that the band would put to superb effect. Thom's vocals on 'Exit Music (For A Film)' were swathed in a ghostly echo, having been recorded on a stone staircase; 'Let Down' was taped at 3 am in the ballroom. As Thom Yorke explained:

A lot of the sounds on the record are a result of limitations imposed on us by a mobile set-up... In a big country house, you don't have that dreadful '80s 'separation'. Some of the best-sounding records from '66 to '74 were made by bands playing live in a room. There wasn't a desire for everything to be completely steady and each instrument recorded separately.[12]

The house was also in the middle of nowhere, meaning that they had no choice but to focus on the job in hand. However, the atmosphere of St Catherine's Court, and the sheer age of the surroundings, forced Thom to become obsessed with his own mortality and the possibility of ghosts.[13] Although this was clearly damaging to his mental equilibrium, it helped him to focus on the eerie, sometimes horrific subject matter of the songs.

Although Radiohead didn't set out with a coherent concept in mind, they soon realised that a number of themes were predominating in the music they played: machines; pressure; madness. Thom Yorke characterised his most pressing concern as "fridge buzz" (see Chapter 8), the combination of incessant information and background noise that always threatened to overwhelm him. An early idea for the title was *Ones And Zeroes*, a reference to the raw material for all digital data. It's a neat and appropriate idea: anything from the latest CD or DVD, to the manuscript of this book, can be broken down into a massive string of binary notation[14] that would seem as meaningless as the fridge buzz that was tormenting the singer.

Yorke also claimed later to have considered calling the new album *Your Home May Be At Risk If You Do Not Keep Up Payments*, a standard warning in literature relating to mortgages and secured loans, and a possible reference to the threatened domestic environments in 'Climbing Up The Walls' and 'No Surprises'. However, in the end the album took its title from a song that had been inspired by a band visit to the Californian 'city of the future' in March, 1996. "OK, Computer!" had originally been a remark made by Zaphod Beeblebrox, the anti-hero in Douglas Adams's science-fiction/comedy classic *The Hitchhiker's Guide To The Galaxy*

(1979); the deadpan, slightly despairing humour of Adams' work would crop up elsewhere on the final album (see Chapters 4 and 5). In the end, the song 'OK Computer' became 'Palo Alto', and failed to make the final cut for the album's running order.

The bulk of the recording was finished by November. Strings were added, and mastering and mixing took place in the early part of 1997. The band rested, in preparation for European and North American touring commitments that would occupy them between May and November; Thom and Jonny, however, recorded three Roxy Music songs for the Todd Haynes movie *Velvet Goldmine*, under the supervision of Michael Stipe.

Despite the ghosts and the cats and the embarrassment of having to entertain fans of Alanis Morisette, the band were quietly satisfied with the whole process, and with the way that Nigel Godrich had settled down into his new production role. Ed O'Brien later described the focused working methods the band had used on *OK Computer*, and contrasted them with the way the previous albums had been recorded.

> When we go into the studio it's about finding a soundscape for the song. When you rehearse you think it sounds great but when you consign it to tape it's like, "Oh God, this sounds awful". So we spent quite a lot of time trying to find the right sounds. On *Pablo Honey* and *The Bends* we ummed and ah-hed: it was a lot more vague. This time we knew fairly early whether it was right or not. The stuff we were vague about didn't make it onto the album. We're coming up to our twelfth year together as a band, and we're playing much better.[15]

The executives from Capitol were less happy, however. Already irritated by the relative failure of *The Bends*, they simply didn't understand the new offering, and while they didn't refuse to release the album in North America, they did reduce their initial commitment, from two million copies to 500,000. The band's insistence on releasing a six-and-a-half-minute epic called 'Paranoid Android' as the first single simply confirmed their instinct that the Brits just weren't serious about making it on that side of the Atlantic.

Radiohead played dates in Portugal, Spain and Canada, before travelling to Randall's Island, New York, for a concert on June 7, to publicise the plight of Tibetans living under Chinese occupation. The band had lent their collective voice to worthy causes before, but this was the first time they'd made such a specifically political statement. It certainly wouldn't be the last. The other acts on the bill – U2, Björk, the Beastie Boys, the Foo Fighters, Blur – offered a pretty representative cross-section of the alt-rock aristocracy of the time, and if anybody doubted Radiohead's claims to join their ranks, nobody heard over the din of the crowd.

OK Computer was released in Japan on May 21, the UK on June 16, and in the US on July 1, 1997. But the people who had created it were too busy to take much notice of the fact. They had embarked on a touring schedule that would help to raise their global profile to unprecedented heights – and, at the same time, would come close to destroying the band.

Notes:

[1] The extraordinary ability of film-makers to choose music that is entirely inappropriate to the subject matter is worth a book on its own. Think how many times 'You're Gorgeous' (1996) by Baby-bird, a song about the dehumanising effect of the beauty myth, has been used (with no apparent irony) over footage of blank-eyed fashion models on the catwalk.

[2] Randall, p. 89.

[3] Clarke, p. 63.

[4] Doheny, p. 49.

[5] Mark Paytress, *Radiohead: the Complete Guide to their Music* (London: Omnibus, 2005), p. 31.

[6] This self-referential stance would be continued in 'Exit Music (For A Film)'; see Chapter 6.

[7] Pat Blashill, 'Radiohead – Band of the Year', *Spin*, January, 1998.

[8] Andy Richardson, 'Boom! Shake The Gloom!', *NME*, December 9, 1995.

[9] Clarke, p. 105.

[10] Randall, p. 139.

[11] Clarke, p. 107.

[12] Aidin Vaziri, 'British Pop Aesthetes', *Guitar Player*, October, 1997.

[13] Randall, p. 140.

[14] 'Radiohead', for example, is '01010010 01100001 01100100 01101001 01101111 01101000 01100101 01100001 01100100'.

[15] 'The Making Of *OK Computer*', *The Guardian*, December 20, 1997.

CHAPTER 3

'AIRBAG' –
CONTRADICTIONS AND COLLISIONS

Here in my car,
I feel safest of all.
—Gary Numan, 'Cars'

The car has been a staple of the rock 'n' roll lyric for almost as long as the genre had existed. For some musicians 'the car song' has become a running motif in their repertoires: think of Chuck Berry ('Maybellene', 'No Particular Place To Go'); The Beach Boys ('Little Deuce Coupe', 'Fun Fun Fun'); Bruce Springsteen ('Pink Cadillac', 'Stolen Car'). Cars tie in with all the myths of post-war America that energised rock in the first place: freedom; youth; sex (on the back seat, or wherever's comfortable).

Thom Yorke, unsurprisingly, never seems to have bought into the rockist myth of glinting chrome and scorched rubber, although that's not to say that he's entirely swerved clear of bringing cars into his art. One particularly vibrant party during his student years culminated in the dismantling of an old vehicle, which was then recycled into musical instruments and a makeshift Chinese dragon.[1] However, most of the automotive references have been less happy. Yorke's perspective has been clouded by a well-documented incident in his teenage years, when he was involved in a serious car accident. Rather than hymning the view from the Pacific Coast Highway, his musical response to the internal combustion engine seems to be caught in a tailback on the A40 outside Oxford. His songs include the likes of 'Stupid Car' (on the early *Drill EP*) and 'Killer Cars' (released in various forms and formats on the 'Creep', 'High and Dry' and 'Just' singles).

Despite the title of *OK Computer*'s opening salvo, and Yorke's previous form as a compulsive autophobe, the immediate impact of 'Airbag' comes not from the subject matter, but from the music. The track kicks off with a distorted guitar line that might have found a home on either of the band's two previous albums. And then the drums come in, and it's clear that Radiohead have turned some kind of corner.

At first listening, in fact, it's not entirely clear whether there is a conventional drum kit on 'Airbag', as opposed to synthesized rhythms. This is especially true of the instrumental break that begins at about 3:32, where the percussion seems to become part drum machine, part human beatbox, part spitting cobra. The reality is somewhere in the no man's land between analogue and digital. Phil Selway played a conventional drum part for 15 minutes, which was then recorded, sampled and hacked back to a few seconds of essential rhythm. This in turn was manipulated to create the unruly backbeat to the album's opener. It was a technique borrowed quite shamelessly from the American turntablist DJ Shadow, whose work opened up new possibilities for fusion between hip-hop, techno, rock and other genres; Thom Yorke would work with him the following year. Ed O'Brien, however, diffidently acknowledged that Radiohead were then still rookies when it came to sonic manipulation. "'Airbag' is great," he said, "but it's full of approximations, because we can't program."[2]

Of course, Radiohead were not the first band to combine rock music with dance music (a distinction which, in any case, would have made no sense to early rock musicians such as Chuck Berry). In the late 80s and early 90s, British rock bands such as The Stone Roses, Happy Mondays and Primal Scream had attempted to infuse traditional alt-rock dynamics with the democratic spontaneity of acid house. For a couple of years, any band whose drummer was able to approximate the shuffling beats of Clyde Stubblefield (James Brown's stickman in the 60s) would feel entitled to make the hackneyed claim that "there's always been a dance element to our music". Radiohead, however, were among the first rock bands to realise that it was possible to plunder elements from dance music without feeling obliged to make the end result in any way danceable. (Somebody may have danced to 'Airbag' at some stage, but it must have been a pretty weird party.) The likes of Shadow and Massive Attack had, of course, been doing this quite happily for several years.

This was not the first time Radiohead had used sampling technology; for example, the rhythm track for 'Planet Telex' on *The Bends* is based on a sample of the drums from 'Killer Cars'. Even earlier, back in the days of On A Friday, Thom Yorke had cobbled together a Prince-influenced track called 'Rattlesnake', based on a single taped drum loop.[3] But on 'Airbag' you can *hear* the influence of dance music. It's the point at which, as Mark Paytress suggests, Radiohead found that unlikely common ground between Van Der Graaf Generator on one hand, Aphex Twin and DJ Shadow on the other[4]. The odd thing is that, apart from the wild and crazy drums, 'Airbag' doesn't break all that much sonic ground. There's a Mellotron, mandolin-toned guitars, and even cellos, echoing the menacing undertow of the Beatles' 'I Am The Walrus'. All are very much in the classic rock tradition. The track even ends, as it begins, with a big, rockist guitar chord, which fades away to silence. The only thing (other than the drums) that steps outside the self-imposed box of Caucasian rock is Colin Greenwood's loping bass, echoing the dub experimentalism of 70s reggae producers such as King Tubby and Lee 'Scratch' Perry. Those lessons were clearly paying off.

In fact, despite the rhythmic debt to the genre imprecisely known as 'dance music', 'Airbag' has antecedents that go back even earlier, well before the advent of digital recording. George Martin helped The Beatles to destroy and rebuild tape as a medium, one notable example being the fairground sounds on 'Being For The Benefit Of Mr Kite' (1967). A much more direct influence on Radiohead was Teo Macero's production work on Miles Davis' *Bitches Brew* (1970); tracks were assembled from segments of live studio performance, creating a synthesis of 'the real' and 'the artificial', to the point where neither term makes much sense. The uninformed listener doesn't know where Davis stops and Macero begins, adding to the unsettling vibe of the whole album (see Chapter 5).

It's interesting to contrast the studio version of 'Airbag' with a live performance, such as the one preserved on the second 'No Surprises' single (recorded in November, 1997, at Huxley's Neue Welt in Berlin). Although Selway makes a valiant attempt to replicate the funky rhythmic twists that came out of the studio Apple Macintosh, it's a much more conventionally 'rocky' take. Good, old-fashioned feedback takes the place of the percussive reptile with a aching head; Yorke's sullen vocal, meanwhile, is replaced by a sore-throated howl, embellished with a touch of melisma[5] (3:18) and, a minute later, a bit of screaming. The closing, dying chord is all present and correct. It's also worth noting that, despite the technical differences, the structure and tempo of the song remain almost unchanged. The studio and live recordings each clock in at a few seconds off four-and-three-quarter minutes.

Rather than being admired simply as a piece of studio-based experimentation, 'Airbag' should be taken seriously as a song, despite its startling studio innovations. The immediate influences when Yorke came to write it were apparently a magazine article called 'An Airbag Saved My Life'[6] and Sogyal Rinpoche's tome, *The Tibetan Book of Living and Dying*. The latter, by a Tibetan monk who studied at Cambridge University, is one of the most successful attempts to communicate Buddhist philosophy to a mainstream Western audience, and in 'Airbag' Thom fuses imagery of traffic accidents with notions of reincarnation (see Chapter 8). However, the language used here (the repeated "I am born again") seems more relevant to Christian theology, and the notion of being 'reborn' through baptism. In fact, Yorke goes one better with his triumphant "I am back to save the universe!!", following the leads of David Bowie (the "leper Messiah" of 'Ziggy Stardust') and The Stone Roses ('I Am The Resurrection') to take on the ironic mantle of Christ.

Death is often a presence in classic car songs, but it's usually presented in sentimental terms, as in the case of the teenager who crashes the stock car he's racing to pay for a wedding ring, in Ray Peterson's camp masterpiece 'Tell Laura I Love Her' (1960). If 'Airbag' has any place in the great car song continuum, it's as a response to Gary Numan's 1979 hit 'Cars', in which the sometime Thatcherite smugly trumpeted his cocooned security. A similar mind-set to Numan's prevails in Bowie's 'Always Crashing In The Same Car', from *Low* (1977), in which the narrator is "never looking left or right"; although, to be fair to Dame David, that was probably the drugs talking.

Yorke later skewered these attitudes by alluding to the delusions of invincibility that car travel instils in drivers. "Your average expensive German car gives you the feeling that you can't die," he said. "And that's a fraud."[7] Rather than allow himself to be fooled by this conspiracy of complacency, Yorke was eaten up by the danger:

Airbag is more about the idea that whenever you go out on the road you could be killed. Every age has its crazy idiosyncrasies, crazy double-think. To me, for our era it's cars. I always get told off for being obsessed about it, but every time I get in my car I have to say to myself that I might never get out again. Or I might get out but I won't be able to walk.[8]

But the lyrics of 'Airbag' are rather more than an anguished reminder to observe road safety rules, with or without the religious overtones. The key line, as it appears in the CD booklet, is ">in a deep deep sssleep of tHe inno$ent/~~completely terrified~~". Yorke is railing not against selfish drivers in particular, but about all of us, selfish wage zombies who accept the mantras of industrial capitalism (that dollar sign) without a second thought; sssleepdriving or sssleepwalking, it's all the same. Fear is crossed out by the safety of one's own metal box, just as a house, a job and a credit card can inoculate us against the dangers of reality, provided we stay on the economic treadmill.

In other words, the link that 'Airbag' has with the classic car songs of Berry and The Beach Boys is that it's not really about cars. There's a key difference, however: the earlier writers were exploring the seemingly infinite possibilities of America in the Eisenhower/Kennedy era, using cars as the obvious metaphor. Springsteen, writing from the perspective of post-Vietnam collective trauma, expresses a rather more bruised variety of romanticism. For Yorke, even the Boss' moral ambivalence is a dangerous lie. The military-industrial complex, under cover of Californian fun, fun, fun, is set to take over all our lives. Humans are reduced to interchangeable parts on the great assembly line of capitalism. And who invented the assembly line as we know it? Henry Ford, who used it to build his Model T, the bedrock of the great American car myth. According to Yorke, people are often their own worst enemies, allowing themselves to be exploited and even destroyed:

So much of the public's perception revolves around illusion. That's what 'Airbag' is about, the illusion of safety. In reality, airbags don't really work and they go off at random. It's exactly the same as when you're on a plane. Everyone should really sit backwards. It's the safest way possible to face the back of the plane as you take of. But because people don't like the idea, and they feel a bit sick, airplanes have always been done the other way around, which is fucked. Anyway, if you're plummeting down to earth at 1,000 miles per hour, there's no way you're going to stand a hope if you sit there with your head between your legs with your seatbelt on. In the end, we're all just fucking bits of meat.[9]

If 'Airbag' has any specific heritage, it comes not from Radiohead's musical forebears, but from the world of cinema. Jean-Luc Godard's *Week End* (1967) uses the metaphor of an interminable traffic jam to represent the corruption and futility inherent in capitalism, as the witless bourgeoisie contend with revolution, murder and cannibalism as they attempt to get out of Paris. "What a rotten film," says one of the main characters, Roland, "all we meet are crazy people." It's an exasperated moment of self-awareness that could just as easily slot into a Radiohead song.

Yorke's fear and loathing of mechanical transportation resurfaces periodically throughout *OK Computer* ("motorways and tramlines" in 'Let Down'; the "tyres that grip in the wet" of 'Fitter Happier'; the aircrash in 'Lucky'; the final invocation in 'The Tourist' to "slow down"). The newfound sense of musical innovation, however, permeates the whole album. There is a key paradox at work here: the musicians and producer are delighting in the sonic possibilities of modern technology; the singer, meanwhile, is railing against its social, moral and psychological impact. As Nick Kent suggested, if *OK Computer* does have a coherent 'message', it's about finding "a humane set of values amid the numbing paraphernalia of the lap-top mind-set."[10] And at the same time, they're not only using that paraphernalia, they're revelling in its use, pushing all its buttons and seeing what it can do.

It's a contradiction mirrored in the culture clash of the music, with the 'real' guitars negotiating an uneasy stand-off with the hacked-up, processed drums. This classic dialectic[11] produces an unlikely, uneasy synthesis; the first inkling for the listener that *OK Computer* would be more than just another rock album.

Notes:

[1] Clarke, p. 21.
[2] Randall, p. 150.
[3] Clarke, p. 17.
[4] Paytress, p. 38.
[5] The vocal technique of stretching a syllable over several notes; it's a trademark of African-American gospel singing. Mariah Carey does it. Lots.
[6] In its early incarnations, the song was called 'Last Night an Airbag Saved My Life', a nod to In-Deep's club classic 'Last Night a DJ Saved My Life' (1983).
[7] Doheny, p. 60.
[8] Phil Sutcliffe, 'Death Is All Around', *Q*, October, 1997.
[9] Interview, http://cokebabie.tripod.com/page31.html
[10] Nick Kent, 'Happy Now?' *Mojo*, June 2001.
[11] Dialectic is a philosophical process that counters a statement or proposition (the thesis) with contradictory statements (antithesis) to form a third position (the synthesis). I've been wanting to use that since I learned it in a history lesson when I was 17. Thanks, Mr Thompson.

CHAPTER 4

'PARANOID ANDROID' –
JONNY HATES PROG

"Life," said Marvin dolefully, "loathe it or ignore it, you can't like it."
—Douglas Adams, *The Hitchhiker's Guide To The Galaxy*

Punk rock killed prog rock. It's one of the cornerstones of the Great Pop Mythology. At the end of 1975, all British teenagers, without exception, were still wearing Army surplus greatcoats and drinking patchouli by the pint while they listened to songs about invisible hobbit wars, enlivened by drum solos lasting about five months. A year-and-a-half later they all had short, spiky hair and listened to bands formed by people with unpleasant names who'd mastered almost two chords. Prog, the sort of self-indulgent nonsense upon which John Lydon bestowed the magnificent adjective 'twaddly' (presumably a chance meeting between 'twaddle' and 'wibbly') was shunted offstage with indecent haste.

As with many successful myths, there's an element of truth in there, but not much more. For a start, progressive rock – the sort of thing that Pink Floyd, Genesis and Yes were doing – was always a minority interest, even at its peak of popularity in the mid-1970s, and it was never the real target anyway. If punk had any ideological foes, it was people such as Mick Jagger and Rod Stewart, who once claimed to embody youthful rebellion, but were now bloated rock aristocrats, surrounded by a coterie of bodyguards, groupies and accountants.

More significantly, the more intelligent punk performers rather admired some of their proggy counterparts, even if they didn't make a big noise about it at the time. Lydon may have wangled his way into the Sex Pistols with a t-shirt proclaiming "I HATE PINK FLOYD", but he was happy to sing the praises of Van Der Graaf Generator's Peter Hammill, Krautrock pioneers Can and the French space-jazz combo Magma. Steve Diggle of Buzzcocks and Clash/PiL guitarist Keith Levene were Yes fans; Captain Sensible of The Damned was a devotee of Canterbury organ trio Egg.[1]

That said, the punk virtues of brevity, simplicity and lack of overt pretension persisted even after punk had morphed with indecent haste into new wave, and then into the genre of guitar-based music known as indie or alternative rock. As devotees of The Pixies and The Smiths, Radiohead were heirs to this tradition. Six-and-a-half minute, three-part epics about neurotic robots were not the sort of thing they were supposed to do, and they knew it.

So it was something of a gamble to put exactly that sort of thing on their latest album; even more risky to release it as the first single. Radiohead had already demonstrated that they weren't just another indie band, but what the hell did they think they were up to?

'Paranoid Android' screams its geek credentials right from the title. The original paranoid android was Marvin, the depressive, cybernetic anti-hero of *The Hitchhiker's Guide To The Galaxy* and its various spin-offs on radio, TV, print, tea towel and, several years after *OK Computer*, a movie. He was the creation of Douglas Adams, a man who shamelessly admitted a fondness for Procol Harum and The Eagles, and who once jammed with Pink Floyd (the post-Roger Waters version, when they were *really* dull). Despite these lapses in taste, Adams, who died in 2001, was surely one of the greatest comic writers of the 20th Century, although his comedy is often laced with bemused concern about the bizarre behaviour of humanity; particularly its preference for religion and superstition over science, and its disregard for the environment. He also provided the title for *OK Computer* itself, of course.

'Paranoid Android' matches, and even exceeds Adams' level of displeasure at the insanity of modern society; the humour, although present, is a little less overt. The genesis of the song, like so much on *OK Computer*, lies with The Beatles' self-titled double LP of 1968, better known as 'the White Album'. Thom Yorke was inspired by the structure of John Lennon's 'Happiness Is A Warm Gun', which is essentially three different songs grafted together. However, as with many of the nominal influences on the album, Radiohead's finished product used the original inspiration as a springboard to something new and dangerous.

For a start, the song, as heard on *OK Computer*, is more than twice the length of Lennon's[2]. It begins with a mid-tempo, strummed

acoustic guitar over shaken percussion. Treated electric guitar si-
dles in, to be joined by Thom Yorke's high voice, sounding like a
surly choirboy. The sound builds gently, with some barely distin-
guishable 'robot voices' hovering in the background.[3] At 2 minutes and 43 seconds, Jonny Greenwood begins an axe assault that
stands comparison with his feedback fest on 'Creep'. The soloing
continues until 3.33, when it is abruptly replaced by multi-tracked
voices that sound almost Gregorian in their sadness. Thom sings
over this, a little like a secular preacher fronting a gospel choir, the
effect heightened by the drawled "God loves his children". At 5.38
there's a brief return to the acoustic riff, before another incendiary
bout of guitar improvisation that takes us to an abrupt halt, harking back to the brutal truncation of 'Just' on Radiohead's previous
album, *The Bends*.

What remains from The Beatles track is the combination of
acoustic prettiness and electric brutality, and a set of lyrics that
create images through hints and implications, rather than coherent
depictions. Yorke offers fragments of dialogue, speaking in numerous voices, creating fleeting images of alienation and disgust,
rather than any kind of coherent narrative. One possible interpretation is that a simple request for release from noise (the plea that
pervades the whole album) ends in some kind of confrontation
with wealthy, successful people; this provokes the protagonist
to entreat God for some sort of actual or spiritual cleansing. So
what's happened? Has that nice Thom Yorke finally snapped and
emptied an assault rifle into a packed wine bar, like the deranged
caller to a radio shock-jock show in Terry Gilliam's *The Fisher
King* (1991)? Is he asking for forgiveness? Absolution? Understanding? Or should we all just applaud?

Any deeper probing into the objective 'meaning' of the lyrics in 'Paranoid Android' is probably fruitless because they work
on the basis of connotation, not denotation. It's what they refer to,
what they're *about* that matters, not what they say. To begin with
the most famous line, "kicking squeeling (sic!) Gucci little piggy".
Thom's story about the origins of the image, when he saw a coked-
up Los Angeles yuppie reacting with demonic rage when someone

spilled a drink on her[4], is well known. But the single word "piggy" sets off all sorts of alarm bells. Since the song had its genesis with The Beatles' 'White Album', we're inevitably led to George Harrison's song 'Piggies', a sarcastic assault on bourgeois society and also one of the tracks that Charles Manson took as a cue for his sadistic murder spree in California in 1969.[5] Harrison's pigs become cannibals, a concept that Yorke touches on with his later reference to crackling skin.

But the echoes don't stop with The Beatles. Roger Waters also equated humans with pigs on the Pink Floyd album *Animals* (1977). It can't have been accidental that two of the images lifted from the *OK Computer* artwork to decorate the sleeve of the 'Paranoid Android' single are direct references to Pink Floyd: the floating pig from *Animals* and the handshaking stick figures that parody the businessmen on the cover of *Wish You Were Here* (1975).[6]

The other key image on the single sleeve is the vast dome crowned with the line "God loves his children, yeah!" What is this construction? St Paul's Cathedral? The Dome of the Rock? Some tent-like megachurch in the Nevada desert? The scrawled lyric is surely ironic, although it should be read in conjunction with Yorke's invocation of rain. The idea of weather as a great cleanser, to nourish the good and wash away the evil, is a common Biblical motif: for example, the story of Noah and the flood.[7] This, in turn, was the imagery that Travis Bickle invoked in Martin Scorsese's *Taxi Driver* (1976) when he called for a rain to wash the scum off the streets.

So is this the persona that Yorke has selected – a vengeful slayer of all those who have turned their backs on God? In a neat political twist, the wrongdoers in this universe are not the dealers and pimps of Scorsese's New York, but the superficially respectable agents of capitalism who consume the drugs and whores that the 'scum' supply. In fact, Yorke's targets may be even more exalted than we first realise. The sneering lines suggesting execution have a faint echo of a remark attributed to the pre-pubescent Prince William, who is alleged to have told a servant: "When I am King, I am going to send my knights around to kill you."

Yorke's depiction of a man screaming soundlessly within a moral vacuum also suggests the greatest modern depiction of urban despair, T.S. Eliot's 'The Waste Land' (1922). "The dust & the screaming" paraphrases Eliot's promise of "fear in a handful of dust"; the barman ejecting the narrator from the yuppie hangout has a counterpart in the "HURRY UP PLEASE IT'S TIME" refrain. More significantly, like 'Paranoid Android', 'The Waste Land' is composed of cultural fragments: Hindu myth sits alongside Tarot cards, Shakespeare and birdwatching guides. The two works part company at the end, however. Eliot eventually reaches some level of contentment with the final word, "Shantih", the Sanskrit for "the peace which passeth understanding"; Yorke's assertion of divine love is at once sarcastic and desperate.[8]

So, 'Paranoid Android' is long and complicated and potentially difficult, drawing on diverse sources and images that aren't usually to be found in the pop vocabulary. But is it really progressive rock, in the tradition of the long, complicated, difficult albums that devout punks attempted to burn, or at least hide at the back of the wardrobe?

Some people close to the band seemed to like the idea that Radiohead were dabbling in proggy waters, or had at least created something akin to a concept album. Nigel Godrich insisted that, "You have to sit through the whole album because it's a whole piece": Keith Wozencroft, the A&R man who had signed the band to Parlophone, argued that, "If people say Radiohead play prog rock, that's good, because it means they're moving forward."[9]

Jonny Greenwood, for one, rejected the accusation. "I've been trying to find lots of good prog rock," he said in 1997, "but unfortunately it's all awful… I was curious. But it is better off dead."[10] He later expanded on why he disliked the philosophy underlying progressive rock, and how he thought Radiohead's music was something different entirely:

I think progressive rock was a very big mistake, to be honest. The idea that rock music and classical music were as good as each other, and trying desperately to fuse the two was very misguided. I don't think we're doing that, we're just really bored; bored of what we hear and bored of what's around. We're not trying to educate people, or push things forward, we're just alleviating boredom, really.[11]

Thom Yorke, meanwhile, despite having sardonically described the version of 'Paranoid Android' played on the Morisette tour as "a Pink Floyd cover",[12] had a pungent response to insinuations of prog tendencies once *OK Computer* was released: "They're talking bollocks."[13]

OK then, no hobbits here. But the "is-it-prog?" controversy seems to be based on a narrow, reductive perspective about what prog really was. Of course it was often fey and self-indulgent, with a tendency to favour form over content. And it's true that Rick Wakeman of Yes boasted of ordering, receiving and consuming (onstage) an Indian takeaway meal while drummer Bill Bruford played a solo. But some progressive groups, such as Pink Floyd, King Crimson[14] and Van Der Graaf Generator, produced material that made pretty pertinent and caustic observations about contemporary society; music that could be as bleak as the glummest songs of Joy Division, Nirvana or, indeed, Radiohead. Even Emerson, Lake & Palmer, now derided (with plenty of justification) as the most self-indulgent manifestation of the genre, released a four-part song ('Karn Evil' on the 1973 album *Brain Salad Surgery*) that dealt with the way in which technology was getting the better of humanity. Sounds familiar? The existence of a mispressed run of Dutch *OK Computer* CDs that play Floyd's *The Dark Side Of The Moon* is sheer coincidence, but will doubtless keep the conspiracy theorists occupied.

Maybe in the post-punk universe, simply having a song (a hit single, no less) that was so long and so complex, seemed self-indulgent and arty by comparison with what was going around it. Remember that the really big hit singles of 1997 included the eminently disposable 'MmmBop' by Hanson and 'Barbie Girl' by Aqua; and the bland, sentimental tedium of Puff Daddy's 'I'll Be Missing You' and Elton John's 'Candle In The Wind 1997', both tailor-made for maudlin, suburban funerals. Oasis seemed to show a bit of ambition by releasing 'D'You Know What I Mean?' a song that was over a minute longer than 'Paranoid Android'; but it was essentially a repetitive terrace chant that could equally have lasted two minutes or two hours without requiring any more input in the songwriting department.

Dai Griffiths compares 'Paranoid Android' with 'I Know What I Like (In Your Wardrobe)' from Genesis' 1973 progressive album *Selling England By The Pound*[15]; Mark Paytress places the track within a tradition that includes the aforementioned Van Der Graaf Generator, and their 20-minute 'A Plague Of Lighthouse-Keepers' (1971), but also encompasses such milestones as Queen's 'Bohemian Rhapsody' (1975), The Beatles' 'Strawberry Fields Forever' (1967) and The Beach Boys' 'Good Vibrations' (1966)[16]. These last three tracks may or not be 'prog', in the bad-hair meaning of the word, but are without doubt 'progressive', in the sense that they helped to push forward the notion of what could be done with the medium of the single, and with the whole technology of record-ed sound. Significantly, they were also commercially successful, a quality they shared with 'Paranoid Android', which reached third place in the British singles chart.

Radiohead's reluctance to be given a label that might suggest pretension and self-indulgence was understandable; they resented a common media perception of the band as a gang of posh, intro-verted intellectuals, and doing something as perverse as harking back to the Mellotron-twiddling dinosaurs of the mid-70s would only have served to reinforce that.[17] However, there's little doubt that, with *OK Computer*, they were taking rock music into new realms, just as Emerson, Lake and Palmer thought they were doing 25 years before.

Let's give Radiohead the benefit of the doubt, and agree that 'Paranoid Android' is not prog rock, at least in the ELP sense. But one important question remains. Who actually is the paranoid an-droid of the title? Is it the narrator/Yorke, who feels dehumanised by the "unbornchikkenvoices" that keep him from sleep? Is it the Gucci-bedecked yuppie, driven over the edge by a cocaine-fuelled persecution complex? While we're at it, maybe it's the child-loving, rain-making God. Marvin, the original paranoid android, claimed to have a brain the size of a planet, which sounds pretty close to divine omniscience.

With its combination of social comment, religious overtones and non-specific menace, there's little doubt that 'Paranoid Android' will have earnest students debating its meaning over instant coffee and other substances at 3am for many years to come. And sorry, Jonny, but that sounds like pretty good evidence of prog tendencies to me.

Notes:

[1] John Robb and Kris Needs, 'The Secret History', *Mojo*, June 2006.

[2] When 'Paranoid Android' was first played live, on Radiohead's support slots with Alanis Morisette, it was often twice as long again, with Jonny Greenwood taking the spotlight for Hammond organ and glockenspiel solos. See Doheny, p. 62.

[3] The indistinct, repeated line is "I may be paranoid, but not android". The voice is created on a Mac, in the same way that the lines on 'Fitter Happier' (see Chapter 9) were produced.

[4] Randall, p. 152.

[5] David Quantick, *Revolution: The Making of the Beatles' White Album* (London: Unanimous, 2002) pp. 185-196. Manson's other cue for mayhem from the album was 'Helter Skelter', which also finds an echo on 'Paranoid Android': the riff that follows the "piggy" line sounds suspiciously close to McCartney's "do you, don't you want me to love you". And if you think that's far-fetched, Dai Griffiths (*OK Computer*, p. 53) reckons the "from a great height" section borrows from Mendelssohn's Hebrides Overture.

[6] The pig as a symbol of the doomed bourgeoisie makes a further appearance at the end of 'Fitter Happier'. And never underestimate the influence of George Orwell (whose pigs became symbols for

the corrupt leaders of the Russian Revolution in *Animal Farm*) on English public schoolboys with anti-establishment leanings.

[7] Genesis 7. Also: "…for it is time to seek the Lord, till he come and rain righteousness upon you." (Hosea 10:12)

[8] T.S. Eliot, *Collected Poems, 1909-1962* (London: Faber and Faber, 1963), pp. 61-86. 'The Tourist' is another track that echoes Eliot; see Chapter 14.

[9] 'The Making Of *OK Computer*', *The Guardian*, December 20, 1997.

[10] Randall, p. 146.

[11] Roger Scott, interview, SpinOnline, September, 1997.

[12] Clarke, p. 107.

[13] Clarke, p. 128.

[14] Crimson's '21st Century Schizoid Man' (1969) isn't a million miles from 'Paranoid Android' in terms of title or content.

[15] Griffiths, 'Public School Music: Debating Radiohead', in Tate, pp. 165-166.

[16] Paytress, p. 39. Another structurally diverse hit single of the same era was 'Something In The Air' by Thunderclap Newman (1969).

[17] Yorke's solo performance of 'Paranoid Android' at the Bridge School Benefit in 2002, accompanied only by his own acoustic guitar, demonstrates how strong *the song* is when stripped of all its sonic trimmings.

CHAPTER 5

'SUBTERRANEAN HOMESICK ALIEN'
AND THE POETRY OF PERSPECTIVE

Another thing tormented me in those days: the fact that no one else was like me, and I was like no one else. I am alone, I thought, and they are everybody.
—Fyodor Dostoevsky, *Notes From Underground*

The idea of the outsider, the individual who is physically part of everyday society, but feels alienated and rejected by its norms and rules, is core to the whole genre of alternative music from which Radiohead came. Part of the appeal of performers such as Ian Curtis of Joy Division, Morrissey of The Smiths and Kurt Cobain of Nirvana is their essential 'otherness'. They didn't sound or look the way that normal pop stars were supposed to.

Of course, this outsider chic didn't begin in the aftermath of punk. It's an artistic and literary model that goes back several hundred years; it's possible to see Shakespeare's Hamlet as a precursor to self-absorbed indie kids who think too much, and can't properly engage with the mundane unpleasantness of life around them. From the mid-19th Century on, writers such as Dostoevsky, Kafka, T.S. Eliot, Hemingway and Scott Fitzgerald created protagonists whose identifying characteristic was that they simply didn't fit. But it was the Second World War and its aftermath that spawned pop-existentialist heroes, such as Meursault (in *The Outsider* by Albert Camus) and Holden Caulfield (in J.D. Salinger's *The Catcher In The Rye*), who would become archetypes for writers, artists, movie-makers, musicians and countless angst-ridden teenagers who, like Hamlet, wore "customary suits of inky black".

Thom Yorke had felt like an outsider from an early age; his size, his lazy eye, the numerous operations he endured, and the resulting bullying, meant that he saw life in a different way – both metaphorically and literally. Confronted with the meat-headed thuggery of his contemporaries, his attitude flip-flopped between abject self-loathing and a feisty assurance that the problem was with the world, not with him. As he said in 1996, "I'm surrounded by a world of grinning idiots and I don't think I want to be another one."[1]

So there must have been some resonance when an English teacher at Abingdon asked him to imagine himself as an alien that had landed in the middle of Oxford. The task was almost certainly inspired by the poem 'A Martian Sends A Postcard Home' (1979), by the poet, critic and academic Craig Raine. In it, the alien sender of the card describes everyday, familiar objects in terms that are bizarre, almost surreal, but all make some sort of sense.[2] Books, for example, are "mechanical birds with many wings" that "cause the eyes to melt or the body to shriek without pain". The poem in turn spawned a short-lived school of 'Martian poetry' that sought to use extreme, often comical metaphors to shake English verse from the grip of cosy familiarity.

The idea of turning the alien imagery into a song didn't occur to Yorke until he was driving through the Oxfordshire countryside one night, and struck a pheasant. Precedent might suggest that this would provoke another anti-car lyric (see Chapter 3), but for some reason he conceived the idea of writing about hovering extra-terrestrials. In any case, although clearly influenced by the Raine poem (or at least the question it posed), Yorke's finished lyric doesn't occupy the point of view of the spaceman. Instead, the human narrator lives in an anodyne town "where you can't smell a thing", and imagines aliens hovering above, observing *homo sapiens* and, as he put it in 1998, "pissing themselves laughing at how humans go about their daily business."[3] If there's a direct influence here, it's the puppet spacemen who peopled the Smash commercials on British television in the 1970s, chuckling merrily as foolish housewives chose to peel, boil and mash fresh potatoes rather than enjoy the delicious wallpaper paste on offer in handy plastic packets.

In the second verse, Yorke occupies a different archetype, the human taken up into a flying saucer. This is an extremely common occurrence in modern folklore, and is probably most familiar from Whitley Strieber's (supposedly factual) book *Communion* (1987), in which the author describes being abducted by non-humans, presumably extra-terrestrials. Yorke's narrator looks forward to viewing "the world as I'd love to see it" from the alien craft but knows that if he ever told his earthbound acquaintances, he'd meet with scorn and disbelief, and finally be locked up; a return to the classic existential, indie-kid outsider once more.

In many ways, the narrator acts out the desires of the other voices on *OK Computer*. Many of them appear to be suburban wage-slaves, seething with indignation at their lot, and the madness that surrounds them, but unwilling or unable to make the necessary leap. The voice in 'Subterranean Homesick Alien' is that of the little boy who points out the emperor's nakedness. This time nobody believes him; but he's right, and this gives him a sense of moral leverage over the people who just keep their heads down and wait for the next pay cheque.

Of course, Radiohead weren't the first band to use science fiction imagery in popular music. Novelty records such as 'Flying Saucer' by Buchanan and Goodman (1956) and 'Telstar' by The Tornadoes (1962) responded to the contemporary excitement over the space race. By the late 1960s, a whole 'space rock' genre began to coalesce: Hawkwind are the band most associated with the phrase, although some of Pink Floyd's music from the same period has been included under this heading. While space rock often used imagery borrowed from science fiction, it's as much to do with the mental spaces that were opened up by the use of LSD and other psychedelic drugs. Some of the shoegazing bands with which Radiohead were associated in their early days shared many musical characteristics with the early space rockers, especially the use of soaring, phased guitar lines; the conceptual angle was picked up by bands as diverse as Funkadelic and ELO, both of whom used flying saucers as part of the stage sets. A number of other performers made their own supposed interplanetary associations a key element of their public identities: jazz bandleader Sun Ra was, according to his publicity, born on Saturn; the cult musician Lucia Pamela claimed to have been the first person to record an album on the moon (1969's *Into Outer Space With Lucia Pamela*); David Bowie also toyed with a number of astronaut and alien alter egos (see footnote 2).

Many of these performers used astral imagery as a means of expressing huge, unwieldy concepts; in 'Subterranean Homesick Alien', on the other hand, the evident banality and insignificance of the situation is key. The narrator hasn't really been abducted by space monsters; he's just bored out of his mind. Despite Radiohead's reputation for glum self-loathing, they were clearly having fun here. As with the previous track on the album, the spirit of Douglas Adams is at work. Arthur Dent, the hero of *The Hitchhiker's Guide To The Galaxy*, is rescued from the imminent destruction of Earth by hitching a ride on a Vogon spaceship; another key character is Ford Prefect, a correspondent for the eponymous guide, who observes Earthlings while pretending to be, not from a small planet near Betelgeuse, but from Guildford (a dull city not far from London). The title, too, indicates that nothing should be taken too seriously. It clearly refers to Bob Dylan's 'Subterranean Homesick Blues' (1965), but as with that classic of surrealist rock/pop, the link between title and lyric might be a little tenuous.[4] In any case, the original title for the Radiohead song was 'Uptight', a word that reflects the seething inner life of the narrator, but not the warm, almost drowsy feel of the music.

It's as if, while creating the lyrics, Yorke has taken an initial idea, then played with it over and over again until most traces of the original concept (the Martian's view of Oxford) have become vague smudges. The music followed a similar path. Originally performed by Yorke and Jonny Greenwood alone, on acoustic guitars, the arrangement on *OK Computer* came about when the singer forced himself to listen to *Bitches Brew* (1970), the seminal jazz-rock album by trumpeter Miles Davis; this was despite his notorious initial belief that the record was nothing but "nauseating chaos".[5] Apart from the prominent electric piano, there seems to be little obvious musical link between the two works, with 'Subterranean Homesick Alien' still clinging to the indicators that tie it to classic rock. The chiming 12-string guitars have something of The Byrds about them; the piano run beginning at 1:52 sounds a little like 'Riders on the Storm' by The Doors. It's more the feel and structure of the piece that echoes Davis, with smooth, bubbling runs disturbed by brief flashes of violence (in the case of 'Subterranean', by the urgent 'uptight!' choruses). Jonny Greenwood suggested that by attempting to emulate a particular sound, and failing, something else interesting might happen:

> Sometimes a guitar plugged into an amplifier isn't enough. So you hear sounds in your head or you hear sounds on a record and you say, 'I want it to sound like this,' and sometimes it won't, for whatever the reason. I can't play the trumpet so it's not going to sound like *Bitches Brew*... But at least you can try and emulate the atmosphere. You aim for these things and end up with your own garbled version.[6]

This, then, seems to be the Radiohead formula: take a half-remembered creative writing assignment inspired by a surreal, science-fiction poem, a 27-year-old piece of jazz rock created by a man in insane sunglasses, attempt to copy them both, and fail. And yet, at the same time, it works.

This really was turning out to be a mighty peculiar record.

Notes:

[1] Krishna Rau, interview, *Shift*, June, 1996.

[2] Of course, the idea of an outsider bringing an ironic perspective to society also goes back several centuries: for example, Thomas More's *Utopia* (1516); Jonathan Swift's *Gulliver's Travels* (1726); and Thomas Bage's *Hermsprong* (1796). But the concept really came into its own with the advent of science fiction as a specific genre. The movie *The Day The Earth Stood Still* (1951) has the alien Klaatu astonished at the barbarism of humankind; Walter Tevis's 1963 novel *The Man Who Fell To Earth* (filmed by Nicolas Roeg in 1976, with David Bowie) similarly presents earthbound madness through extraterrestrial eyes. A further refinement of the idea comes in Mark Haddon's *The Curious Incident Of The Dog In The Night Time* (2003) which has a first-person narrative with the 'alien' perspective of an autistic teenager; avoiding the "cracks in the pavement" is a classic autistic behaviour.

[3] Doheny, p. 64.

[4] And the aliens aren't subterranean, of course. They stay in their spaceship, which is presumably above the ground, rather than under it.

[5] Paytress, p. 40.

[6] Randall, p. 147.

CHAPTER 6

'EXIT MUSIC (FOR A FILM)' –
THIS IS NOT A DEATH SONG

Romeo: *Here's to my love! O true apothecary!*
Thy drugs are quick. Thus with a kiss I die.
—William Shakespeare, *Romeo And Juliet*

Ceci n'est past une pipe (1926) is one of the most famous paintings by the Belgian surrealist René Magritte. It's a very simple picture. There's a pipe, on a pale brown background. Underneath, in somewhat childish script, is the title, which translates as "This is not a pipe."

Which is ridiculous. Of course it's a pipe. Until you slap your head and make that Homer Simpson noise – of course it's not a pipe! It's a *picture* of a pipe. Magritte's just painted it. He didn't carve it; you can't smoke it. It's made of paint and canvas. And from then on, you look at all art in a different way.

Radiohead pull a similar stunt with the fourth track on *OK Computer*. It wasn't a new song: it was written specifically for the soundtrack of Baz Luhrmann's 1996 Shakespeare adaptation *Romeo And Juliet*. It plays over the final credits, after Romeo (Leonardo DiCaprio) and Juliet (Claire Danes) have committed suicide.

Which explains the title. It's 'exit music' in two senses: death, the leaving of life; and the end of the film, as the audience makes for the EXIT signs.[1] And it's clearly for a film. Which is all pretty self-evident, until you consider the effect the title has on the way you hear the rest of the song.

Yorke began work on 'Exit Music' having seen nothing of Luhrmann's film except a 30-minute rough cut; he was, however, inspired by the 1968 adaptation of the play, directed by Franco Zeffirelli.[2] Superficially at least, they are very different versions. Luhrmann plays around with time and place, relocating the action from 16th Century Verona to modern Venice Beach and replacing daggers with handguns. Romeo's wisecracking sidekick Mercutio becomes a black transvestite; his nemesis Paris is, for some reason, rechristened 'Dave'. At the same time, it's not a 'realistic' situation: the actors speak in Shakespeare's iambic pentameter rather than California slang; the costumes and settings are intense and gaudy, fixing the film in the hyperreal tradition of Luhrmann's other works, *Strictly Ballroom* (1992) and *Moulin Rouge* (2001).

Zeffirelli's film seems, on the surface, to be less ironic, more 'straight'. The actors are dressed in Renaissance costumes; there are no cars or guns; and that's really Italy you see there. But is it actually 'real' as we usually understand it? These are still actors, mouthing lines written by someone else. In fact, they're not even actors: what we see is flashes of light representing actors, on film or tape or the ones and zeros of a DVD. Luhrmann, it could be argued, is more honest, more 'real' in the way he draws attention to the artificiality of what he's doing.

Similarly, Magritte can be seen as more honest than an artist striving scrupulously after realism, because he makes it quite clear that what you are looking at is a clever distribution of pigment on canvas. And Radiohead make the rare move, for musicians, of putting big inverted commas around their song before they've even started.[3]

So, you know what you're going to get, and what you're going to get is film music. Since Radiohead were enjoying themselves at the time with diverse influences beyond the indie-rock clichés, it seemed obvious to take inspiration from one of the greatest film composers of all time, the legendary Ennio Morricone, best known for his work with the director Sergio Leone. In best postmodernist tradition, there are also references to Radiohead's own 'Fake Plastic Trees', from *The Bends*; 'Hushabye Mountain' from the 1968 film *Chitty Chitty Bang Bang*; and the 1991 art-disco single 'Crucified', by the camp, Swedish subversives Army of Lovers.[4]

The track starts with sparse, strummed guitar, which hints at Leone's spaghetti westerns, but owes more to Bob Dylan's soundtrack for Sam Peckinpah's *Pat Garrett And Billy The Kid* (1973) and the prison recordings of Johnny Cash. The big, mournful sound of Morricone comes in at 1:26, with a celestial choir, maybe summoning the doomed lovers to eternal rest. This is replaced by the indecipherable chatter of children, reminding us that the "star-cross'd lovers" are little more than kids. Phil Selway's soft cymbals chime in at 2:35, heralding the lurching arrival of the full drum kit a few seconds later – a trick that Morricone pulled off on his track 'Chi

Mai', which reached No. 2 in the UK charts in 1981, and also served as the theme to the BBC drama series *The Life And Times Of David Lloyd George*. It's the sign for all the emotional stops to be pulled out, as Yorke's voice soars against a backing of mandolins and Colin Greenwood's filthy fuzz bass; before we return to the voice, the guitar and the distant children.

It's a deeply emotional, almost draining experience for the listener; but is that really the effect that Radiohead want? From the title to the influences, the track screams out that it's been written, not as a spontaneous outpouring of teenage angst, but as a commission, a job of work. It's 'For A Film'. Indeed, until it appeared on *OK Computer*, it was only for a film; Radiohead did not allow its use on the *Romeo + Juliet* soundtrack album, where it was replaced by a remix of 'Talk Show Host', from the era of *The Bends*.

The lyrics are appropriate, but hardly autobiographical: Thom is not a 16th Century teenager, and he's performing a role in just the same way that Leonardo DiCaprio performs in the film. In fact, the lyrics offer a superb summary of the narrative arc that Shakespeare's lovers follow: they wake into realisation of their love; they try to escape the tentacles of the family feud that keeps them apart; they fail, and through a combination of misunderstandings, become "one in everlasting peace"; and their death becomes a reproof to the warring Montagues and Capulets, expressed brilliantly in terms of opposing supporters willing a penalty-taker to miss – "we hope that you choke". "I can't do this alone," he sobs; he can't live or love alone, but equally he can't die alone, and Juliet will have to follow him. It's adolescent, inarticulate language that makes the listener remember how young the protagonists of Shakespeare's play really were; Juliet is only 13 years old, a fact that's usually glossed over in modern interpretations, for obvious reasons. Fortunately, Thom resisted his initial instincts to use actual lines from Shakespeare. Cole's Notes be damned; this is as fine a précis of the plot as has ever been written.

The production is superbly atmospheric – Yorke's vocal was recorded in a stone porch in St Catherine's Court to obtain the right ambience – and the arrangement, building to and falling from a soaring, searing peak, can leave you light-headed. But listen closely. That choir of angels is clearly Jonny Greenwood playing a Mellotron.[5] And Yorke's singing is imperfect, with pops and sibilants all over the shop; it makes the performance real, and reminds you that there is a human being here, singing into a microphone, as a producer watches and presses the right buttons. By 3:25 it's clear that, in technical terms, Yorke's pipes really aren't up to the job, as the orchestral opulence swamps him. But it's right: he's choked, just as Romeo and Juliet choked on their poison; he stops breathing; he's frail and imperfect, like all Shakespeare's tragic heroes; and, once again, he's real, with an existence beyond the four minutes and 24 seconds in which this song exists.[6]

In 'Exit Music (For A Film)', Radiohead have created what literary theorists call a metafiction – a narrative that draws attention to its own fictionality. In the same way that Magritte never lets the viewer forget that it's a painting, and Luhrmann throws cinematic artificiality in your face every other frame, the listener is always aware that this is a pop song. Emotional involvement is possible, but you are asked to maintain some level of distance. Complete absorption in the emotional nuances will create nothing but sentimentality; the big evil addressed on the next track.

Notes:

[1] As if to hammer the point home, it's also the last song heard on Grant Gee's Radiohead documentary *Meeting People Is Easy*. Possibly coincidentally, EXIT is a former name for Dignity in Dying, the British pressure group that campaigns for the legalisation of voluntary euthanasia.

[2] Paytress, p. 40. There's ample evidence to suggest that the sexual preferences and fetishes of British males who were at secondary school in the 1970s and 80s can be traced back to the Shakespeare plays they were forced to study for O-level or GCSE. Those who did *Romeo and Juliet* got the memorable chest of the nubile Olivia Hussey; those who did *Macbeth* were presented with the equally attractive bottom of Francesca Annis, in Roman Polanski's 1971 adaptation. Choices, choices...

[3] Other examples: the theme song for the 1980s sitcom *It's Garry Shandling's Show*, which announces, "This is the music that you hear as you watch the credits"; George Harrison's droll, underrated contractual obligation number, 'Only A Northern Song', from The Beatles' *Yellow Submarine* (1968); 'This Is Not A Love Song' (1983) by Public Image Limited; and, of course, Radiohead's own 'My Iron Lung' (see Chapter 2).

[4] Allan F Moore and Anwar Ibrahim, 'Identifying Radiohead's Idiolect' in Tate, p. 144. Army of Lovers were rumoured to be threatening legal action for alleged plagiarism, but it would appear that they forgave Radiohead; by the end of 1998, AoL member Mattias Lindblom was including 'Karma Police' in his solo performances.

[5] Curtis White, 'Kid Adorno', in Tate, p. 13. The question as to whether this artificiality matters depends on one's emotional involvement with the music. Was it important to the young, Smiths-loving Abingdonians that the 'Hated Salford Ensemble' that played the tracks on *The Queen is Dead* by the Smiths (1986) was really Johnny Marr doodling on an Emulator?

[6] Kevin Dettmar, in the Foreword to Tate's anthology (p. xx), summons up the preposterously whiskered ghost of Nietzsche to argue that Radiohead's greatest strength comes in the moments when they're "human, all too human".

CHAPTER 7

'LET DOWN' –
SENTIMENTALLY HANDICAPPED

But it's too much for a young heart to take,
Cos hearts are the easiest things you could break.
—The Jesus and Mary Chain, 'Some Candy Talking'

For many years, Radiohead have banged their heads against the tendency of the music industry to put all performers into neat little marketing boxes; but if a shotgun were put to their heads, they'd probably admit to some allegiance with bands in the camp variously identified as 'indie' or 'alternative'.

By the time *The Bends* was released, it was clear that they were keen to test the boundaries of this designation, a process that continued on *OK Computer*, and went to startling extremes later on *Kid A*. In 1996/7, Radiohead were still essentially a guitar/bass/drums outfit, proudly displaying their allegiance to the heritage of The Smiths, Nirvana, Magazine, Elvis Costello and The Pixies. However, they'd never felt any kinship with the Luddite nostalgists who had embraced the (by now) stultifying 'Britpop' tag.

One of the things that makes *OK Computer* so intriguing is the constant battle between indie-rock roots and a wider, more ambitious musical picture that inhabits the sonic corridors that lead between doors marked 'DJ Shadow' and 'Miles Davis', 'Ennio Morricone' and 'Krzysztof Penderecki'. As each track starts, the listener doesn't know which influence will ease its way between the notes, to challenge the orthodoxy of Rickenbacker feedback and mumbled self-deprecation.

As 'Let Down' begins, it seems that the indie kids have already won, with a knockout in the first round. The instrumental set-up is appropriately raw and primitive: the floor-toms and tambourine echo the minimalist drumming of The Velvet Underground's Moe Tucker, and Bobby Gillespie on *Psychocandy* (1985), the first album by The Jesus and Mary Chain. Guitars jangle and chime, and Thom Yorke sighs and slurs like a student dragged from his celibate bed to a lecture on Sartre on a dull Wednesday morning.[1] With a few tweaks, the first minute could have been plucked from the notorious *NME C-86* compilation, a cassette (remember them?) that gave an identity, for good or evil, to a whole school of guitar bands variously defined (by besotted fans as well as contemptuous critics) as 'twee' and 'shambling'.

But things aren't necessarily as they first appear. Yorke's lyrics avoid the smack-addled solipsism of his black-clad forebears. Instead, we're back into his pet gripes: technology; transport; the crushing (literal in this case) of the dissenting individual. It's a stream of consciousness that's on offer here, rather than a coherent narrative; vaguely connected sentences, rather than full sentences, create a word picture of disappointment and disillusion. "Don't get sentimental," insists the singer, "it always ends up drivel". As Yorke explained:

> Sentimentality is being emotional for the sake of it. We're bombarded with sentiment, people emoting. That's the Let Down. Feeling every emotion is fake. Or rather every emotion is on the same plane whether it's a car advert or a pop song.[2]

He later expanded on this, discussing how the language of advertising had hijacked the legitimate expression of emotion and feeling for its own ends:

> One of the satisfying things about doing *OK Computer* was that I felt we'd gotten to a state where I didn't have to get emotional about what I was doing. The best vocal takes I did were usually first takes where I hadn't gotten into it yet. So I wasn't trying to be emotional. It seems like the most overtly emotional things now tend to be adverts and gospel music... In the advert, the emotions aren't genuine. But if they were – if there was a camera in front of two people genuinely feeling that way, well, everyone's already seen the car advert, so that genuine emotion has been circumvented forever. There are certain emotions you think are trite, certain things you'd never say to your partner because it's corny. Because it's been stolen to sell products.[3]

'Let Down' expresses this need to avoid corny expressions of feeling. In an effort to protect himself from the bullshit of contemporary culture, Yorke (or the narrator whose voice he adopts) must grow a shell that wards off emotional attachment to things that really don't matter. But his emotional protection is nothing more than the fragile carapace of an insect, and he's obliterated beneath the careless boot of capitalism. His startling imagery sums up the resulting mess: "shell smashed, juices flowing, wings twitch".[4]

A constant criticism of the traditional indie mindset was that it encouraged listeners to wallow in self-pity, rather than engaging in the real problems in the wider world. It's also a charge that's been levelled at Radiohead, possibly with some justification when it's applied to early tracks such as 'Creep'. However, by the third album, the band's perspective had expanded beyond frustrated love and tearful self-abasement. In 'Let Down', Yorke and his bandmates seem to be breaking free from the up-its-own-arse attitudes of the genre, without severing all the musical links. Guitars still jangled in St Catherine's Court, after all. The track also retains a crucial paradox of classic indie pop, in the apparent contradiction between the form (chiming, soaring guitars, expressing optimism, even triumph) and the content (lyrics about disappointment and dying insects). As the critic David Stubbs put it, 'Let Down' is "a rapturous, cathedral-like tribute to utter misery."[5]

However, the finished track, which was recorded live at three o'clock in the morning, actually reveals itself to be far more complex, musically as well as lyrically, than the endearing minimalism suggested by the introduction. This is light years on from the sort of thing that The Pastels and The Shop Assistants might have come up with 10 years prior. Jonny Greenwood solos in a different time signature from the rest of his bandmates; the second verse is repeated in the background (presumably by Ed O'Brien) while Yorke mumbles the third; the *Bitches Brew* electric piano hovers under the guitar arpeggios. Structure and sense and decorum are being uprooted before our ears, to mirror the perversity that the lyricist sees unfolding around him.

And by this stage, the 10-year-old alt-rock blueprint is looking distinctly crumpled. The track's lasted well over four minutes, flouting the less-is-more aesthetic of the C-86 generation; and then, as if from nowhere, comes a wibbling synth line that sounds, if anything, like the intro to The Who's 'Baba O'Riley' (perhaps now better known as the theme music for the forensic detective show *CSI: NY*). The defeated indie kids, never handy in a fight, shamble – fists stuffed into their cardigan pockets – back to their bedsits, where they listen to early Primal Scream bootlegs and await their turn. Which never comes.

'Let Down' was an early candidate to be the single that trailed the release of *OK Computer*. The fact that 'Paranoid Android' was chosen instead hints at the conceptual leap that the band were making at the time. 'Let Down' expands upon and extends the model of the indie-pop genre, but it could still conceivably have appeared on *The Bends*, two years previously. The Radiohead of 1995 would simply not have been able to conceive of something like 'Paranoid Android'. This feeling of a band in transition, moving from alt-rock certainties to the scary territories of experimentation, is one of the key components in the success of *OK Computer*.

When, in 2006, the *NME* polled its readers to find out the tracks they'd like Radiohead to play for their first British festival appearances in three years, 'Let Down' finished in second place, pipped only by 'Just', from *The Bends*. Stephen Dalton hinted sardonically at the irony of tens of thousands of people revelling in their own isolation and despair: "One can but hope that we all get to sing along in unity to the delightful line about being 'crushed like a bug in the ground',"[6] he quipped. This is the essential paradox of the indie/alternative mentality: it thrives on difference, alienation, otherness; and yet all these alienated others enjoy meeting up in fields to proclaim their otherness, etc, to a whole bunch of people who are dressed pretty much the same. Can a song still function as a soundtrack to loneliness if everyone appears to know all the words?

Despite the potential of 'Let Down' for this sort of collective expression of self-abasement, Thom Yorke's own performance on the song is relatively restrained and low-key: he sings from a position of cool, clear-eyed detachment, freed not just from sentimental drivel, but from all emotional entanglements. He observes; he describes; he doesn't get involved. It's an attitude that provides the philosophical core of the next track on the album.

N o t e s :

[1] But then the indie aesthetic was always more to do with an attitude and a haircut than a particular way of tuning a guitar or whacking a drum. See Tim Footman, 'Notes Towards... a Definition of Indie', *Careless Talk Costs Lives*, Jan/Feb, 2003; Andrew Collins, 'Wan Love', *The Word*, October 2006; Alistair Fitchett, *Young and Foolish* (Exeter: Stride, 1998), pp. 114-115; and Chapter 24.

[2] Phil Sutcliffe, 'Death Is All Around', *Q*, October, 1997.

[3] Mary Gaitskill, 'Radiohead: Alarms and Surprises', *Alternative Press*, April, 1998.

[4] Randall (p.156) suggests a link with another indie/outsider icon, Kafka's Gregor Samsa (in the 1915 novella *Metamorphosis*), who wakes up to find himself "transformed in his bed into a monstrous insect". Another existential hero comes to mind: Sam Lowry in Terry Gilliam's *Brazil* (1985), who, in his dreams, flies clad in a silver suit of armour, like some kind of metallic dragonfly; but always falls back to earth.

[5] *OK Computer: A Classic Album Under Review* (Sexy Intellectual DVD, 2006). See also Chapter 12.

[6] Stephen Dalton, 'The National Anthems', *NME*, August 19, 2006.

CHAPTER 8

'KARMA POLICE' –
LISTEN TO THE VOICE OF BUDDHA

A young Thai man, believed to be mentally ill, almost completely destroyed one of Bangkok's most revered religious images, the statue of Brahma, the Hindu god of creation, at the Rajprasong intersection early yesterday morning, after which he was beaten to death by a group of angry bystanders. The Erawan shrine housing the statue is one of the city's most popular tourist spots and regularly attracts crowds of worshippers, both locals and tourists. Two street sweepers from Pathum Wan district office have been arrested and charged with the second-degree murder of Thanakorn Phakdeephol, whose father Sayant said he had a history of mental illness and had received psychiatric treatment six years ago when he was 21.

—*The Nation* (Bangkok), March 22, 2006

Thanks to such globally revered figures as Mahatma Gandhi and the Dalai Lama, many westerners perceive Hinduism and Buddhism, the ancient religions that came out of India before the time of Christ, to be one big, fluffy ball of laughter and loveliness. The jolly, fat Buddhas that sit alongside waving cats in Chinese restaurants probably give credence to this view. But it's not that simple.

Without delving too deeply into Comparative Religions 101, these Vedic religions share the concept of *karma*. This can be seen as the spiritual energy that attaches to a person through his or her actions. In a moral sense, it can be positive or negative. A good action – feeding a stray dog, making an offering at a shrine – enhances ones karmic load; an evil action – kicking a dog, desecrating a shrine – drags it down. Since Buddhists believe that a life is merely one link in an eternal cycle of reincarnation (*samsara*), such karma can affect the nature of one's next life. Good people become princes; bad people become insects.

But, in another sense, all karma, positive or negative, is bad, because it ties the individual to the physical realities of the world. The aim of a good Buddhist should be to transcend these realities and attain a state of *nirvana*, where the soul is freed from the cycle of reincarnation.

Karma just happens. It doesn't need someone to impose it: there isn't really a Buddhist equivalent of the Roman Catholic Inquisition, or the Taliban's Ministry for the Promotion of Virtue and the Suppression of Vice. Many Thai Buddhists would argue that the unfortunate man who destroyed the statue was ultimately killed, not by two street-sweepers, but by the torrent of karma that he'd unleashed through his sacrilegious action.

So the notion of a karma police force is nonsensical; which is probably a heavy enough hint that the sixth track on *OK Computer* is not to be taken entirely seriously.

For a start, the song was inspired by an in-joke: whenever someone had attracted the collective wrath of members of Radiohead, someone would call for retribution at the hands of the "karma police". The offenders identified in the lyrics aren't entirely unexpected: the man who "buzzes like a fridge" represents the background noise of industrial technology that provides the overriding theme in *OK Computer*; the girl with a "Hitler hairdo" is surely the same "Gucci little piggy" that Yorke encountered in Los Angeles and described in 'Paranoid Android' (and possibly the snack-packet face on the back cover of the CD booklet; see Chapter 15).

So far, so funny. 'Karma Police' is in the venerable tradition of self-referential (some would say self-indulgent) pop, where the band sings a song about the life of the band, and the audience, in thrall to the whole rock 'n' roll myth, laps it all up: other examples include 'Creeque Alley' by the Mamas and the Papas (1967); 'Smoke On The Water' by Deep Purple (1972); 'Jam-Master Jay' by Run DMC (1984). This time, though, the music tells a slightly different story.

In structure and arrangement, 'Karma Police' is yet another tip of the hat to The Beatles' 'White Album', with particular reference to 'Sexy Sadie'. This, along with 'Helter Skelter' and 'Piggies' was one of the songs believed by Charles Manson to be a signal to launch his campaign of terror (see Chapter 4); Manson, who made one of his acolytes change her name to Sadie, sometimes described his atrocities as "levelling the karma"[1]. But the original target of the song was Maharishi Mahesh Yogi, the guru whose teachings captivated The Beatles in 1967 and 1968 (essentially, between the release of *Sgt. Pepper's Lonely Hearts Club Band* and *The Beatles*), but whose own failings caused John Lennon to walk away in disgust.[2] The Maharishi's creed of Transcendental Meditation encouraged devotees to search for a form of ego death, in which the self was submerged into a greater whole.

Dai Griffiths points out that 'Karma Police' is a song of two halves.[3] It begins at a conventional, medium tempo, with hints not just at 'Sexy Sadie' (the piano being the most obvious element) but also to Radiohead's own 'Exit Music (For A Film)' (see Chapter 6: the acoustic guitar intro; the choir of analogue angels; the delayed return of the drums at 1:37). At about 2:10, Yorke has a moment of revelation: "this is what you get". His voice changes register, as if he's trying to outdo the angels, in preparation for the second key line, "Phew, for a minute then I lost myself". In turn, he's pushed aside by a magnificent display of feedback from Ed O'Brien, the *Pablo Honey* days of "polite guitar" finally behind him.

So what have we got? A song that's quite consciously influenced by the story of an allegedly corrupt guru. A first half of mundane, earthbound reality, distinguished from the second by a moment of clarity, of awareness. "This is what you get when you mess with us" is as succinct a clarification of the law of karma as has ever occurred on a multi-million-selling mid-90s alt-rock masterpiece. You do X, and Y happens. You kick a dog; you come back as a dog.

And then, we're back down to earth. "For a minute there I lost myself," gasps Yorke, blinking. Has he just been dreaming? Or has he actually experienced, however briefly, the loss of self that the Maharishi described as ego death, and classic Buddhist tradition calls *nirvana*, the state at which the soul is freed from all the ties of existence and identity. In English, 'nirvana' is often used in a loose sense, almost as an equivalent to the Judeo-Christian 'paradise' or 'heaven'. It isn't – the soul that attains nirvana is freed from sadness, but also from happiness. Comedy, tragedy, love and hate are left behind. It's a fair bet that the first band to call themselves Nirvana, the Anglo-Irish duo that recorded the pop-psychedelia gem 'Rainbow Chaser' in 1968, opted for the looser, hippy-dippy definition. It's also more than likely that Kurt Cobain was in a less cheery state of mind when he came to name his own band.

Despite the hippy implications, Buddhism can be considered as the ultimate indie rock religion; nirvana as the ultimate punk state of mind. Punk, the creed and aesthetic that informs *OK Computer* and all indie rock before and since, is about blankness, apathy, freedom from the mundane cares, the 'nothing' that generations of rock fans have experienced through the medium of screaming feedback, as they become submerged in the baying crowd. There's a standard phrase that Thai people often use when disaster befalls them or others, and you hear it every day on the Bangkok streets where Thanakorn Phakdeephol met his messy end: "*mai pen rai*". Which translates, very roughly, as "it doesn't matter" or, as Kurt Cobain put it, "oh well, whatever, never mind". Some first-generation punks took the nihilism/nirvana equation to its logical, transcendent conclusion: for example, Poly Styrene of X-Ray Spex, who eventually became a devotee of Hare Krishna. Her demands that we should "Get rid of the synthetic life... Go back and be natural," echo the anti-technology tone of *OK Computer*; her prediction that her music might "turn into the sound of a Hoover"[4] is Yorke's 'fridge buzz', 19 years before its time.

But 'Karma Police' is all a joke, isn't it? Thom Yorke has described the song as "not entirely serious"[5]. As Dai Griffiths points out, the "phew" that prefaces the last line seems to add a layer of irony between the listener and the apparent spiritual connotations in the song; or it takes everything into the territory of a comic strip, or a bedroom farce.[6] It's a joke that seems to have got enough people laughing, though: 'Karma Police' reached number eight in the British charts when released as a single in September, 1997, thus becoming the best-selling comedy Buddhism song since Culture Club's ribtickling 'Karma Chameleon' (1983). It seems on the face of it to be in the long tradition of pop music that adopts the superficial trappings of Eastern religion, without properly engaging with it.

And yet Yorke has described himself as a "hippy" and a "shameless dabbler" in Buddhism[7] who meditates to stave off the madness of touring, until "all the crap has seeped out of my brain"[8];

he's acknowledged *The Tibetan Book of the Dead* as an influence on *OK Computer*[9]; he's played benefit concerts in support of the rights of Tibetan Buddhists against the Chinese authorities, an action that has led to Radiohead being banned from the People's Republic. He even agonises over his own political outbursts, on the Buddhist principle that evil will somehow return to the evildoer. As he explained in 2006:

> I have a problem when I make personal attacks; I always say, "Well, they don't make personal attacks on me." It's bad karma doing that shit. But at the same time, they're pretty good at racking up their own bad karma. I find it very difficult to worry about that level of karma when they're still preaching about democracy.[10]

If 'Karma Police' is indeed a joke song, there seems to be something deeper in there, alongside the gags. Maybe the fat, chortling Buddha in the Chinese restaurant has something to add to the debate after all.

N o t e s:

[1] Paytress, p. 41.
[2] In fact, the charges of sexual misconduct now seem to have been exaggerated; see Quantick, pp. 135-136.
[3] Griffiths, *OK Computer*, p. 61.
[4] Jim Irvin & Colin McLear, *The Mojo Collection* (Edinburgh: Canongate, 2003), p. 415.
[5] Phil Sutcliffe, 'Death is All Around', *Q*, October, 1997.
[6] Griffiths, *OK Computer*, p. 62.
[7] Sylvia Patterson, 'Let's Try and Set the Record Straight', *NME*, 19 May, 2001.
[8] Nick Kent, 'Ghost in the Machine', *Mojo*, August, 2006.
[9] Paytress, p. 37.
[10] Brian Raftery, 'Bent out of Shape', *Spin*, August, 2006.

CHAPTER 9

'FITTER HAPPIER'
AND THE STRANGE DEATH OF
THE ROCK STAR AS WE KNOW IT

That's not writing. It's typing.
—Truman Capote, on the work of Jack Kerouac

Near the beginning of Grant Gee's documentary *Meeting People is Easy*, which chronicles Radiohead's fraught touring existence during and immediately after the release of *OK Computer*, we hear a voice. It's a pleasant voice; the voice of a youngish, educated Englishman. He sounds middle-class, but not posh; there are enough dropped *t*'s to imply that he'd be able to get into the ground of any Premiership football club without being beaten up (although maybe he'd prefer the expensive seats where, according to the former Manchester United captain Roy Keane, they eat prawn sandwiches). This is what the Englishman says:

> Hi, this is Colin from Radiohead and you're listening to 1040 Australia… playing Europe's biggest hits, this is Colin from Radiohead reminding you that you're listening to the Euro-chart Hot 100… What does 'generic radio ID' mean? [A female voice clarifies, there's a brief babble of apology, and the main voice picks up again.] Hi, this is Colin from Radiohead and you're listening to Radio Mix FM 102.7… Hello, this is Ed from Radiohead and you're listening to Radio Centrus… Hi, this is Jonny from Radiohead…[1]

So, who is this nice young man? Colin, the bass guitarist, we presume. He's just playing around, you see, bored with the drudgery of the publicity treadmill, taking off and landing, meeting and greeting but never really talking to anyone, and certainly not able to take in the surroundings of Berlin or Philadelphia or Tokyo. But if the listeners to Radio Centrus heard their customised soundbite in isolation, they'd think it was Ed, the unfeasibly tall guitarist. And why should anyone contradict them? The plot thickens when Colin (or 'Colin' as we'd better call him; for all we know, it could be anyone) gets bored and hands the script over to 'Ed' who reels off his lines in a voice that (if you were half-listening to the radio while driving a car or doing the dishes or painting the ceiling of the Sistine Chapel) would sound pretty much the same as 'Colin'. Maybe it was 'Ed' all along. Or 'Phil'. Who knows?

Despite Thom Yorke's voice-of-a-generation persona (to be fair, not one with which he seems to be happy), Radiohead are a group first and foremost. Writing credits are split five ways; Griffiths' ironic creation of their 60s alter egos as "Tommy York and the Radioheads"[2] was never going to be on the agenda. Thom, Colin, Ed, Jonny and Phil may have specific roles within the organisation, but for each of them their primary identity is as one head of a quintuple hydra. From taking on each other's identities, it's a short step to subsuming any individual notion of identity into the group itself.[3] *OK Computer* is the first Radiohead album where the band members' musical responsibilities (Thom: voice; Jonny: noisy guitar, etc) are not explicitly defined in the accompanying credits. Their significance is limited to membership of something bigger. The rock band; the rock star; the rock guitar hero; even that butt of the best rock jokes, the drummer; all begin to disintegrate before our eyes, as they become absorbed into some indefinable *other*. In *Star Trek* terms, it's a bit like the Borg.

The fact that the radio ID sequence in *Meeting People is Easy* comes immediately after a rendition of 'Fitter Happier' suggests that the latter is placed there for a particular reason: it's more than just background noise. Of all the tracks on the album, 'Fitter Happier' is the furthest from what we have come to define as 'a song', and the recording marks the point at which the sense of each individual contributing a discrete part begins to unravel. (This would, of course, become the standard model for the music on Radiohead's next album, *Kid A*.)

The otherness of 'Fitter Happier', its difference from the rest of the songs on *OK Computer*, is flagged up even before the listener has penetrated the shrinkwrap. In the listing on the back cover, we skip directly from Track 6 ('Karma Police') to Track 8 ('Electioneering'). 'Fitter Happier' appears to be hovering, small and alone, out of synch with the other tracks, of them and yet not quite of them. What's actually happened is that the title has been put into superscript, as if it refers to a footnote. The implication being, of course, that this is what the song is: a footnote; an afterthought; an addendum; a free gift that nobody in their right minds would buy if it were at full price.

It's in lower-case text as well, unlike the other titles, which are in BLOCK CAPITALS.

The idea of certain parts of an album having some sort of 'auxiliary' status was pioneered, inevitably, by The Beatles. Their acid-spiked inventiveness around the time of *Sgt Pepper's Lonely Heart's Club Band* (1967) seemed so uncontainable that it spilled over into the play-out groove (the endless loop variously deciphered as "I could not be any other" and "Fuck me like a superman"). In December of the same year, The Who trumped this with *The Who Sell Out*, which was dotted with satirical advertisements and radio announcements between the songs proper. The Beatles subsequently put an entire un-listed song, 'Can You Take Me Back?', on the 'White Album'.[4]

By the 1990s, the whole phenomenon seemed pretty run of the mill, although some acts were prepared to offer a new slant on the idea. Nirvana, for example, added a track called 'Endless Nameless' to the end of pressings of *Nevermind* (1991), but the listener had to wait about 10 minutes from the end of the 'real' (listed) final track, 'Something In The Way', to get there.

But is 'Fitter Happier' really an extra track? Once you open the case, even before you take the disc out, the situation is unclear. On the inside front cover (ie the back cover of the CD insert booklet) is a handwritten list of songs. 'Fitter Happier' is there, its title written the same size as the others; it's just next to 'Karma Police', rather than after it. In jotting down the listing, someone (Thom Yorke) has temporarily forgotten it; an omission that's harder to disguise when writing with an analogue ballpoint than with a computer keyboard. It seems that the designer, Stanley Donwood, has simply transferred the format of the written notes into typed form.

The status of 'Fitter Happier' was even less ambiguous to pur-chasers of the vinyl double-LP version of *OK Computer*, by 1997 a Luddite minority. For them, the track was in prime position, the opener for the second disc. Apparently, the band even toyed with the idea of opening the whole album with it, until they decided that would be "right over the boundaries of what's decent"[5]. Surely Ra-diohead wouldn't subject a fragile 'non-song' to such an exposed, precarious existence?

And then you listen to it.

At the heart of 'Fitter Happier' is a monotonous, electronic voice that seems to be reciting a list of phrases, forming a checklist for anyone wishing to be a healthy, wealthy member of the consumer society. To start with, these sound like the sort of bland platitudes that pepper the health pages of mid-market newspapers. We are enjoined to take regular exercise, moderate our drinking and cut back on saturated fats; to keep in touch with our friends and our bank statements; to drive safely and give to charity. But pretty swiftly (the track lasts less than two minutes) the prescription begins to change. Entreaties to be kind to animals shift in emphasis, so that the listener identifies with a tortured cat, then a drugged-up pig. The model citizen has, in a matter of seconds, become trapped. He is "fitter, happier and more productive" but only when there is "no chance of escape". Life is not like the brochures; it's "frozen winter shit".

Although these phrases are supposedly disconnected, and pretty much randomly arranged, when put together they create their own reality: the materially comfortable, morally empty embodiment of modern, Western humanity, half-salaryman, half-Stepford Wife, destined for the metaphorical farrowing crate, propped up on Prozac, Viagra and anything else his insurance plan can cover.

The method is not new, of course. In Zürich during World War One, the Dadaists turned sliced-up texts into poetry, a technique rediscovered in the 1950s by the American writers William Burroughs and Brion Gysin. Major modernist works such as T.S. Eliot's *The Waste Land* and James Joyce's *Ulysses* are, in a sense, collages; they pull together texts from numerous sources, to create something that is greater than the sum of its parts. Surreal, apparently disjointed wordplay litters the oeuvres of David Bowie and Bob Dylan (see 'Subterranean Homesick Blues', which leads us back to…)

Of course, this shouldn't suggest that the ordering of the found material in 'Fitter Happier' is in any way random. There's a definite sense of progression, as the listener is lured in gently with the deceptively banal (health advice) via the disturbing ("no chance of escape") to the horrific (the caged pig). The phrases themselves may have an air of randomness, but Yorke gives them a specific structure and order, for maximum political effect. In this regard, his method is similar to that of the Situationists, the Paris-based artistic and political movement that used apparently paradoxical slogans and commercial images to highlight the banality and corruption of contemporary life.[6]

Setting self-help platitudes to music is not new either. 'Fitter Happier' can be seen as the bleak flipside to 'Desiderata' ("Go placidly amid the noise and haste"), the hippyish prose poem that Les Crane made into a Top 10 hit in the United States in 1971.[7] The 1983 single 'Kissing With Confidence' by Will Powers (actually the photographer Lynn Goldsmith, with assistance from Carly Simon) is a more satirical take on the phenomenon; it's interesting to compare Goldsmith's vocoder-treated vocals with the 'Hawking' voice on 'Fitter Happier'. And a couple of years after *OK Computer* was released, Baz Luhrmann (who had, of course used Radiohead's 'Exit Music (For A Film)' in his *Romeo and Juliet* movie) made the frankly bizarre 'Everybody's Free (To Wear Sunscreen)', which topped the UK charts in 1999 thanks to (despite?) lyrical entreaties to "stretch", "floss" and "get plenty of calcium".[8]

These efforts were, deliberately or not, comedy records. 'Fitter Happier' is satirical, but it's satire with a sneer, and that's borne out by the music. Underneath the android nightmare of empty language there are indecipherable snippets of conversation, guitar effects that could have come out of a cheap science-fiction movie, and a slow, sketchy piano line with backing strings, the closest thing to 'a tune' on offer. The guitars bear fleeting resemblances to offcuts from 'Airbag' and 'Let Down' and the piano seems to be from 'Exit Music', although Dai Griffiths hears echoes of Noel Harrison's song 'The Windmills Of Your Mind' from the movie *The Thomas Crown Affair* (1968).[9] Thom claims to have copied the dialogue onto a MiniDisc, from a hotel TV showing the 1975 Sydney Pollack thriller *Three Days Of The Condor*, starring Robert Redford.[10] Hummable, it all ain't. The text itself seems to be: "This is the Panic Office. Section 917 may have been hit. Activate the following procedure."

The lyrics themselves were written (if that's the right word) during a three-month bout of writer's block, during which Yorke could only compile lists, rather than coherent songs. Faced with a collection of mostly fatuous statements on his computer screen, he used the voice synthesizer within the SimpleText application to 'read' it. Since this application is only ever used by blind people and bored people, and Yorke (despite his childhood eye problems) has OK vision, it's pretty clear what his state of mind was when he came up with the idea. Incidentally, the flat, midatlantic tones of the voice synthesizer are similar to the one used by the physicist Professor Stephen Hawking, who lost his natural voice to the effects of motor neurone disease in 1985. This led to the urban myth that it is Hawking himself on the track.[11]

Dai Griffiths has pointed out that, because the synthesized voice removes any possibility of inflexion or intonation from the lyrics, the only way to delve beneath the surface of the borrowed words, and deduce what he really means (if he means anything) is by the use of parentheses in the printed lyrics that form part of the CD packaging.[12] This does make a difference: in the line "will frequently check credit at (moral) bank", the distinction between moral and financial credit is highlighted by the key word being set aside from the rest of the text.[13] It may also be significant that the designer Dan Rickwood (aka Stanley Donwood) has been assigned a share of the copyright for the lyrics – at least in their printed form. How they look, in this case, appears to be as important as how they sound.

So, what have we got? Lyrics borrowed from multiple sources; vocals from a machine; sounds taken from existing songs, or sampled from the television (and subsequently misattributed in the album credits). Is there anything here that can be described as original work by Radiohead, in the way that 'Creep' or 'Fake Plastic Trees' or 'Paranoid Android' is 'by' the band?

Well, like the Dadaist cut-up poems, it's 'by' Radiohead in the sense that the band members chose to put specific sounds together in a specific way, and release the results under their collective name. In the strictest sense, their working method is little different from that of Shakespeare or Bach or Rembrandt, who put words or notes or pigments together in a way that seemed to work. What threw a digital spanner in the works was technology; specifically, sampling technology, a process that makes it possible to use someone else's recorded work as easily as Bach used a single key on the harpsichord.[14]

On the other hand, musicians were playing around with recorded and found sounds way before the advent of sampling. The obvious precedent is 'Revolution #9', which fills a similar role on *The Beatles* to that played by 'Fitter Happier' on *OK Computer*; if only in that they are (without justification) probably the most-skipped tracks on their respective albums.

'Revolution #9' is a confection of sound effects, spoken words and music that is, in some ways, even more challenging to the average listener than 'Fitter Happier' because a) it's four times longer and b) it lacks the unifying thread that the synthesized voice gives to the Radiohead track. What the two have in common is that they challenge the idea of a pop record consisting of a written song that is performed by one or more people; that performance being captured on tape or other medium.[15] Without the supporting evidence printed on the record or CD and their packaging, how can we know that it's The Beatles or Radiohead that we can hear? (In fact, 'Revolution #9' does offer some hints as to its origin. In the section where popular dance crazes of the 1960s are discussed, it's quite clearly John Lennon and George Harrison talking; although it might, of course, have been the actors who provided their voices for the *Yellow Submarine* movie.)

Now we're back to poor old Colin Greenwood and his "generic radio ID". Perhaps the ideal of recorded music being the preserve of identifiable, credited performers and/or writers is just a temporary blip. As Baudrillard put it: "Only with our modern civilization did we find ourself forcibly inducted into this individual existence."[16] We know, pretty much, who recorded *OK Computer* and who wrote *Hamlet*. But further back, there are songs and stories and other great works, the authorship of which is unclear, at least in the sense of having one person entitled to put his or her name on the front cover. Maybe we're returning to a similar situation, where it's become so easy to move digital material around the world, that notions such as authorship and copyright and originality will become so complicated, they cease to have any real meaning. Add to this the rising power of transnational megacorporations; and if what we make and do can disappear into a soup of ones and zeroes and dollars signs, maybe what we are – the sense of humans as individuals – this is Colin, this is Ed, this is Jonny – will disappear in a similar manner.

Again, what Radiohead are doing here is not entirely new. Kraftwerk denied their own existence as musicians, preferring to present themselves as androids or dummies; The Residents similarly lost themselves under their eyeball masks. But for Radiohead, a band with personalities in the public domain, who'd been on the treadmill of tours and promos and interviews and meet 'n' greets, to wipe out their identity as people, as musicians, as stars, is radical and, for the consumer, disorienting.

And yet, at the same time, it's entirely appropriate that they begin the process of losing themselves[17] on this track. Any individual line within 'Fitter Happier' is anonymous, even banal in itself, but gains from its context. Similarly, the impact of the song derives as much from its situation – where it is, sandwiched between two rock songs, on an album released by a major band on a legendary label – as from what it is, what it sounds like.

'Fitter Happier' is not just *about* the death of individuality in the face of global capitalism; it even *becomes* the death of individuality. Not bad, especially when you get change from two minutes.

Notes:

[1] *Meeting People Is Easy: A Film By Grant Gee About Radiohead* (Parlophone, 1998). See also Marshall McLuhan, *Understanding Media* (London: Routledge and Kegan Paul, 1964; Routledge Classics 2001), p. 83.

[2] Griffiths, *OK Computer*, p. 81. In the days of 'Creep', washed-up Australian teen idol Jason Donovan proclaimed his admiration for a new band called 'the Radioheads'. Griffiths is joking: Donovan, probably not.

[3] The Beatles were surely not alone among rock bands in developing the ability to copy each other's autographs faultlessly.

[4] It should be noted that the identity of 'Can You Take Me Back?' as a full song is not accepted by everyone. Quantick (p. 150) includes it; Ian MacDonald, in *Revolution in the Head: The Beatles' Records and the Sixties* (London: Pimlico, 1995, p. 233) dismisses it as a "fragment of between-takes ad-libbing"; it isn't identified on the album's tracklisting. The fact that it segues into the sonic playground of 'Revolution 9' (of which more shortly) adds to the ambiguity.

[5] Clarke, p. 122.

[6] While working on *OK Computer*, Yorke was reading about the Situationists and their finest hour, the Paris riots of May 1968. Paytress, p. 37.

[7] 'Desiderata' was written by Max Ehrmann in 1927; there is an earlier recorded version by, of all people, Leonard Nimoy, under the title 'Spock Thoughts' (1968).

[8] The lyrics were apparently based on a graduation speech by a student at the University of Chicago.

[9] *OK Computer: A Classic Album Under Review*.

[10] The sleevenotes refer to *Flight of the Condor*, although the only film of this name that I could unearth was a 1985 documentary about the Andes, with very annoying panpipe music.

[11] Hawking does appear on the track 'Keep Talking', on Pink Floyd's 1994 album *The Division Bell*. His words are sampled from a television commercial.

[12] Griffiths, *OK Computer*, p. 65.

[13] The blurred distinction between banks and churches was satirised by Samuel Butler in his proto-science fiction novel *Erewhon* (1872); the book also hints at themes of mechanisation and artificial intelligence, which crop up throughout *OK Computer*.

[14] Silent Gray's cover version of 'Fitter Happier' (see Chapter 20) seems to make use of exactly the same voice synthesizer as Radiohead used, meaning that this part of the record is sonically identical; copying the original recording directly would have had the same effect. Does this make it a sample?

[15] Authorship and performance credits for 'Revolution #9' are also a thorny issue. MacDonald (p. 230), accepts the contractual authorship of Lennon and McCartney, and avoids breaking down the tapes by attributing the performance to "Sound collage". Quantick credits "Actual writers: John Lennon/Yoko Ono/George Harrison" (p. 151) and namechecks the same three as performers of "tape loops, spoken vocals" (p. 154). This is not one of the tracks for which Paul McCartney (who had no involvement in the track, much to his annoyance) has asked to have his name placed first in the credits.

[16] Jean Baudrillard, *The Intelligence of Evil or the Lucidity Pact* (Oxford: Berg, 2005), p. 56.

[17] A process to which they refer in 'Karma Police', and would explore further as a musical activity on *Kid A* and *Amnesiac*.

CHAPTER 10

'ELECTIONEERING' –
DON'T VOTE, IT ONLY ENCOURAGES THEM

Mixing Pop and Politics, he asks me what the use is.
I offer him embarrassment and my usual excuses.
—Billy Bragg, 'Waiting For The Great Leap Forwards'

Radiohead are a political band. Collectively or individually, members have made clear their views on globalisation, fair trade, the environment, the Iraq war, the Chinese occupation of Tibet and more. Thom Yorke in particular has been highly vocal in his withering assessment of the political and economic elites that run the world, while at the same time expressing ambivalence about his right as a mere musician to hold forth on subjects beyond the normal limits of his job description. At the same time, politicians have been keen to have some of his glamour and integrity rub off on them, although the singer has been wary of such approaches. In September, 2005, he turned down a chance to meet British Prime Minister Tony Blair, citing his environmental policies and his conduct of the Iraq War as reason enough to refuse. In May the following year, Conservative Party leader David Cameron suggested on the BBC Radio 4 show *Desert Island Discs* that Thom and Jonny played 'Fake Plastic Trees' at his request during a Friends of the Earth benefit, a claim that was dismissed out of hand by Radiohead.[1] They do politics, but they don't do politicians.

But there's a paradox. Yorke's explicit pronouncements are mainly restricted to interviews; only rarely do Radiohead's lyrics express specific political arguments or ideas. They hint; they suggest; there's clearly a political aspect to, for example, 'Paranoid Android', but there's no sign of a coherent viewpoint, let alone an ideology or a strategy. 'Electioneering' is a big, loud exception – or so it seems.

The song begins with a rattle, maybe keys against bars, with a faint hint of the self-referential prison effects that kick off The Rolling Stones' 'We Love You' (1967). Jonny Greenwood's nagging introductory riff is equally Stonesy: indeed, it could have decorated the work of pretty much any guitar band since The Kinks began playing with feedback in 1964. Greenwood's power chords do battle with Phil Selway's clattering, cowbell-enhanced wallops until about 2:35, when he slows for 20 seconds, gearing up for a balls-out solo that would have fans of any other band making that funny heavy-metal, devil's-horn sign with their fingers. The whole package might have slipped neatly onto *Pablo*

Honey, although it probably wouldn't have been so unashamedly macho back then.

In its gleefully derivative *rawk*-ness, 'Electioneering' offers a startling contrast with the preceding track, the arrhythmic, synthesized 'Fitter Happier'. The lyrics, too, seem to be offering an explicit message, as opposed to the implied socio-economic critique contained in the previous song.

But how political is it? Yorke is inhabiting the persona of a corrupt politician seeking votes, who "will stop at nothing" to ensure his grip on power. Buzzwords are thrown in: "voodoo economics" (a phrase popularized by independent candidate Ross Perot in the US Presidential election of 1992); the "riot shields" and "cattle prods" used against anti-globalisation protesters; and the whole reality behind the smoke and mirrors of representative democracy is "just business".

Yorke claims to have been influenced by the writings of three critics of capitalism, the Britons Will Hutton and Eric Hobsbawm, and the American Noam Chomsky.[2] Although they all point out the flaws in big business and global trade policies, the three men differ widely in their perspectives: Hutton is a mainstream social democrat who supports a mixed economy; Hobsbawm offers a more traditional Marxist critique; and Chomsky's views are coloured by the American New Left of the 1960s and a persistently negative view of US foreign policy. If the three were placed in a room together, they'd probably argue with each other as much as focusing on the mutual enemy.

So any argument based on these three sources is unlikely to be coherent; instead, we just get a list of things that are simply 'bad'. Strip the style away from the content and 'Electioneering' and 'Fitter Happier' are essentially the same song. They consist of an ironic voice speaking disconnected phrases that are intended to set off a negative response in the listener.[3] 'Electioneering' simply has more of a tune.

Does this mean that the political aspect of 'Electioneering' is deceptive? It's clearly *about* politics, in the sense that flecks of political discourse are being spat into the microphone. But its structure, like that of 'Fitter Happier', owes something to the Situationist techniques of Guy Debord. Slogans are batted around until they're deprived of meaning, or at least the meaning that nominally adheres to them. Of course, in our current soundbite culture, such techniques aren't restricted to the outer fringes of politics. Phrases such as "voodoo economics" or "free market" or "war on terror" may have had a meaning at one stage, but they quickly become rhetorical tools rather than containers of any particular truth.

The problem is that even when an artist is using words that are intended to be meaningless, there should still be a reason for having them. The refrain "when I go forwards you go backwards and somewhere we will meet" is particularly problematic. James Doheny guesses (presumably after some pretty rigorous chin-stroking) that it might be a hint at Tony Blair's 'Third Way' doctrines that combined the social policies of the Labour Party with free market economics[4]; Dai Griffiths on the other hand admits: "I don't quite follow – are we going to do the hokey cokey?"[5] Ambiguity might be a virtue in the art of the personal, but when dealing with political matters, it just sounds as if Yorke is putting his cross in the box that says 'Don't Know'. Curtis White, however, is more charitable, suggesting:

> Radiohead's aesthetic strategy is not to avoid the enemy but to inhabit it and reorient its energies… this strategy has been taken up less through an explicit 'message' in the lyrics while the music remains more or less standard pop-rock (even if very good pop-rock) and gets taken up more integrally in the textures of the music itself.[6]

This is the case with tracks such as 'Airbag', 'Fitter Happier' and 'Climbing Up The Walls', and it's a state of affairs that came to dominate *Kid A*. The music is so disturbing, so opposed to what rock music tends to be, that it makes us think and feel in new ways, thus creating a political impact of its own, independent of words.

Of course, Radiohead weren't the first or last musicians to do this. The political and social upheavals of the 1960s were as much to do with the alien sound of Jimi Hendrix's guitar as they were about Bob Dylan's lyrics. And when it comes to defying genuinely totalitarian regimes, it's often oblique strategies that work best. During the 1970s, opposition to the Communist government in Czechoslovakia coalesced round a band called the Plastic People of the Universe, who didn't sing about human rights or free speech or the brutal corruption of the Soviet lackeys who ran the country; their influences were Captain Beefheart, Frank Zappa and The Velvet Underground, whose dissidence was expressed via peculiar time signatures, surreal lyrics and pure noise. Tom Stoppard's play *Rock 'n' Roll* is set between the Prague Spring of 1968 and the first Rolling Stones gig in the city, in 1990, after the fall of Communism. In it, Jan, an unwilling dissident who loves The Beach Boys, says:

> What difference does long hair make? The policeman is angry about his fear. The policeman's fear is what makes him angry. He's frightened by indifference. Jirous doesn't *care*. He doesn't care enough even to cut his hair. The policeman isn't frightened by *dissidents*! Why should he be? Policemen *love* dissidents, like the Inquisition loved heretics. Heretics give meaning to the defenders of the faith... But the Plastics don't care at all. They're unbribable. They're coming from somewhere else, from where the Muses come from. They're not heretics. They're pagans.[7]

It was the Plastic People of the Universe that helped to provoke the foundation of the Czech human rights organisation, Charter 77; a process that led eventually to the chain-smoking, Lou Reed-loving playwright Vaclav Havel becoming President after the Communist government had collapsed. Meanwhile, in Britain, the likes of The Clash and Billy Bragg saw Margaret Thatcher elected to three successive terms, and her Conservative Party hanging on to power until 1997; at which point they were replaced by Tony Blair – essentially Margaret Thatcher with a Fender Stratocaster and a marginally better haircut.

So history seems to suggest that it's not words that change minds, but sounds. In Plato's phrase (constantly reiterated during the 1960s): "When the mode of the music changes, the walls of the city shake."[8] Unfortunately, 'Electioneering' doesn't change modes. Nothing much changes, in fact. It's a perfectly decent little post-punk workout, which is very effective in a live setting. The musicianship on display, particularly from Jonny Greenwood and Phil Selway, is excellent. Considered as a whole, however, it's not new and it's not different. No walls were shaken during the making of this music. Not only could it be a Radiohead track from five years before; with a different singer it could be any one of a dozen guitar bands from the 1990's. Oasis, say; or Nirvana. Maybe even Stereophonics. Martin Clarke describes it as "Radiohead's most difficult song"[9], which is preposterous. The only difficult thing about it is wondering what the hell it's doing there.

Actually, that's not entirely fair, and the Stereophonics dig was a bit harsh. 'Electioneering' serves two specific purposes within *OK Computer*: it provides a few minutes of breathing space, positioned as it is between the two most challenging songs on the album; and it demonstrates the overall range to which Radiohead can aspire. Returning once again to the model of The Beatles' 'White Album', mind-blowing tracks such as 'Happiness Is A Warm Gun' and 'Revolution #9' seem even better because they're bundled with mundane rockers like 'Helter Skelter' and one-joke efforts such as 'Rocky Raccoon'. It's all right; it's served its purpose.

Simon Reynolds identifies *OK Computer* as the moment where the band defined themselves against the "anti-intellectualism and vacant hedonism"[10] represented by the likes of Oasis. 'Electioneering' is the exception; as another band might have put it, it's pretty vacant.

Lapsing back into politician-speak, can we draw a line under this, please?

Notes:

[1] Craig McLean, 'All Messed Up', *Observer Music Monthly*, June 2006.
[2] Paytress, p. 43.
[3] Throughout *OK Computer*, Yorke speaks in various voices that aren't his own (see Chapter 16). Only in 'Fitter Happier' and 'Electioneering' does his character express views that are diametrically opposed to what he actually means. ('Climbing Up The Walls' is too ambiguous to call.)
[4] Doheny, p. 75.
[5] Griffiths, *OK Computer*, p. 69.
[6] White, 'Kid Adorno', in Tate, p. 13.
[7] Tom Stoppard, *Rock 'n' Roll* (London: Faber and Faber, 2006), p. 48. See also Richie Unterberger, *Unknown Legends of Rock 'n' Roll* (San Francisco: Miller Freeman, 1998).
[8] First he quotes Baudrillard and Deleuze, now it's Plato. Jesus.
[9] Clarke, p. 122.
[10] Simon Reynolds, 'Dissent into the Mainstream', *The Wire*, July, 2001.

CHAPTER 11

'CLIMBING UP THE WALLS' - THE HORROR, THE HORROR

*Later, after I had fallen asleep with the jungle in my ears,
I dreamed of knives and faces, and gigantic alien creatures which
were half-lobster and half-wasp.*
—Richard Lloyd Parry, *In The Time Of Madness*

'Climbing Up The Walls' is the scary one. But I didn't really
understand how scary until I met Richard Lloyd Parry in an Irish
pub in Bangkok. It was a fortnight or so since Thanakorn Phakdeephol (see Chapter 8) had his unpleasant interview with the karma
police, only a couple of kilometres away.

Richard is the Asia editor for *The Times* of London, and the
author of *In The Time Of Madness*, an eye-witness account of the
fall of Indonesia's mystic dictator President Suharto, and the mas-
sacres on East Timor. We'd been earnestly dissecting Asian politics
and the future of blogging, and then I told him that I've just signed
the contract to write a book about Radiohead.

"When I was in Indonesia," said Richard, and for a few seconds, he seemed somewhere else. By the end of the week he would
be in a Tokyo hospital with malaria, but neither of us knew this yet.
"When I was in Indonesia in 1997, *OK Computer* was my soundtrack. I played 'Climbing Up The Walls' over and over again. The
lyrics… That sound at the beginning. Insects, helicopters. It just…
fitted."

'Climbing Up The Walls' does indeed sound as though it's
coming through the jungle with murderous intent. The twitchy electronic stabs that hint at unfriendly insects that you never studied in
school biology lessons; and then the relentless, metallic percussion.
The listener becomes Marlow in Joseph Conrad's *Heart Of Darkness* (or his counterpart Willard, in Francis Coppola's 1979 movie
Apocalypse Now). But then you realise that it's not a real jungle,
a specific area in Congo or Vietnam; it's the unspecified jungle of
our nightmares, and the equally ill-defined intruder who inhabits it.

Yorke's voice enters about half a minute in, high and distorted, like a herald angel gone to the Dark Side. Apart from a distant
acoustic guitar, he's the only thing that provides a noticeable tune;
the rest is atmosphere, effects. And then, at about 1:31, we hear

strings, playing a nagging, insistent riff that builds alongside the clanks and chirrups until, at 3:07, Yorke howls (in anguish or terror, or maybe even delight) and we're thrown into a brief, chaotic guitar solo. The singer staggers back for a final, primal bellow, but then we return to the jungle again, with only the drums and the strings and those bloody insects.

It's a profoundly disturbing soundscape that's more than matched by the lyrics. But both work on the basis of implication and connotation, rather than outright shock value.

'Climbing Up The Walls' seems, on the face of it, to be about an intruder, potentially a killer, who is able to enter a family home. This is not some opportunistic raider; he seems to be a watcher, a stalker.[1] Yorke inhabits him totally, distinguishing the 'I' character (associated with penetrative, invasive imagery: "I am the key to the lock"; "I am the pick in the ice") with the 'you': the listener; the potential victim; the one whose duty is to "tuck the kids in safe to-night". This is the mindset of Little England (and Middle America), it would appear. A neat little domestic haven, disturbed only by the threat of 'the other', which might be represented by burglars, pae-dophiles, immigrants, asylum-seekers, terrorists, drug-dealers, the European Union, the United Nations, disease, traffic wardens, mo-bile-phone masts... any or all of the threats that assail decent, hard-working families in these dangerous times, if we believe middle-market, tabloid newspapers and their equivalents in other media. Do *you* know where your child is?

But it's not that straightforward, is it? Go back. Listen again. "The key to the lock". Would an outsider have a key? "You'll only see my reflection". Whose face do we only see as a reflection, never as a reality? "Open up your skull".

Every few months a horror story erupts, somewhere in the world, about a happy child being abducted by a stranger, sexually abused and, almost invariably, killed. Not surprisingly, such crimes provoke horror and revulsion and anger. It's not only that pain and degradation has been inflicted on an innocent child; it's a blow against the stability and comfort that most of us enjoy in the de-veloped world. The instinct is to put up defences, install panic but-tons and alarms, not to let our children play outside. And we expect our governments to do something. In 1996, the year that 'Climbing Up The Walls' was recorded, Congressman Dick Zimmer authored United States Public Law 104-105, known as 'Megan's Law' in reference to the rape and murder of seven-year-old Megan Kanka in New Jersey, two years before. This federal law requires states to develop procedures for advising residents when a convicted sex offender is living nearby.

Which may help parents sleep more soundly, and may well have protected little Megan Kanka, but it rather misses the point; that the majority of sex offences and acts of violence are committed not by strangers, but by people known to the victim. They're people who can't be kept out, because they already have "the key to the lock in your house". After a few listens, you realise that the 'I' and the 'you' in 'Climbing Up The Walls' are one and the same. You tuck the kids up. They trust you. They love you. But your smile is waning; it's all getting too much for you; you're climbing up the walls. What happens when the light is off? From the earliest myth of Adam and Eve to the latest post-postmodern theorists, we are all capable of evil. At the risk of provoking the wrath of Dai Griffiths, I'll bring in Baudrillard one more time: "In the 'intelligence of evil' we have to understand that it is evil that is intelligent, that it is it which thinks us – in the sense that it is implied automatically in every one of our acts."[2]

However, as with most of the tracks on *OK Computer*, this isn't 'about' any one specific thing. Yorke has suggested that the roots of the song lie in the period when he worked in a mental hospital, although 'madness' is distributed much more widely than the inhabitants of those Gothic edifices. "Some people can't sleep with their curtains open," says the lyricist, "in case they see the eyes they imagine in their heads every night, burning through the glass."[3] There's a man born to tell ghost stories.

As in 'Subterranean Homesick Alien', Yorke flips between identities and perspectives, creating a situation where the listener can only grasp at snippets of description, rather than build up a coherent narrative. And as with several of the other tracks on *OK Computer*[4], there's something cinematic about it. It plays with a number of traditions: the slasher movie of the sort that was mercilessly spoofed by *Scream* (Wes Craven, 1996) and its various sequels and variants; the explosion of films that followed the lead of *The Usual Suspects* (Bryan Singer, 1995), playing tricks with identity and morality (and thus with the emotions and reactions of the audience)[5]; and, of course, the film from which both these traditions spring, Alfred Hitchcock's *Psycho* (1960).

Psycho – and here's a big, fat SPOILER ALERT if, by any chance, you haven't seen it – is a film that whips the narrative rug out from under the viewer's feet, not once, but twice. It begins as the story of a woman who has stolen money from her employer; then turns into the story of a mysterious, barely-seen old lady who murders her; and finally resolves itself as having been the story of an insane young man who inhabits the identity of his dead mother when he feels the urge to kill.[6] The traditional cinematic morality of heroes and villains is upended; we begin the movie rooting for the adulterous thief, and end feeling sorry for a psychopath. In a similar way, 'Climbing Up The Walls' runs a strong magnet over our moral compasses, as we find ourselves inside the mind of (presumably) someone who is about to deliver "15 blows to the back of the head" of a sleeping child.

The *Psycho* association is accentuated by the string arrangement on the track, which seems to echo Bernard Herrmann's film score. However, its roots lay in the work of the Polish composer Krzysztof Penderecki, in particular his *Threnody to the Victims of Hiroshima* (1960)[7]. Although Jonny Greenwood's string arrangement manages with just 16 instruments (Penderecki wrote for 52), he maintains the technique of having instruments playing a quarter-note apart from each other, exacerbating the horrific effect. The insect noises at the beginning of 'Climbing Up The Walls' also owe something to a discordant passage that erupts about a minute into the *Threnody*.[8]

The use of strings on pop records had become something of a cliché: as Jonny himself put it, "I got very excited at the prospect of doing string parts that didn't sound like 'Eleanor Rigby', which is what all string parts have sounded like for the past 30 years."[9] When playing the song live, and deprived of strings, Greenwood tunes a transistor radio to local classical music and talk stations, augmenting his bandmates' guitars and drums with random sounds. The technique was pioneered in the 1950s by avant-garde composers such as John Cage; these in turn influenced The Beatles, who used 'found sound' on tracks such as 'Tomorrow Never Knows', 'I Am The Walrus' and 'Revolution #9'.

Oddly, for a recording that relies so much on its overall sound and arrangement, as much as on its strengths as a song, 'Climbing Up The Walls' is the only track from *OK Computer* to have been issued in a remixed form (the two bonus tracks on the second CD single of 'Karma Police'). The version by Zero 7 is pretty awful. Snippets of Astrud Gilberto recast the song as some kind of coffee-franchise jazz, the sort of not-quite-jazz that might one day end up on a *Café del Mar* compilation; Groove Armada without groove; Air (the band) deprived of oxygen. Those Penderecki strings turn up towards the end, but by that time we've downed our overpriced Frappuccino®s and left the building. Fila Brazillia, in their offering, seem to have more of a grasp of the mood and atmosphere behind the song, infecting it with a wheezy, dubby ambience, maybe Augustus Pablo on a very off day; at one point, Yorke's voice transforms into something like the computer tones of 'Fitter Happier'. It's interesting, but doesn't add that much to the original, which remains one of Radiohead's greatest, most unsettling recordings; not just on *OK Computer*, but across the band's whole career.

In the final analysis, the song's impact derives from its vagueness. It alludes to unspeakable evil, without offering specifics. In this instance, it's similar to the work of one of Thom Yorke's favourite authors, the deadpan Japanese fabulist Haruki Murakami. As the singer says of Murakami's books: "In them are all these shadows which are like this malignant force. He never comes into contact with it, but it's pushing people."[10] This lack of contact, lack of engagement, lack of definition can at first seem like a cop-out, but in the long run it makes Murakami's – and Yorke's – images of evil seem even more terrifying.

Although 'Climbing Up The Walls' is imprecise about the true source of the terror at its core, it dares to confront the terror itself. Yorke can be maddeningly allusive in his lyrics, but he doesn't shy away from topics simply because they are difficult or unpleasant. As he told the *NME* in 2001:

> The reason you create music or art or write is in order to put things in a way you can possibly deal with. And death is one of those areas. But we don't seem to spend much time with it, do we? If you're accused of being morbid or bleak then you're onto a good thing, I'd say. 'Cos our culture is the most fucking desperate culture desperately trying to avoid anything vaguely depressing, which is alarming, because what's the result? Well, we all know what that is, don't we? We're at a time when we are being presented with undeniable changes in the global climate and fundamental issues that affect every single one of us, and it's the time we're listening to the most hokey shite on the radio and watching vacuous bullshit celebrities and desperately trying to forget about everything. Which is fine, you know, but personally speaking, I can't do that. With what I do, it's not even to do with necessarily taking yourself seriously, it's just to do with, 'Well, no, I think we use music as a way of turning bad energy into good energy. Or making something out of inexpressible emotion, which could be useful'.[11]

Notes:

[1] David Stubbs suggests a link with the stalker anthem 'Every Breath You Take' (1983) by the Police; *OK Computer: A Classic Album Under Review*

[2] Baudrillard, p. 160.

[3] Paytress, p. 44.

[4] 'Subterranean Homesick Alien' again; 'Airbag', slightly; 'Exit Music', obviously; 'Lucky'.

[5] These include: *Face/Off* (John Woo, 1997); *Fight Club* (David Fincher, 1999); *The Sixth Sense* (M. Night Shyamalan, 1999); *The Others* (Alejandro Amenabar, 2001). But, you say, most of these were released after *OK Computer*. Go on, read the introduction again. That bit about Philip K Dick.

[6] *Psycho* was based on a 1959 novel by Robert Bloch, whose short story 'Enoch' (1946) has a number of parallels with 'Climbing Up The Walls'. It is narrated by a serial killer, who claims his crimes are the responsibility of someone or something called Enoch, who lives inside his head. Enoch's modus operandi is to bore into the skulls of his victims and eat their brains.

[7] The piece had previously been sampled by the Manic Street Preachers on their single 'You Love Us' (1991).

[8] Doheny, p. 77. Penderecki's music was also used on the soundtracks of two other classic chillers: *The Exorcist* (William Friedkin, 1973); and *The Shining* (Stanley Kubrick, 1980).

[9] 'The Making Of *OK Computer*' *The Guardian*, December 20, 1997.

[10] Mat Smith, 'Big in Japan', *Arena*, September 2003. Samuel JP Shaw's interesting comparison between Radiohead and Murakami is at Joseph Tate's site, http://www.pulk-pull.org/essay/where-murakami-ends-and-radiohead-begins-a-comparative-study-by-samuel-jp-shaw/

[11] Sylvia Patterson, 'Let's Try and Set the Record Straight', *NME*, 19 May, 2001.

CHAPTER 12

'NO SURPRISES' AND THE BEAUTY OF DESPAIR

Sometimes days go speeding past,
Sometimes this one seems like the last.
—Sparklehorse, 'Sad And Beautiful World'

After the psychological torment of 'Climbing Up The Walls', the next track appears, initially at least, to offer some sort of relief. Ed O'Brien's gently picked guitar is joined by that most childish of instruments, the glockenspiel, providing a hypnotic, restful refrain. Thom Yorke's voice enters at 0:25, soft and subdued. The rhythm section hovers in the background; wordless vocal counterpoint and soft, synthesised strings weave in and out of the melody. It's like a Belle & Sebastian song played by intelligent eight-year-olds, and it's quite lovely.

But in Radioheadland, of course, nothing is quite what it seems. With 'No Surprises', the first song from *OK Computer* recorded at Canned Applause, we return to the realms of middle-class domesticity, a place previously hinted at on *Pablo Honey*'s 'Vegetable' ("I ran around in domestic bliss") and 'Black Star' from *The Bends* ("I get home from work and you're still standing in your dressing gown").[1]

In fact, Thom had come up with the original idea for 'No Surprises' towards the end of 1995, when Radiohead were supporting REM on their Monster tour. The first draft was called 'No Surprises Please', and in the early stages was performed solely on acoustic guitars. The lyrics were rather different, but what remained consistent between the two versions was the domestic scenario. In 'No Surprises Please', the "no alarms" are literal, the result of the protagonist's clock and watch stopping. There's also a reference to a girl who won't "take off her dress when bleeding in the bathroom", which seems to echo the recurrent blood/menstruation motifs of the American lo-fi songwriter Bill Callahan, aka Smog.[2] The black mood of the original version deepened as the band worked on it; emotional claustrophobia and dissatisfaction with a relationship developed into abject despair.

In the finished, recorded version, the first four words seem to offer love and happiness. "A heart that's full..." is a romantic cliché, full of love, bursting with joy. And then they have to go and spoil it with "...up like a landfill." The safety and security offered by the salaryman's tedious nine-to-five has become oppressive and deadly, choking him so slowly that he barely notices it. He's like Bill Foster, the Michael Douglas character in Joel Schumacher's 1993 movie *Falling Down*: at some point, something's got to give, and the only question is whether he will explode or implode. (Schumacher also uses the supremely Yorkean metaphor of a traffic jam to represent the pressures of Foster's life; see Chapter 3.)

It's still the same anti-capitalist thread that runs through *OK Computer*, but this time on an intimate, human scale. The little man from 'Subterranean Homesick Alien' knows he'll never get a ride in a flying saucer, or even smell "the warm summer air". The jack-nifed juggernauts, the motorways and tramlines have squeezed all the pleasure out of his life. All that's left for him is one final whiff of carbon monoxide, and then silence. It's effectively the same story as 'Climbing Up The Walls',[3] with a slightly different ending; the frustrations of being a tiny cog in the industrial mechanism drive the protagonist to suicide, rather than murder. Dave Thompson traces a thematic link to the death of Kurt Cobain,[4] one of the tortured rock icons whose fate was held up as a warning to Thom Yorke in the early years of Radiohead. But it's not even a romantic, bleakly glamorous rock- or movie-star suicide, of the sort depicted in 'Exit Music (For A Film)'; this is just one more statistic, a nondescript, middle-aged man found slumped across the front seats of a nondescript hatchback in an utterly nondescript suburban garage.

Or is it? Some commentators have suggested that 'No Surprises' deals not with an actual suicide – the ending of a life – but with someone who doesn't live that life to the full. Barney Hoskyns suggests that the message is about taking risks, about daring to confront life's alarms and surprises, and that living without this full-on attitude is fairly pointless. David Stubbs argues that the lyric is about "absenting yourself", and contrasts it with songs such as Ozzy Osbourne's 'Suicide Solution' (1981) that became controversial in the mid-1980s for supposedly encouraging teen suicide.[5] Whether or not the song is about suicide in a literal sense, or about only daring to live an incomplete life, it's clear that Yorke sees such behaviour in a negative light. However, he doesn't blame the character in question; he's a victim of the system.

At the same time, this political angle is only implied, and the one part of the lyric that seems to condemn the system explicitly is the line about bringing down the government. At first this was just a throwaway manifestation of the central character's disillusionment, but it began to attract disproportionate attention at concerts from about 2003, especially in the United States. However, anti-Bush heckling is not the focus of the song. There is indeed a political subtext at work, but it's very subtle, especially when compared to the crass slogans of 'Electioneering'. And herein lies its danger; because of the focus on mundane domesticity, it can feel as if Yorke is having a sly dig at the boring, golfing, *Daily Mail*-reading bourgeoisie.[6] For a quintet of self-confessed posh boys, this is dangerous territory.

What saves the song is the tenderness with which we are allowed to perceive the doomed central figure, and the uncertainty that comes from having such a ravishing, soothing melody coupled with such downbeat subject matter. Joseph Tate identifies Yorke (or the characters he inhabits) as having some psychological problem when it comes to confronting beauty. In 'Creep' he debases himself before the gorgeous object of his affections; in 'No Surprises', "such a pretty house, such a pretty garden" is heartfelt; but a four-bed semi with a two-car garage (the sort of thing that the *Daily Mail* perceives as being emblematic of a successful, stable, respectable life) is, in the final analysis, not quite enough to live for.[7] One of Yorke's original ideas for the album's title (see Chapter 2) explicitly referred to the dream of home-ownership, and its attendant perils. He understands the attraction of such a lifestyle, and isn't damning those who build their world around it.

It's the system that's at fault, not the individual. The illusion of beauty and perfection presented by such glib catchphrases of the free market as "the home-owning democracy" masks the desperation underneath. Yorke said the sonic effect he was after was "the sound of newly fitted double glazing – all hopeful, clean and secure".[8] As with 'Fitter Happier', then, the song becomes its own subject matter, presenting a glossy, hollow edifice that disguises its real identity.

The combination of a beautiful arrangement with a sense of implied regret is common to several of the tracks cited by the band as influences on the song. The opening guitar sound takes its inspiration from The Beach Boys' 'Wouldn't It Be Nice?', on *Pet Sounds* (1966); there are also hints of Louis Armstrong's 'What A Wonderful World' (1968) and 'Sad And Beautiful World', from *Vivadixiesubmarinetransmissionplot* (1995) by Sparklehorse. Dai Griffiths suggests a link to The Smiths' 'Girlfriend In A Coma' (1987), another song with a bitter lyric bundled up in a gorgeous tune; Alex Ogg calls 'No Surprises' "an anti-nursery rhyme".[9]

Whether or not 'No Surprises' is a suicide song as such, the mood of depression is inescapable. Such themes have led to the glib, but somehow understandable suggestion that Thom Yorke himself suffers from depression, or some other mental health problem. He has dismissed these intimations many times, while admitting to being moody, thin-skinned, pessimistic and prone to worry. As he said to *Spin* magazine in 2006: "I have many bleak thoughts. Don't get me started, man. It's one of my specialties." He lashed out at the idea of taking antidepressants: "GlaxoSmithKline's legacy to the world is these poor bastards who can't get off Prozac. That's a fucking evil organization." But as for depression itself? "Maybe. I mean, I can never work out if it's depression or just lack of energy."[10]

The wintry strain of melancholy made 'No Surprises' an appropriate choice for a release in January 1998. Despite the fact that the album had by that time been available for six months, something clicked with British record-buyers who were enduring their own customary post-Christmas comedown, and the single achieved a top-five placing.

Notes:

[1] Doheny, p. 79.

[2] For example, 'Bathroom Floor' from *Wild Love* (1995).

[3] The lyrics for 'Climbing Up The Walls', as printed in the CD booklet, include the line: "do not cry out or hit <<the panic button>>hit the Al Arm", although many of these words do not seem to be included in the final, recorded version. Compare this with the repeated "no alarms" in 'No Surprises'.

[4] Dave Thompson, *Alternative Rock* (San Francisco: Miller Freeman, 2000), p. 575.

[5] Both comments from *OK Computer: A Classic Album Under Review*. Judas Priest's song, 'Better By You, Better Than Me' (1978) also provoked a court case when it was alleged to have provoked two teenagers to shoot themselves; in a less rowdy vein, 'Asleep' by The Smiths (1985) was criticised for appearing to glamorise suicide.

[6] An accusation that has also been made about 'Piggies', on the 'White Album'. See Quantick, p. 112; MacDonald, p. 253.

[7] Tate, p. 8.

[8] Paytress, p. 44.

[9] Both comments from *OK Computer: A Classic Album Under Review*.

[10] Brian Raftery, 'Bent out of Shape', *Spin*, August, 2006.

CHAPTER 13

'LUCKY' –
HOLDING OUT FOR A HERO

"He is a decent fellow, the President, isn't he?" he asked
Chance.
"Yes," said Chance, "though he looks taller on television."
—Jerzy Kosinski, *Being There*

By the time *OK Computer* was released, 'Lucky' was two years old. The tune has its roots in some soundcheck strumming that Ed O'Brien extemporised while Radiohead were playing a string of Japanese dates in June, 1995; within weeks it had become a fully-fledged component of the band's set-list. However, they had no immediate intention to record it until a request came from former Roxy Music member/Bowie collaborator/U2 producer/inventor of ambient music, Brian Eno; he wanted a contribution to an album he was organising for War Child, a charity helping children affected by the war in Bosnia.

Radiohead were more than happy to offer their assistance in such a worthwhile cause, but at the same time they were uneasy about re-entering the recording studio so soon after the fraught experiences they'd had while making *The Bends*. To add to the pressure, the album had a central concept (or, if you prefer, gimmick). All tracks were to be recorded on one day, Monday, September 4, 1995;[1] the CD was scheduled for release the following Saturday. The band's unstructured, deadline-free, see-how-things-go approach seemed totally unsuited to these restrictions, but in the event they adapted well to the change in methodology.

In artistic terms, the album – entitled *Help* – didn't quite come off. In keeping with the mid-90s vibe, there was lots of adequate, guitar-based rock-pop, whether it was Britpop (Oasis, Blur, The Boo Radleys) or bands that could fit into the Britpop box without too much squeezing (The Stone Roses, The Charlatans, Manic Street Preachers, Suede, Radiohead themselves). A few dance-influenced acts (Orbital, Portishead, Massive Attack) provided variety; but there were a lot of cover versions, and rather too much celebrity back-slapping. (Noel Gallagher brought Johnny Depp in to play on the Oasis track, and then formed an impromptu supergroup with Paul Weller and Paul McCartney for a reworking of The Beatles' 'Come Together'.)[2]

It wasn't, on the whole, the sort of company with which Radiohead tended to feel comfortable; and, appropriately enough, 'Lucky' sounds quite unlike anything else on the album. Not that it doesn't share Britpop's retro tendencies, but it points them in a different direction; 'Lucky' is a wholehearted nod to classic album rock. At times the song seems to represent how a guitar shop must have sounded in about 1974: it starts like Neil Young in acoustic mode; erupts into a soaring, space-age lead of the sort that Bernie Leadon provided for The Eagles;[3] calms slightly into something more like David Gilmour of Pink Floyd; then a virtual Jimmy Page rushes in, straight from his day job with Led Zeppelin. The whole thing wouldn't be out of place on one of those compilations with a big American car on the cover.

Further listening to 'Lucky' indicates that it's closer to the Radiohead template than it might appear. Before the guitar heroics start up, there's a peculiar, synthesised texture, not unlike the insects and strings they would later use on 'Climbing Up The Walls' (see Chapter 11). The end is odd, too; there's no big, climactic chord, or even a faded solo. Thom just stops, as if in mid-sentence. And the lyrics are rather different from the sort of thing that Don Henley or Robert Plant might utter.

The context is rather similar to that of 'Airbag'; an unnamed narrator survives a transport catastrophe. But this time, it's bigger and more spectacular, as he is pulled from that modern emblem of the fragility of life, the air crash. When airliners crash, it makes the international news; when it's a juggernaut, it's usually only a local story, unless it causes major traffic problems, or if something amusing – tomato ketchup, say, or sunblock – ends up spread across the road. Of course, since 9/11, we think of air crashes as something more than a simple loss of life. There is inevitable media speculation about terrorist activity; and even if this is disproved, the event forces us to reconsider the fragility of the modern, industrial world, and the place of humanity in it. The artist Damien Hirst clearly overstepped the mark when he said that the 9/11 terrorists had created something "visually stunning" and "a kind of artwork in its own right",[4] but at the same time it's possible to see a degree of truth in his arguments. In a jaded, visually numbed cultural environment, people often only respond to something as terrible and spectacular as a plane disaster. The phrase "car-crash TV" was coined to describe something so bad (in an aesthetic and/or moral sense) that people are compelled to watch against their better instincts. Perhaps now, a car crash isn't quite enough.

Moreover, the air crash is a truly rock 'n' roll way to go. Think Buddy Holly; think Lynyrd Skynyrd; think Otis Redding who, like Yorke's character, was pulled out of a lake. The difference being that, in 'Lucky', the narrator survives and becomes "a superhero". The Christ-like hero of 'Airbag' is redefined as a muscle-bound fantasy figure in tights; although, of course, what are Superman and Batman today if not secular Christ substitutes?

In the event, little of superheroic proportions seems to happen. He is "standing on the edge"... of what? Who is the mysterious Sarah who is asked to kill him (again, just to reinforce the immortality motif)? He is summoned by the head of state, but doesn't have the time. There's an obvious thematic link with cinematic survivors such as Jeff Bridges' Max Klein in *Fearless* (Peter Weir, 1993), who walks away from a plane crash and, on the movie poster, is depicted "standing on the edge" of a skyscraper. A later example is David Dunn, in M. Night Shyamalan's *Unbreakable* (2000). Dunn, who survives a train crash that kills everyone else, proves himself to be a genuine hero (well, he *is* played by Bruce Willis), but the protagonist of 'Lucky' sounds more like a fantasist; maybe the cousin of the man picked up by extra-terrestrials in 'Subterranean Homesick Alien' (see Chapter 5). Rather than the square-jawed heroes of Marvel and DC comics, the protagonist seems to be closer to some distinctly anti-heroic archetypes, little men who find themselves, accidentally, on a big stage: think *Zelig* (Woody Allen, 1983); *Forrest Gump* (Robert Zemeckis, 1994); Chance the gardener in Jerzy Kosinski's novella *Being There* (1971), filmed by Hal Ashby in 1979, with Peter

Sellers.[5] Chance is a simple-minded man, a holy fool, whose sole contact with the world has been via television and whose meaningless platitudes are taken as profound insights by the major business and political players in whose company he now moves. The power of mass media, and of slogans; and the moral vacuum at the heart of global capitalism; it's a very Radioheady book.

'Lucky' was chosen as the lead track of a *Help*-related EP (alongside tracks by PJ Harvey and Guru that had not appeared on the album). Released two months after the album, and not long after 'Just' (the third single from *The Bends*), it stalled at number 51 in the UK charts. At first, the band resisted the idea of including it on *OK Computer*, and considered the compromise option of remixing it. Yorke, however, realised that the original recording seemed to tie in, thematically and musically, with the other songs they were laying down. "'Lucky' was indicative of what we wanted to do," he said. "It was like the first mark on the wall."[6] The song had more success, albeit at arm's length, when a live version (recorded in Florence, Italy, in October, 1997) appeared on the second CD single of 'No Surprises', which reached number four in the British charts in early 1998; the original version of 'Lucky' was released as a single in France at the end of 1997.

There must have been a strong temptation for the band to end the album with 'Lucky'; it's a big, emotional track, and with its lyrical references harking back to the first track, there would be a sense of neatness and circularity; possibly even highlighting the notion of *OK Computer* as a (whisper it not) concept album. But Radiohead have never liked to do the obvious thing; moreover, since they had so many qualms about including it at all, they would have been wary to put it in such an exposed position. Instead, that honour goes to...

Notes:

[1] An exception was made for Sinéad O'Connor's cover of Bobbie Gentry's 'Ode To Billy Joe', which arrived late. But, considering Ms O'Connor's various endearing misdemeanours over the years, this was nothing.

[2] Radiohead would be one of the few acts to contribute to both the original *Help* album and its 2005 sequel, *A Day in the Life*, for which they provided the track 'I Want None Of This'.

[3] For example, 'Journey Of The Sorcerer', on *One Of These Nights* (1975), perhaps better known as the theme music to *The Hitchhiker's Guide To The Galaxy* (see Chapter 4).

[4] Rebecca Allison, '9/11 wicked but a work of art, says Damien Hirst', *The Guardian*, September 11, 2002.

[5] The derisive subtitle 'Waster' that appears on the lyric sheet (but not the track listing on the back cover) seems to reinforce this.

[6] Randall, p. 161.

CHAPTER 14

'THE TOURIST' –
DEAD RINGER

Vladimir: Well? Shall we go?
Estragon: Yes, let's go.
*   (They do not move.)*
—Samuel Beckett, *Waiting for Godot*

So, if you've rejected the obvious ending for your album, how do you end it? The final choice was 'The Tourist', which brings the pace of *OK Computer*, which has been on a fairly consistent downward trajectory since the agit-punk frenzy of 'Electioneering', to a new, almost druggy low.

The music was written by Jonny Greenwood after he saw an American tour party travelling at breakneck speed through the French countryside, without pausing long enough to take anything in. Appropriately, Thom Yorke wrote the lyrics in the Czech capital of Prague, a beautiful city in which drunken young British men enjoy debauched stag weekends while studiously ignoring St Vitus' Cathedral and the Charles Bridge.

We're still in Pink Floyd territory, with specific reference to the meditative guitar work on *Wish You Were Here* (1975). The closest the track comes to intensity is when Thom Yorke enters into the "hey man, slow down" refrain, joined by a synthesised choir similar to the one used in 'Exit Music'. The second time this happens, he's succeeded (3:50) by some typically intense fretmanship from Greenwood; Yorke then returns, with choir intact. There's a brief, restrained drum solo and then – but we'll get to that shortly.

There's another Floydoid animal link (see Chapter 4) in the lyrics, but it's a dog this time, rather than a pig. And immediately there's an enigma. If the dog barks only at me "like it's seen a ghost", might I be a ghost? And what are these sparks it sees? Is Yorke still in his superhero persona (from 'Lucky'), but this time as Johnny Storm, the Human Torch from the Fantastic Four? Or are they just metaphorical sparks, like jagged lines above a character's head signifying anger in a comic strip? Is he literally "overcharged", in the electrical sense (which would explain those sparks)? Or is he another of *OK Computer*'s faintly tragic wage slaves, his suit sweaty, his tie at half-mast, complaining that the bumbling assistant at the sandwich shop where he goes during his 19-minute lunch hour hasn't given him the right change?

Only halfway through does the title make sense, and the immediate influences on the writers make themselves known. The narrator is simply travelling too fast, at "1000 feet per second". Like most of the personas that Yorke adopts through his lyrics, he's passive: things happen, and all he can do is to watch. Colin Greenwood has suggested that in this instance at least, there's some sort of correlation between the lyricist and the characters that people his narratives:

> Thom's lyrics are sort of like a running commentary on what's happening in the world, almost like you're looking out of the window of a Japanese bullet train and things are sort of flying by. It's like a shutter snapping in succession.[1]

Greenwood's explanation of his colleague's creative method appears to follow the same analogy that keeps cropping up throughout the album, with transport representing the various kinds of movement that modern life imposes on humanity. The character doesn't have to be literally in motion; he's just running to keep up, on the work-sleep-eat treadmill of capitalism. The voice of hippydom, the pastoral, pre-industrial ideal, implores: "hey, man, slow down." And the music, of course, obeys.

'The Tourist' has come in for criticism, much of it justified. The lyrics seem to be just thrown together without due care and attention; and wasn't "hey man" the sort of language that punk was sent to eradicate? Above all, the whole thing's just too *long*: of all the tracks on *OK Computer*, only 'Paranoid Android' is longer, and that's effectively three songs. The Ghost of Prog-Rock Past just won't stay down.

Dai Griffiths is particularly harsh, dubbing 'The Tourist' "too soft and comfortable" and reserving particular scorn for the closing triangle strike: "The world ends with a whimper not a bang, assuredly, but there just seems something a bit 'youth orchestra' about that triangle."[2]

There's some truth in this analysis. But try thinking of the triangle (which has been hovering in the background through much of the recording) not as what it *is* but as what it *sounds like* and *represents*; a bell. It's a pretty feeble, anaemic bell, but a bell nonetheless. It's a sound that resonates, literally and metaphorically, through the most unlikely byways of British culture. It's the sound with which Basil summoned the inept Catalan Manuel in the legendary sitcom *Fawlty Towers*. It's the sound of an old-fashioned cash register signalling a sale, as heard in that slightly-less-legendary sitcom *Are You Being Served?*, and also repeatedly on the track 'Money', on Pink Floyd's *Dark Side Of The Moon* (1973). It's the sound made when you hit the carriage return on an old-fashioned manual typewriter. (Ask your dad.) Middle-class families, of the type from which the members of Radiohead emerged, would recognise it as the sound with which the avuncular, erudite, combed-over Robert Robinson marked a new word in the none-more-bourgeois BBC2 game show *Call My Bluff*. The bell signals closure, ending, completion of a transaction, and sometimes a new beginning; the guest has signed in; the sale is completed; the line is finished; the round is done. Further afield, many American bartenders and waiters use it to signify a generous tip; and of course, according to Clarence in the Hollywood classic *It's A Wonderful Life* (Frank Capra, 1946), it's the sound of an angel getting his wings.

Also, coming from a devoutly Anglican establishment such as Abingdon, bells must have had specific connotations; not simply the bells that demarcated their timetables, but the bells that marked all significant endings and transitions. The boys would have had the symbolism of church bells rung into them in English lessons: "The curfew tolls the knell of parting day";[3] "…and therefore never send to know for whom the bell tolls; it tolls for thee."[4] It's the mournful, solitary sound of the Church of England bidding farewell.

So, a bell symbolises death, ending and, in that ghastly therapy-speak aberration, 'closure'. But why such a small sound, and not the sonorous chime with which, for example, AC/DC marked the passing of singer Bon Scott at the beginning of 'Hell's Bells', on *Back In Black* (1980)? Why end – to take Griffiths' paraphrase of (the Anglican) T.S. Eliot[5] and mangle it even more – not with *Kerrang!*, but with wimp-rock?

James Doheny compares 'The Tourist' to 'Good Night', the final track on – stop me if you've heard this one before – the 'White Album'.[6] It's a lush, orchestral, but ultimately disposable lullaby; John Lennon demonstrated his ambivalent attitude to his own composition by giving it to Ringo Starr to sing. Rather than ending with the echoing, apocalyptic piano chord that closed 'A Day In The Life' (the final track on their previous album, *Sgt Pepper's Lonely Hearts Club Band*) they edge out politely, almost apologetically. And this has two effects. One is the manner in which the downbeat tones of 'The Tourist' highlight, by means of dramatic contrast, the churning angst of some of the other tracks. 'The Tourist' may not be one of Radiohead's strongest songs, but like the equally second-tier 'Electioneering', it serves a particular structural purpose within *OK Computer*. The morbid, narcotic, introspective atmosphere is similar to the directions that were being pursued by some of the band's non-Britpop contemporaries, such as The Verve and, especially, Spiritualized. There's a faint echo as well of The Doors in their less bellicose moments, especially the final track of their debut album (from 1967). This is the end, my beautiful friend, but I'm a creep…

The other is the way in which 'The Tourist', in common with 'Fitter Happier' and 'No Surprises', takes on the identity of its own lyrical content. It's not about tourism, it's about life; the small, sad, mundane lives that people feel the need to live, pressured by advertising and social expectations. The central figure in 'The Tourist', in common with the characters in many of the songs on *OK Computer* ('Subterranean Homesick Alien'; 'Let Down'; 'No Surprises' again) is an insignificant figure, a hamster on a corporate wheel. Like Beckett's bowler-wearing tramps, Vladimir and Estragon, in *Waiting For Godot* (1952), there's an illusion (and a delusion) of movement and purpose, but nothing ever happens. The spaceship will never pick you up; Godot will never arrive. However fast you travel, wherever you're going, you'll never reach your ideal destination, so why not just slow down? It's existentialism set to music (see Chapter 5). The end of life is, inevitably, an anticlimax; not the melancholy knell of a church bell, but the barely-there *ting* of a school triangle.

But is it truly the end? Is that final note simply a miniaturised church bell, or is it something else? Could it be the small bell of Buddhist and Hindu ritual, the *ghanta*, representing wisdom and the feminine, warding off evil? Or maybe the bell that is sounded at the beginning and end of rituals at the *butsudan*, the Japanese family shrine, symbolising wisdom and unity? Might Radiohead still be "shamelessly dabbling" in Buddhism (see Chapter 8)? It's important, because this would suggest not an ending, as with the Christian funeral bell, but simply a marker on the circular journey of reincarnation; not a full stop, but a comma, or an ellipsis, the trusty three dots, trailing off into...

As Eliot said: "In my beginning is my end."[7] So, we're back to the beginning, or even to Chapter 3. But if you do make that journey, slow down, or your juggernaut might jacknife.

Notes:

[1] Chuck Klosterman, 'No More Knives', *Spin*, September, 2003.
[2] Griffiths, *OK Computer*, p. 75.
[3] Thomas Gray, 'Elegy Written In A Country Churchyard' (1751).
[4] John Donne, 'Devotions Upon Emergent Occasions: XVII' (1623). The quotation was later used by Ernest Hemingway, for his Spanish Civil War novel *For Whom The Bell Tolls* (1940).
[5] From 'The Hollow Men' (1925); Eliot, p. 92.
[6] Doheny, p. 81.
[7] 'East Coker' (1940); Eliot, p. 196.

CHAPTER 15

PICTURES DRAWN BY DUMB COMPUTERS –
ARTWORK AND DESIGN

Pile on many more layers and I'll be joining you there.
—Pink Floyd, 'Shine On You Crazy Diamond'

By the time *OK Computer* was released in the middle of 1997, the compact disc had become the dominant medium for the delivery of music to consumers. Launched in 1982, the format was intended to offer better sound quality and be more durable than vinyl or cassette tape. Record companies were delighted by the enhanced profit margins available; the newness of the format and its hi-tech image enabled them to raise the retail price of an album, often luring consumers away from other formats with CD-only bonus tracks, taking advantage of the 74-minute playing time available on the discs. It also offered an opportunity to reissue the material in their back catalogues, much of which had not been commercially available for years. CD proved that the ultimate capitalist fantasy – millions of consumers prepared to buy something they already owned – was entirely real. By 1988, CDs were outselling vinyl LPs, and the cassette album's brief period of market dominance had ended by the early 1990s.

From the point of view of the consumer, especially the serious consumer of rock and jazz albums, there was a major disadvantage to the new format, no matter how good the sound was. The decline in size, from a 30-centimetre (12-inch) disc to a mere 12.5 centimetres (5 inches), meant that the packaging – still widely known as a 'sleeve', but in most cases a slim, transparent, plastic case with paper inserts – had also shrunk. Ignoring the peculiar margin/spine affair on the left hand side of the case (too small, too oddly-shaped to do much with), standard CD packaging now had a front surface area of under 160 square centimetres, as opposed to 900; roughly one-sixth of the previous dimensions. And this mattered. Apart from the fact that the old album sleeves were the perfect size for rolling joints,[1] the artwork was often seen by the listener as an integral part of the album experience.

The first record company to fully understand the importance of sleeve design was the US jazz specialist Blue Note which, from the mid-1950s, used the graphics of Reid Miles and the photography of Alfred Wolff to create a cool, innovative look for its hard bop albums. By the late 60s, however, rock musicians (with The Beatles, inevitably, at the forefront) were releasing albums, the sleeves of which were prone to as much interpretation as the music contained within. A record sleeve was not simply the means by which an album could be made to stand out on the shelves; it became a crucial component of what would now be defined as the record's branding. Sleeves began to take on an artistic life of their own; the most notorious instance being when imagery on several of the later Beatles albums, especially *Abbey Road* (1969), was believed to contain hidden clues about the reported death of Paul McCartney.

In some instances, the designers of album sleeves were regarded as associate members of the bands themselves. Examples include Roger Dean, who designed many covers for Yes albums; Storm Thorgerson of Hipgnosis (Pink Floyd); and Vaughan Oliver, who was behind the visual identity of the 4AD label (Cocteau Twins, Pixies, Throwing Muses, etc). Since 1995, Stanley Donwood (real name Daniel Rickwood) has been responsible for all of Radiohead's cover art, often with the assistance of Tchocky (aka Thom Yorke).

Donwood's work tends to be expressionistic and atmospheric; images bear little explicit relevance to the subject matter of the songs on the recording. However, the sleeve design clearly has 'meaning'; or the consumer of the album will probably infer a meaning; otherwise what's the point of the sleeve at all, beyond protecting the contents?

OK Computer was originally release in four formats: the double vinyl LP; compact disc; tape cassette; and the almost-forgotten MiniDisc, the great lost format of recorded media. Although the sheer size of the LP sleeve shows Stanley Donwood's work to its best, this chapter will concentrate on the packaging of the CD, the format that was produced in the highest volume, and can be considered 'the norm'. And, just as it makes most sense to consider the music in the order in which it will probably be heard, at least on the first listening (track 1 to track 12), it is probably best to consider the various components of the packaging in the order in which they will be viewed.

Pictures and words

Which leads us, inevitably, to the front cover. The dominant colour is white, and the main image is of a section of motorway, tinted in blue and apparently scratched with some sort of stylus. This defacing technique reappears throughout the packaging; could it be a visual manifestation of the 'fridge buzz' that permeates the album itself? Immediately, the transportation/industrialisation motif ('Airbag', 'Let Down', 'The Tourist') is in evidence. As Dai Griffiths points out, we are watching the scene from above, from a distance, which gives a sense of the album's all-encompassing sweep. Griffiths compares this to *The Wanderer Above The Mists*, by the German romantic painter Caspar David Friedrich, which depicts a lone, black-clad, defiantly indie figure "standing on the edge", looking down on a rocky landscape.[2] I think of a scene from Carol Reed's 1949 film *The Third Man*, in which the similarly dressed existentialist anti-hero Harry Lime (Orson Welles) looks down on Vienna from a Ferris wheel and talks about how nobody would have any scruples about killing someone from that distance, since the people seem as small as insects ("crushed like a bug in the ground"?).

The album's title and the band name appear in the top, left-hand corner of the cover, almost disappearing off the side. The word "RADIOHEAD" is in the same typeface in which it appeared on the cover of *The Bends* and its associated singles; "OK COMPUTER" is in a very ordinary, bold, san serif font. The only other text is the phrase "Lost Child", which appears twice (once obscured) towards the top right. Each occurrence is accompanied by an imperfect logo representing a child, suggesting that the whole design was acquired from a sign used in a public place (an airport, maybe, or a supermarket), to indicate a location where separated parents and children can be reunited; thus emphasising the domestic aspect of the album ("tuck the kids in safe tonight") as well as the industrial, money-oriented, motion-obsessed perspective. As if to comfort the lost child(ren), there's also the shadowy, blue-orange outline of what looks like a mother and child;[3] and, back to the transportation theme, the nose-cone of an airliner, along with people effecting an escape from it. Almost obscuring these tiny figures is a black cross on a blue background, of the sort used to designate irritating or harmful materials.

At first glance, then, the cover seems to 'fit' the music. It's appropriately smudgy and distorted; and the key lyrical themes are represented, in a suitably enigmatic and oblique manner. Jake Kennedy suggests that "it's like somebody's taken an album cover and put it in the wash";[4] the streaky texture also suggests the rain-soaked urban hell of Ridley Scott's 1982 movie *Blade Runner*. There's nothing so crass as a picture of the band[5] or, god forbid, an actual computer. So far, so (relatively) straightforward.

The back of the packaging (probably the next 'page' that the potential consumer looks at – you can still see this part without piercing the shrinkwrap, or busting that peculiar security clip) seems to maintain the thematic approach. It's transportation again, "motorways and tramlines"; or, more specifically, a diagrammatic cross-section of an underground railway station. There seems to be an evacuation going on, similar to the passengers leaving the aeroplane on the front; there's also a tiny logo of a man who seems to be availing himself of the piped oxygen that appears when an aircraft hits trouble (and the logo is 'in flames', which might hint that his lungful of air at the airline's expense is pretty useless). But closer examination reveals that some of the minuscule figures are running away from the train and platform, while others are apparently running towards it. Is it just rush hour – literally?

The back is also where the necessary bits and pieces end up: the barcode, with manufacturing details; the Parlophone label, that implicitly links Radiohead to The Beatles; the copyright declaration. The band name and album title is repeated; there's a track listing (with 'Fitter Happier' hovering in no-song's-land – see Chapter 9); there's also a quotation from 'Exit Music'. But there are other elements, the meaning of which is less obvious.

"18576397" is, according to fanboy mythology, the precise time and date on which the final mix of the album was completed (6:57 pm, on the 6th of March, 1997) although nobody connected with the band has confirmed this. "1=2" may be a hint towards George Orwell's *1984*, in which the Party forces Winston Smith to acknowledge that "2+2=5", a concept later explored on Radiohead's *Hail To The Thief* (2003).[6] But it also suggests the man who "talks in maths" in 'Karma Police'; there's a notorious algebraic trick that unscrupulous maths teachers have used to persuade students that 1 does indeed equal 2.[7] There's also a small red triangle, the symbolic meanings of which could fill a book on their own; one, that may or not be relevant, is the pyramid design on United States currency, which in turn has connections with Freemasonry. Global capitalism and secret handshakes – a pretty Radioheady combination.[8]

So, you've made your purchase, and you open the case (possibly having broken a nail while attempting to get the better of the shrinkwrap). It has the comforting feel of a book,[9] so your eyes alight first of all on what should be the 'front page', but is in fact the compact disc itself. The text and images on the metallic surface are mostly pretty mundane: that Parlophone logo again; copyright and manufacturing details.[10] The only surprise is a couple of round-headed stick figures, apparently shaking hands. They look suspiciously like the men on the cover of Pink Floyd's *Wish You Were Here*; although, of course, *OK Computer* is most certainly *not* a prog rock album, because Jonny says so (see Chapter 4).[11] The original businessmen on the Floyd album (one of whom was on fire) parodied the imagery of business publications: flick through a few websites or magazines aimed at executives and they're always, *always* packed with photographs of men in suits, shaking hands. Maybe there's a quota.

Your next move depends on how impatient you are to play the CD. Take it out of the case, and you're faced with a section of the motorway from the front cover; the Pink Floyd men again; a wonky star in a circle (looking rather like the emblem on the fuselage of United States Air Force craft, if you want to follow the conspiracy theories); and the scrawled message 'against demons'. Who are the demons? The handshaking money men? The American military? The devil that possesses the narrator in 'Climbing Up The Walls'? The non-specific sense of dread that permeates the album?

Opposite this inner 'page' (although forming the back page of the actual insert booklet) is, just to confuse things further, the image of an open book. As Dai Griffiths points out, the designers of CD packaging soon came to the conclusion that they had two options when expanding their domain beyond two or three 12-centimetre squares of paper; the long, thin, many-folded oblong, forcing the reader to become "something of a piano accordionist"; or the stapled booklet, "inviting comparison with art books".[12] This latter connection may be a leap too far; most CD booklet inserts resemble comics or leaflets rather than art books. And is there any connection between the choice to present CD artwork in 'accordion' or 'book' format and the perceived difficulty or 'artiness' of the relevant music? In the case of *OK Computer*, there does seem to be a conscious decision to present the artwork as a book; the individual pages exist as self-contained squares (albeit with connections through repeated imagery) rather than as one big painting.

The main body of the back page of the booklet is a skyscape, presumably viewed from an aircraft; at the top right is another sky scene, with grass and a lone tree; "the smell of the warm summer air" perhaps? The book's pages are dominated by what looks like a sketch for some sort of three-dimensional display, apparently relating to 'Lucky'. Other text hovers around; a handwritten track listing; references to "people with bird-like faces" and the cryptic "in time square in nuclear fallout reflective clothing in his personal space". It appears to be Thom Yorke's notepad, where he jots down potential lyrics and visual ideas. There's reversed text, in what appears to be Greek; and the logo for Sabritas, a popular Mexican brand of potato chips. The latter is slightly defaced by stray text and a dark rectangle that looks not unlike a moustache; the "Hitler hairdo" in 'Karma Police', maybe?

On removing the booklet, you find that 12 of the pages are devoted to lyrics and production credits, which may come as something of a relief. That, after all, is what CD packaging is 'supposed' to contain. But that still leaves a further 10 squares dominated by images.

Some of them offer more of the same. There's aeroplane/air crash imagery; images of domesticity (red houses; couples with children; someone pasting wallpaper); the Sabritas face and the Greek text; and another nod to Pink Floyd (the red pig, suggesting the flying porker on the cover of their 1977 album *Animals*). Many of these images were repeated further in the packaging for the three singles that were taken from the album.[13] There are further connections with the lyrics: the statue of Jesus (from the Mormon Visitors' Centre in Salt Lake City, Utah), reminding us that "God loves his children"; the pig is also the "Gucci little piggy". An arm reaches up, suggesting the big, empty gestures of an electioneering politician; on the facing page is a hand in a similar position, poking desperately out from a hole in "Thin Ice" ("pull me out of the lake"?).

Again, text is interwoven with the images, from the self-help platitudes of Emile Coué ("Every day in every way I am getting better and better") to barely visible instructions on preparing a McDonald's hamburger (on the page with the large, red handshake image). On the same page are four symbols, three of which have accompanying text in Esperanto;[14] Yorke's early hero and influence Elvis Costello used this invented, universal language in the sleeve text of his 1986 album *Blood and Chocolate*.

Words and pictures

Even when you reach the pages containing the lyrics, there's still ambiguity and apparent confusion. Although there's some stylistic consistency (white, sans serif font on a black background, rather resembling a primitive computer screen; song titles in blue), from then on, typographical rules are thrown to the digital wind. Line breaks and tabs are scattered at random, and the text for 'Let Down' and 'Electioneering' is flipped through 90 degrees; syllables are elongated (25 extra 'a's before the line "ambition makes you look very ugly" in 'Paranoid Android'); text is crossed out; sometimes the text even diverges from the recorded lyric ('Climbing Up The Walls'). The only lyric that is displayed in a 'normal' manner is 'Fitter Happier'; the track that diverges most radically from what we understand to be a 'normal' song. And there are rogue clusters of seemingly random text; each song title has a virtual 'subtitle'[15] that ranges from the superficially sensible ("waster", in the case of 'Lucky') to kitten-on-the-keys random (the first 'word' alongside the title of 'Electioneering' is "yyyyhngbgyhntthy", which can be constructed from a cluster of six adjacent keys in the centre of a standard keyboard).

There's a hint here of the typographical playfulness introduced by the Dada movement. This 'anti-art' phenomenon, which began in Zürich around 1916, challenged the insanity of war and the stuffiness of bourgeois society, not with logical argument or political campaigning, but by presenting visual art, music and poetry that challenged the fundamental assumptions of beauty and order.[16] In the same way the songs force us to question reality (the voice in 'Fitter Happier'; the nature of the killer in 'Climbing Up The Walls'; the reality of the extra-terrestrials in 'Subterranean Homesick Alien'), the printed lyrics force us to contemplate the relationship between words and their meaning. When words are torn from the safety zone of grammar, spelling and layout, you have to think harder about their meaning. Try to remember the first time you received a txt msg.

There is an added layer of confusion when text is pulled out of context in this way; it makes us suspicious of all text, even that used in a conventional, contextualised way. The front cover of Grant Gee's 1998 documentary *Meeting People Is Easy* is an example. Designed by Stanley Donwood to maintain thematic links with the *OK Computer* (pale blue on white, line drawings, transport imagery, those little handshake guys) it also contains decontextualised text ("avoid peril"; "Hand hold on the wheel"; "YOU ARE A TARGET MARKET", etc). Underneath this is the line "This film contains stroboscopic effects that may adversely affect epilepsy sufferers". Presumably the reader is expected to take this seriously; but when it's juxtaposed with the other text (especially the lines that also express warning, and care for the purchaser's safety), its impact is lost. Do we accept it in the same, cynical way that we read the injunctions to get out of bed as soon as we hear the alarm clock, or way we hear the bland utterances of 'Fitter Happier'? We can no longer make any assumptions about *any* messages, even if – especially if – they appear to be provided for our own wellbeing.

By comparison, *OK Computer*'s list of production credits – the who-did-what section – is much more straightforward: black on white; right justified. The few sucker punches come not from the visual style, but from the content: designers are thanked for "additional complicated artwork skills"; live appearances become "performing monkey bookings"; and of course, the cheeky sideswipe at the niceties of publishing deals, "lyrics used by permission even though we wrote them".

Under this is a strip containing text and images reproduced from various places throughout the packaging, rather like the key that clarifies the symbols on a map. Except that there's no clarification, just repetition. It's as if all the symbols on a map are put in a box, but you have no idea which one represents a B-road, which one is a post office, which one is a coniferous forest. By lining up the symbols, you're presented with an illusion of order and rationality. But nobody explains. You're on your own.

So, what's it all about, then? Should we really be nosing among the handshakes and the air crashes, between Jesus and his lost children, for some form of meaning? Is the red pig a sign that we should be snuffling for Radiohead-scented truffles? Well, yes and no. Feel free to argue until dawn about the precise meaning of the backwards Greek text, the little red houses, or the wallpaper paste. But it's probably best to consider the images in the same way you considered the sounds. It's less about what they *say* or *mean* individually; more about what they *are*, collectively.

In artistic terms, the cover unites two tendencies of sleeve design: the knowing symbolism of 60s and 70s rock, with its enigmatic images and odd juxtapositions; and the consciously messy, hacked-up collage techniques that Jamie Reid and his followers created to offer a visual manifestation of the punk ethos. This, of course, reflects the tensions within the music: the soaring guitar solos and ethereal keyboards, coupled with a pervasive sense of nihilism and anger. Prog meets punk, and the listener gets stuck in the middle.

But to achieve a full understanding, go back to that row of symbols, beneath the production credits. It's full of familiar images, that seem to offer comfort, nurture, support. It looks as if it's supposed to help. As Lisa Leblanc suggests:

> The iconography is familiar, symbols that we have seen before, comforting elements of a basic visual literacy... Donwood relies on the language of wayfinding icons, those we see in subways and malls, guiding us through our lives, showing us the way out, to send us in the proper direction, to steer us from danger... Beware what lurks behind the clear and shiny surface, question everything: 'Thin Ice,' 'Lost Child,' 'Against Demons.' They tell us to proceed with caution, at our own risk, we are being alerted, we are being told to pay attention.[17]

But just being told to beware, to take care (fasten your seatbelts in case of jacknifing juggernauts; tuck the kids in and set the alarms, because you don't know who's climbing up the walls) is not enough. In fact, these warnings accentuate our helplessness and exacerbate our fears – thus putting us more firmly under the control of our political and economic masters. We need knowledge and information and explanation, not scare stories. Just as Yorke's lyrics scratch beneath the surface of the reassuring, mundane images of the modern world, and find a monster beneath; so do Donwood's images. But, still, nobody explains. Still, you're on your own.

Notes:

[1] The rigid plastic of the CD case did provide an excellent surface from which to snort other substances – a change that reflects all manner of social and economic connotations, within the music industry and beyond.

[2] Griffiths, *OK Computer*, p. 87. See also the posters for Peter Weir's *Fearless* (see Chapter 15) and Wim Wenders' *Wings Of Desire* (1987).

[3] The Lost Child was also a recurring theme of the poet and artist William Blake (1757-1827), who argued that industrialisation and science were the enemies of childlike, Christlike innocence, and of the ideal of a pastoral England that he called Albion. Apart from the obvious links with the anti-technology ideas underpinning *OK Computer*, Blake's thoughts have been a major influence on several other rock performers, including Syd Barrett of Pink Floyd, and Pete Doherty of The Libertines and Babyshambles.

[4] *OK Computer: A Classic Album Under Review*.

[5] Radiohead have not used images of themselves on the packaging of their music since the days of *Pablo Honey*.

[6] Joseph Tate, '*Hail To The Thief*: A Rhizomatic Map In Fragments', Tate, p. 182.

[7] Let $a=b$.

$a^2=ab$

$a^2+a^2=a^2+ab$

$2a^2=a^2+ab$

$2a^2-2ab=a^2+ab-2ab$

$2a^2-2ab=a^2-ab$.

$2(a^2-ab)=1(a^2-ab)$

$\therefore 2=1$.

In case you're still there, the proof falls down because it involves dividing by zero, which is arithmetically impossible. This is exactly the sort of mathematical torture with which teachers at schools such as Abingdon have long delighted in persecuting their pupils.

[8] It could, of course, be the triangle at the end of 'The Tourist'.

[9] A connection that Donwood made when he designed the packaging for Radiohead's *Amnesiac* (2001).

[10] Although, on my copy, there's an oddity; an 's' is missing from the word "broadcasting". It's almost certainly a typographical error, but with Donwood and Yorke at work, you can never be entirely sure.

[11] The cover of *Pleased To Meet Me* (1987), by Minneapolis punks The Replacements, also makes reference to Pink Floyd's handshaking plutocrats.

[12] Griffiths, *OK Computer*, pp. 77-78.

[13] Although there's a clear stylistic link between the design of *OK Computer* and the singles that came from it, each single sleeve is tied to its main song by a specific quotation: "God loves his children, yeah!" on 'Paranoid Android'; "Phew! For a minute there" on 'Karma Police'; "Such a pretty house" on 'No Surprises'. Possibly, because the more basic packaging of the CD single offers less space, there is less room for hints and allusions.

[14] The Esperanto translates as: "Syringe"; "Symbol"; "Dangerous Neighbourhood".

[15] These scrawls of letters and numbers have been subject to imaginative interpretation on fan sites. It's commonly accepted in these circles that "1421421", next to 'Airbag', are yet another nod to *The Hitchhiker's Guide To The Galaxy*, in which 42 is the answer to Life, the Universe and Everything. The news that the letters accompanying 'Paranoid Android', "yuc" and "zhd", give the words for "good" and "cardigan" when tapped into a Hebrew keyboard, have achieved less credibility. In 2003, Radiohead bestowed each track on *Hail To The Thief* with a subtitle (eg 'The Boney King Of Nowhere' for 'There There') that seemed to make more sense than those on *OK Computer*; although their relationship to the songs themselves still tended to be pretty tenuous.

[16] The performance aspect of Dada was also a clear influence on the Plastic People of the Universe. See Chapter 9.

[17] Lisa Leblanc, 'Ice Age Coming: Apocalypse, the Sublime, and the Paintings of Stanley Donwood', Tate, p. 86.

CHAPTER 16

THANK YOU FOR LISTENING –
THE ALBUM

Science and technology multiply around us. To an increasing extent they dictate the languages in which we speak and think. Either we use those languages, or we remain mute.
—J.G. Ballard

An album is a collection of songs, wrapped in a cover – essentially, the subject matter of the previous 13 chapters. There may be a bonus video track, or a free poster, but when you hand over your cash, this is pretty much what you get. Except, of course, it's more than that. A successful album depends for its longevity on developing an identity that listeners and potential consumers will appreciate. And truly successful albums (or books, or films, or...) manage to bypass critical language entirely, by becoming definitive markers for describing other works.

In some ways, this means that attempting to describe a work is like describing a colour. We all know what 'orange' or 'purple' are, but do you really see them the same way that I see them? Similarly, when *Dark Side Of The Moon* or *Fear Of A Black Planet* or *OK Computer* become signposts for defining particular movements in the history of popular music, do we really agree on what they mean? Essentially, is your *OK Computer* the same as mine, or hers, or your grandchildren's?

Given the impossibility of a perfect definition of sound in words, we have to call on other resources to create an idea of what those sounds are. It will always be approximate, but a critic's job is something like that of a goalkeeper in soccer or hockey: always try to narrow the angle, to give yourself the best odds. Rock criticism is reborn as a branch of geometry.

There are effectively three components to this sort of analysis: what else does it sound like?; what's it about?; how important is it? The last question will be dealt with in Chapters 23 to 25; the first two have their angles narrowed here

Sounds

Any description or analysis or criticism of a work of art is bound to rely on comparisons with other works, as the preceding chapters have shown. There is a critical consensus about the music that permeates *OK Computer*, although listeners differ in the emphasis they give to each influence. Everyone hears the 'White Album'; I hear less Miles Davis than some critics, maybe a little more Pink Floyd.

It's possible to go all the way down the postmodernist route, and recreate the album entirely from odds and sods of other records, as Paul Morley does, describing it as:

> The worlds of Wire, *Wired* and the World Wide Web all wrapped up in a universe of everything for the boy fan who knows everything, the missing link between a fraud and a masterpiece, between deathly and deathless, between Can and muzak, between the graphic and the non-linear, between the post-rock of Peter Hammill and the rock of Tortoise, between glam and glitch, and for those of you who really do know everything, between Lard Free and Coldplay, or between Yes' *Relayer* and Porcupine Tree, or between Blodwyn Pig and *Aqualung*, or between Don McLean and Don Caballero. In a Robbie Williams sense, the missing link between U2 and Aphex Twin.[1]

Of course, such a description relies for its full effect on the listener having at least a cursory knowledge of everything from the tiresomely obvious (U2, Coldplay) to the chin-strokingly obscure (Lard Free, a mid-70s French prog band led by drummer Gilbert Artman and, yes, I had to Google that). But it does indicate the number and diversity of influences under which Radiohead were operating. This is perhaps the reason why the 'White Album' is so often pulled out as a comparison. It's an undisciplined, everything-bar-the-kitchen-sink production, ranging from gritty blues-rock ('Happiness Is A Warm Gun', 'Yer Blues') to lush schmaltz ('Good Night'), from daft cowboy songs ('Rocky Raccoon') to cheesy cod-reggae ('Ob-La-Di, Ob-La-Da'), with influences stumbling from The Beach Boys to Stockhausen and back again. *OK Computer* doesn't have quite the same range: its most left-field track is clearly 'Fitter Happier'; its most stylistically conservative, 'Electioneering'; indeed, all but three of the 12 tracks have a good old verse-chorus-verse structure.[2]

What *OK Computer* does share with the 'White Album' is the sense of adventure. Just to pluck a few influential names from the preceding chapters: David Bowie; King Tubby; Genesis; The Doors; Ennio Morricone; The Jesus and Mary Chain; The Who; The Stereophonics; Krzysztof Penderecki; Sparklehorse; The Beach Boys; Louis Armstrong; The Eagles. This is one reason I find the explicit link with *Bitches Brew* hard to fathom, beyond the shared use of the electric piano. Davis' album uses similar instrumentation on all tracks, only varying the precise number of pianists and percussionists; *OK Computer*, while still holding onto the basic guitars-bass-drums setup that would eventually be torpedoed on *Kid A* (and resurrected on *Hail To The Thief*), rings the changes with treatments and effects, making especially clever use of various keyboards and synthesisers, as well as paying attention to space and texture. The album also uses fragments of non-musical sound, especially on 'Fitter Happier', and also more subtly on 'Paranoid Android'. The process owes something to the sampling technology that was then being used most imaginatively in dance and hip-hop music, and also to the pioneers of tape manipulation in rock; The Beatles again, and Pink Floyd, who used fragments of taped speech on *The Dark Side Of the Moon*, and an array of bellowed interjections on 1970's *Atom Heart Mother*, on which they were assisted by tape pioneer Ron Geesin.

This is why I'd argue that the biggest single influence on the actual *sound* of *OK Computer* remains the mid-70s output of Floyd, particularly *Dark Side* and *Wish You Were Here*; they share the sense of space and melancholy, as well as the technical innovation. Radiohead themselves deny this, and I can well believe that they weren't the sort of boys who spent their teenage years chilling out to 'Comfortably Numb', let alone 'Several Species Of Small Furry Animals Gathered Together In A Cave And Grooving With A Pict'. But the sonic innovations made by Pink Floyd in these records had a major effect on mainstream rock music well into the 1980s, punk rock notwithstanding; an influence remains an influence, even if it's second-hand.[3] Moreover, Radiohead bring a seething anger and a genuine aura of dread to the sounds, whereas the dominant emotion that hovers over the music of Pink Floyd (at least in the period between 1968 and 1983, when Roger Waters was the chief songwriter), is a sort of grumpy indignation. There, I've said it. Radiohead are better than Pink Floyd. Quote me.

Subjects

Thom Yorke has already told us what *OK Computer* is about: "fridge buzz". It's a good, glib description of his preoccupation at the time: the real and metaphorical background noise that invaded his life. It also describes many of the incidental sounds on the album: in many places on *OK Computer* they smudge the boundaries between what something *is* and what it's *about*; 'Fitter Happier' providing a good example.

But for an album this varied and complex, ten letters isn't quite enough. Fridge buzz in itself is an annoyance: it's where it comes from that's the real problem. Yorke's prime concern throughout the album is the way that the intersection of politics, economics and technology grinds down the individual. It's not the technology itself that scares him; the problem is the social and human effect that the technology might have.

In this, Yorke is following in a noble tradition. His concerns echo those of William Blake (see Chapter 15), who felt that the forces of the Industrial Revolution and Newton's scientific methods were erasing the innocence and beauty of England; and also the early-19th century direct action of the Luddites, who smashed textile machines that they saw to be threatening the livelihoods of working people. These concerns have been revived and amplified for the present day by anti-corporate campaigners such as Naomi Klein, Kalle Lasn and José Bové (see Chapter 21); Yorke has been vocal in his support for their views.

Although he's quite happy to voice his opinions in the public arena, Yorke is more circumspect as a lyricist. Part of the problem is that many of the songs are essentially character pieces, in which he inhabits a narrating persona, rather like an actor. As he told *Mojo*'s Jim Irvin, in an interview to accompany the magazine's review of the album:

> I spent a lot of time trying not to do voices like mine. The voices on 'Karma Police', 'Paranoid Android' and 'Climbing Up The Walls' are all different personas. I think 'Lucky', the lyric and the way it's sung, is really positive, really exciting. 'No Surprises' is someone who's trying hard to keep it together but can't. 'Electioneering' is a preacher ranting in front of a bank of microphones.[4]

So, if the lyricist is going to hide behind a succession of masks, where do we go to find out what *OK Computer* actually means? Does the title offer any help? It's an oddly ambiguous phrase, which hints at the themes of the album, yet never lays them out in full view. The two words – the informal, cheery "OK" (perhaps accompanied by a thumbs-up) and the cool, mechanical "Computer" (suggesting unemotional analysis and calculation) – make an unlikely pairing. But that, in a way, *is* what the album's about: the flawed, flesh-and-blood human, trying against the odds to achieve happiness, or at least OK-ness[5]; pitted against the megalithic power of industry, electricity, ones and zeroes. Apart from the works of Douglas Adams, the overriding image is of Stanley Kubrick's *2001: A Space Odyssey*, in which HAL, the spaceship computer, becomes powerful and deadly by adopting the characteristics of its human creators. Dai Griffiths suggests a more accurate title should be *Domesticity, Transport and Human Freedom* but that misses the sense of opposition and conflict, as well as sounding a little too much like an early 80s synth-pop album.[6]

It is, however, helpful to consider these and other specific themes that come and go through the 12 tracks, adding to the sense of unity and coherence. Some are core to the meaning of a song, while others are more incidental; I've restricted the list to themes that have a significant effect on the understanding of three or more songs.

TRANSPORT/ TECHNOLOGY: 'Airbag'; 'Subterranean Homesick Alien'; 'Let Down'; 'Fitter Happier'; 'Lucky'; 'The Tourist'.

From the front cover onwards, the theme of transport moves through the album like traffic on a five-lane highway. But the treatment of the subject varies. The danger of mechanised transport, one of Thom Yorke's eternal obsessions, is obvious in the crash narratives of 'Airbag' and 'Lucky', and this stems from his well-documented brushes with oblivion when he was younger. As he explained:

> I've been in two accidents myself. One was serious, and I could have died. I was really young, and I had just got a car and spun it off the road, and was very near to being hit by two other cars coming the other way. I missed them by inches. Then you have that thing where you walk away from the car and you just ask yourself, 'Well, why am I lucky? Why am I allowed to walk away from this?' when you constantly hear of friends who die in car accidents for no reason. It fucks with my head completely. The day we have to stop getting in cars will be a very good day.[7]

In 'The Tourist', physical movement is a metaphor for a life that's spun out of control, a man whose desire to 'get on' means that he's lost touch with his surroundings and, implicitly, his own humanity. In 'Let Down' and 'Fitter Happier', transport is just one aspect of the modern Western lifestyle that contributes to its own destruction. It's not simply the danger of travel that disturbs Yorke: it's the stress and boredom and waste that comes from it. As he says: "Sitting in gridlock is not a blissful occupation."[8] Much later, he suggested that the environmental costs of road and air travel might cast into doubt any future Radiohead tours:

> I think it's a necessary part of what I do, to tour or play live, but I find it unacceptable, what the consequences of that are.... Some of our best ever shows have been in the US, but there's 80,000 people there and they've all been sitting in traffic jams for five or six hours with their engines running to get there, which is bollocks... Long haul flights just feel wrong. I'm trying to figure out a way of getting to Japan by train. I quite fancy that Trans-Siberian whatsitsname but apparently it's a bit scary.[9]

But he does understand the attractions of travel and transport, and its benefits. He still drives a car, after all, despite his teenage crash. The "interstellar burst" of 'Airbag' and the "glorious day" in 'Lucky' demonstrate that he can see beauty within the ugliness and disaster; just as many artists have identified a savage beauty in images of exploding space shuttles, or the destruction of the Twin Towers on 9/11. And 'Subterranean Homesick Alien' represents the timeless desire to escape and rise above all the mundane reality of everyday life.

There's a very clear precedent for this in the work of the British author J.G. Ballard, particularly his novel *Crash* (1973, filmed in 1996 by David Cronenberg). In Ballard's story, the characters are so numbed by modern society, they are only able to achieve sexual arousal through technology, especially through car crashes. Ballard, of course, was writing before the advent of voyeuristic TV shows based on footage of real-life police chases, complete with climactic collisions. Yorke is presenting a horror story, one that becomes even more horrific when we realise that we are all complicit in it. Compare his attitude with, for example, Kraftwerk, who seem to luxuriate in the speed and anonymity of the *Autobahn* (1974) and *Trans-Europe Express* (1977), although irony is not a foreign concept to the neatly-dressed knob-twiddlers.

Although images of transportation dominate the *OK Computer* wordscape, they often represent more general themes relating to the increasing mechanisation of modern life. As with Yorke's ambivalent relationship to driving (somewhere on a line between hatred and grudging tolerance), Radiohead warn about the dangers of technology, while shamelessly wallowing in its pleasures and possibilities. The songs on the album are populated by characters desperately trying to maintain their individuality in the face of robotic, industrialised conformity: the sanitised "town where you can't smell a thing" of 'Subterranean Homesick Alien'; the self-help platitudes of 'Fitter Happier'.

This is a theme that has been tackled by artists in all genres throughout the 20th century. Writers such as Upton Sinclair (in his 1906 novel *The Jungle*, about the meatpacking industry in Chicago) and Yevgeni Zamyatin (in *We*, a dystopian satire that influenced George Orwell's *1984*) expressed outrage at the way the industrial process dehumanise people; filmmakers such as René Clair (*À nous la liberté*, 1931) and Charlie Chaplin (*Modern Times*, 1936) made fun of it. However, artists were just as likely to see beauty in the subordination of the individual to industrial conformism. The early-20th Century movements of Futurism and Modernism predicted centrally-planned cities, with citizens wearing uniforms and living in state-run tower-blocks. There's a sense of wonder as well as horror as we watch the hapless workers toiling away on the soaring machines of Fritz Lang's *Metropolis* (1927)[10]; Kraftwerk's attitude to the mechanical dummies that we (they?) have become, *The Man-Machine* of their 1978 album, is as inscrutable as their opinions of roads and railways. The Italian Futurist architect Antonio Sant'Elia called his own, conceptual city of the future "the urban machine"; Thom Yorke's anguish is about the extent to which the machine is not just an environment for living, but is seeping into the human soul itself.

CAPITALISM: 'Paranoid Android'; 'Karma Police'; 'Fitter Happier'; 'Electioneering'; 'No Surprises'; 'The Tourist'.

If Yorke agonises over the extent to which he can dirty his hands with modern technology, we – Radiohead, their listeners, me, my readers – are just as complicit in the second big theme of *OK Computer*, the power of global business and economics. The great satires of Zamyatin and Orwell attacked a state-run, mechanised dictatorship, and the great message of capitalism is that it offers freedom to the individual. Yorke begged to differ.

Radiohead were not perceived at this point to be an explicitly political band; the anti-corporate 'Banana Co', first released as an extra track on the 'Pop Is Dead' single in 1993, was a rare exception. However, by the time *OK Computer* saw the light of day, the political agenda could not be stifled any longer. For the most part, the level of political comment was oblique, often incidental. Radiohead are not a doctrinaire band in the tradition of acts like Crass or The Redskins, whose political dogma (anarchism and Trotskyism respectively) took priority over everything else. So the comment about networking yuppies in 'Paranoid Android' feels like a jibe against a social clique; until you recall that the whole yuppie phenomenon is a by-product of the 'greed is good' mentality fostered by the Reagan and Thatcher administrations of the 1980s, and their free-market, pro-business ethos. Similarly, the line "bring down the government" in 'No Surprises' seems to be a casual aside; but in the context of a man crushed by the system that he has helped prop up, it's bitterly ironic, and integral to the meaning of the song.[11] The little portion of democracy he's allowed every four or five years isn't enough to save him. The protagonist of 'The Tourist' is in the same boat. As David Stubbs suggests, political lyricists such as Thom Yorke differ from their predecessors in the 1970s and 80s, because the developed world is no longer experiencing mass unemployment or other symptoms of economic downturn; instead, they offer a seemingly paradoxical "protest against a time of plenty";[12] the poverty of Yorke's characters – who tend to be affluent and educated, by global standards at least – is spiritual rather than material.

'Fitter Happier' offers a value-free enunciation of the bland catchphrases that prop up this system, and it is only because of the musical context that we know from the start they are being present-

145

ed as a litany of evil; by the time the digital voice gets to the "cat tied to a stick" line we understand fully. 'Electioneering' dispenses with the irony, and provides Radiohead's most full-blooded descent into agit-pop to this point. The fact that the song is second-rate may be the whole point: it seems as if, after all those oblique hints, Yorke can no longer bite his tongue, and feels obliged to unveil the monster without the prettifying addition of a decent tune or an imaginative arrangement.

After the release of *OK Computer*, the band's views became more explicitly political, both in their music ('Optimistic' on *Kid A*; 'Dollars And Cents' on *Amnesiac*; the title of *Hail To The Thief*) and in the extra-curricular activities (in particular in protests against globalisation). But there was still a paradox at work. Radiohead were part of the music industry, agents of the multinational EMI, and thus liable to accusations of hypocrisy. As they acknowledged on 'Karma Police': "we're still on the payroll".

MADNESS: 'Paranoid Android'; 'Subterranean Homesick Alien'; 'Karma Police'; 'Climbing Up The Walls'; 'Lucky'.
Rock music has always had a fascination for various strains of madness and eccentricity. The initial appeal of pioneers such as Little Richard and Screamin' Jay Hawkins was their essential 'otherness', a flash of colourful perversity in the buttoned-up years of Eisenhower and Macmillan. The rock genre is littered with psychological, often drug-afflicted casualties such as Syd Barrett, Arthur Lee and Sly Stone, as well as performers in the realms of 'outsider' music (such as Daniel Johnston, Wesley Willis and Wild Man Fischer) whose mental illnesses become their main attraction and selling point for many fans.[13] But post-punk and indie music was the first to raise depression to the level of art; the gloomy textures of Joy Division and the arch melancholy of The Smiths both influenced the music of Radiohead greatly.

Radiohead have never been icons of mental illness to the same degree, although Thom Yorke has been open about the stress and confusion he suffered in the aftermath of *OK Computer*'s success. Mental illness is a theme on the album; one underlying message is that the whole world's going insane. Compulsive travel is madness; global capitalism is even madder. As Thom Yorke said in 2003, the bizarre world views expressed in the mass media often persuade him to question his own sanity:

> I absolutely feel crazy at times. Anybody who turns on the TV and actually thinks about what they're watching has to believe they're going insane or that they're missing something everyone else is seeing. When I watch the Fox News channel, I can't believe how much nerve those people have and how they assume that people are just going to swallow that shit. And I find myself thinking that I *must* be missing something.[14]

Madness in the more conventional sense – specific disturbances in the mind of the individual – is also a persistent theme, both as a microcosm of the wider lunacy, and as a symptom of it. The characters of Yorke's narratives buy into the system, which in turn drives them out of their minds. The scale of the mental disturbance varies. The speaker in 'Karma Police' seems to be a daydreamer ("for a minute there I lost myself"); those in 'Lucky' and 'Subterranean Homesick Alien' also appear to be deluded to a greater or lesser extent, but the gap between perception and reality is never made clear. As the title suggests, the dysfunction depicted in 'Paranoid Android' is less benign, and teeters on the verge of violence; 'Climbing Up The Walls', taking derangement to the next level, shows what happens when that line is crossed. As Dave Thompson says:

> *OK Computer* could have been made by one of the album's own invented characters; someone who couldn't decide whether to top himself now, or take a few dozen passers-by out first. Making the record was his way of killing time while he made up his mind.[15]

DEATH: 'Airbag'; 'Exit Music (For A Film)'; 'Climbing Up The Walls'; 'No Surprises'; 'Lucky'.

Like madness, death has been a staple subject of rock music from the beginning, although not without controversy: 'Tell Laura I Love Her' (see Chapter 3) was banned by the BBC in the early 1960s for its morbid content. Of course, the blues and country traditions from which rock sprang are drenched with decay and demise. Death songs represented a strain of nihilism and existentialism that, again, came to fruition with punk and the various musical styles that sprung from it. The morbid obsessions of lyricists such as Morrissey ('Suffer Little Children', 'There Is A Light That Never Goes Out', 'Asleep') and Nick Cave ('The Mercy Seat', the *Murder Ballads* album) were a formative influence on indie kids of Radiohead's generation.

Both Morrissey and Cave have risked accusations that they glamorise death, particularly suicide and murder, and this is a criticism that could be thrown at Thom Yorke. The songs of Radiohead, like the fiction of J.G. Ballard, demonstrate that part of the dangerous attraction adhering to technology is the proximity of death and disaster. 'Airbag' and 'Lucky', it could be argued, are less about road and air travel, than about road and air *crashes*; the most effective STOP sign of all. The survivors' brush with oblivion leaves them wild-eyed, exultant, in a state that hovers somewhere between sexual glow and religious fervour.

Yorke himself was self-critical over his attitude to death, seeing it as a product of his late 20th Century, Western background, and the insulation from the realities of the world that it bought:

The way I've been brought up and most of us are brought up, we are never given time to think about our own death. In fact everything you do stems from trying to offset that fear with the idea of immortality. Especially doing what I do. If you're a pop star, all you're trying to do is search for immortality. Or that's the cliché at least. Yet you're constantly a knife-edge away from being killed in a car accident... I don't believe I've encountered death enough. No one close to me has died. Death is very obvious, it's all around us all the time, but I'm aware of how cloud-cuckoo my particular experience is.

I'm 28 and I've never even seen a dead person. So I wonder what a dead person would feel like, that sort of thing. But not in a morbid way.[16]

Real death usually comes more slowly, with plenty of warning: the threat of savage slaughter in 'Climbing Up The Walls'; the downbeat suicide of 'No Surprises'; the more romantic, but still pathetic and pointless suicide of 'Exit Music (For A Film)'. However, *OK Computer* is not strictly 'about' death, at least not in the physical sense. Physical death is a side-effect of the moral, spiritual and environmental death that comes from industrialisation and slavish obsession with economic 'progress'. It is this living death that permeates the album.

SLOGANS: 'Paranoid Android'; 'Fitter Happier'; 'Electioneering'.

Rock lyrics are created to be heard, rather than to be read. As Radiohead's contemporaries Pulp always insisted on their album sleeves, "Please do not read the lyrics whilst listening to the recordings." Moreover, when lyrics are printed, they often dispense with the basic rules of punctuation, capitalisation, and other disciplines that make language readable.[17] The reprinted lyrics for *OK Computer* are no exception. There are few punctuation marks and even fewer capital letters (see Chapter 15). What we're left with are chunks of text, from which it's possible to extract individual words of phrases; these can be quoted in reviews or (heaven forbid) used as chapter headings for books about the album a decade later. Essentially, Yorke has fashioned song lyrics from loosely collected slogans, which drift out of the conceptual babble to be seized by the listener.

Most of the songs, then, contain slogans; but some of them become self-referential, and take slogans as their subject matter. In 'Paranoid Android', this is only part of the overall, hell-on-earth effect, as the random chatter of the yuppies ("the unborn chicken voices" expressing "opinions which are of no consequence") build up to form a fog of oppressive noise, that can only be cleansed by the rain. But still, the banal, empty catchphrase of the televangelist ("God loves his children") remains.

In 'Electioneering', the slogans are to the fore, as Yorke mixes the smug request of the doorstepping election candidate with the violent reality, as well as dropping in a genuine political soundbite ("voodoo economics") as he goes. 'Fitter Happier', of course, is entirely built from them, building a collage that maintains its potency, not through content but through form and structure: the journey from the unexceptional "regular exercise at the gym" to the dosed-up pig is swift and remorseless. These three tracks collectively highlight the banality of language, and the way it loses real meaning, becoming part of the background drone that unifies Yorke's lyrical concerns.

There's a major omission, however. Yorke goes against many decades of tradition, by avoiding the subject of love through most of the album. 'Exit Music (For A Film)' is the closest to a romantic love lyric; but the only use of the word itself, in 'Paranoid Android', is deeply ironic. Of course, punk had made love unfashionable for a brief while (Johnny Rotten argued that it was what you felt for a cat, not a human) but bands such as The Undertones and Buzzcocks had no qualms about baring their emotional sides. Even devotees of gloom like Joy Division admitted to the existence of the L-word, even if it was depicted as a destructive force. On *OK Computer*, Radiohead (whose most successful track up to this point had been a love song of sorts) dispense with the concept. The final victory of the fridge buzz, it seems, is the eradication of all emotions bar fear and despair.

Album sequence

Words and music are, of course, crucial to the success of *OK Computer*. But the choice of material is not the whole story. Selection, sequencing, even the gaps between each track becomes a matter of profound importance.

Thousands of people grew up to the soundtrack of *Sgt Pepper's Lonely Hearts Club Band*, on vinyl, and will remember clearly the first time they heard the album on compact disc.[18] In the sleevenotes was the band's original idea for the sequence of Side One, with the suggestion that, thanks to the programming function of most CD players, you could now shuffle the tracks to see how the album would have sounded in this form. Many tried it (of course) and it sounded utterly *wrong*. 'Being For The Benefit Of Mr Kite!' does not come after 'With A Little Help From My Friends'. It just *doesn't*. 'Lucy In The Sky With Diamonds' does. It's a law as immutable as Pythagoras' Theorem or the Spanish football team's underachievement at every World Cup. Of course, if The Beatles had decided in 1967 to leave 'Mr Kite' as the third track, and put 'She's Leaving Home' at the end of Side One, this order would have become hardwired into our psyches as 'the right one'. Unless, of course, the very art of sequencing is so crucial that a *Sgt Pepper* with 'Mr Kite' as the third song would have entered the critical consensus as a failed attempt to follow *Revolver*, a lame copy of The Beach Boys' *Pet Sounds*, and a sad epitaph for a once-great band, who split up acrimoniously in January, 1968.[19]

Thom Yorke clearly thought the order was important; he spent weeks with the tracks on his MiniDisc player, juggling the sequence over and over. Perhaps a future special edition of *OK Computer*, in some as-yet unknown medium, will identify all the rejected running orders, and we'll play them, maybe with a holographic TY head hovering in front of us, explaining his thinking.[20]

Until then, we have the released version, in the released order. Of course, we can juggle the tracks as we see fit; maybe repeat some; leave others out; mix and match with songs from other Radiohead albums; or other artists; maybe cherry-pick two or three tracks from *OK Computer* for an iPod mix called *Grumpy Songs About Technology, Death And Hopelessness, '96-'98*. But in the back of our minds we will always be aware that the album begins with 'Airbag' and ends with 'The Tourist'. Guitar to triangle.

So, why is this order so significant? Is it just to create an overall balance, so that 'pretty' songs ('Exit Music', 'No Surprises') and 'ugly' songs ('Airbag', 'Climbing Up The Walls') aren't bunched up at one end; the musical equivalent of shuffling a pack of cards? Or is there a meaning? The fact that Yorke was still shuffling the tracks some time after they had been written and recorded indicates that there was no big, pre-ordained 'story' that the album was intended to tell: that *OK Computer* is not a concept album in the style of *Tommy* by The Who, or Pink Floyd's *The Wall*. There are stories and narratives and messages going on, but there is no single authorial voice and no recurring motifs that give an overall structure. Although there are isolated influences from the world of classical music, the model for *OK Computer* is a collection of discrete songs (a path followed by everyone from Frank Sinatra to Britney Spears) rather than a unified, symphonic whole (the model of Beethoven, Mahler and, say, Mike Oldfield).

But there is clearly a pattern at work, and this permutation of 12 songs has an aesthetic and emotional effect that another order would not produce. It's quite possible that the final decision was as much instinctive as considered, and if the story about Yorke and his MiniDisc is true, a product of frustration and despair as well.

But, running the risk of imposing a meaning where there is none, some kind of narrative logic seems to exist. Tracks 1 to 6 present various aspects of modern urban madness; 7 and 8 depict the cause of that madness (consumer capitalism and political corruption). The last four songs are about various ways out, the first three of which are, loosely speaking, religious: 'Climbing Up The Walls' and 'No Surprises' show life on the Abrahamic (Christian-Jewish-Islamic) model, linear, with a beginning and an end (death, in this case violent); 'Lucky', with its theme of resurrection or reincarnation, and its thematic return to the subject matter of the first song, sees life as cyclical, on the Vedic (Hindu-Buddhist-Sikh) model. But the last song offers the key. The message may be existential (there's no God to help) but this does imply that if there is a solution, it's in our own hands. 'The Tourist' may be one of the weaker tracks on the album, but it earns its place by its explicit rebuke to all the *Sturm und Drang* of the preceding 11 songs. As Thom Yorke described it:

> When we chose to put 'Tourist' at the end, and I chilled out and stopped getting up at five in the morning and driving myself nuts, we did find that it was the only resolution for us

– because a lot of the album was about background noise and everything moving too fast and not being able to keep up… That song was written to me, from me, saying 'Idiot, slow down.' Because at that point I needed to… If you can slow down to an almost stop, you can see everything moving too fast around you and that's the point.[21]

It's as if *OK Computer* had become a code, a tangle of tapes and guitar strings and ones and zeroes, that not even its creators could quite understand. In a way, just as some of the individual tracks were self-referential, the album had become what it described: a human creation that had run away from its creators, developing a baleful, dangerous personality of its own. *OK Computer* can be seen as the record of human attempts to crack the code, to tame the beast; an effort mirrored in the singer's solitary holiday in MiniDisc hell. To return briefly to the author who gave the album its title: Douglas Adams constantly deals with computers and robots that fail to fulfil their core function, which is to aid their creators. Deep Thought takes generations to decide that the meaning of life, the universe and everything is 42, which really wasn't what was required. When its successor, Earth, is programmed to make sense of that answer by calculating the appropriate question, all it can come up with is a sum that is, inevitably, wrong. ("What's six times nine?") Marvin the Paranoid Android is a self-absorbed git; and even Eddie, the shipboard control mechanism to which the phrase "OK Computer" is addressed, refuses to protect the craft and crew from certain disaster because it's more interested in working out why humans like to drink tea.[22]

And the eventual answer reached by both Adams and Yorke was the same. "Slow down." It's a message that they both followed in deed as well as word: Adams by devoting much of his energy towards environmental and ecological concerns; Yorke by his increasing involvement in battling globalisation and its attendant ills. The fact that both men remained unabashed about their fondness for some aspects of technology and progress is a paradox; but this does suggest that this is one urgent debate where the arguments aren't entirely black and white.

Notes:

[1] Paul Morley, *Words and Music: A History of Pop in the Shape of a City* (London: Bloomsbury, 2003), p. 197.

[2] 'Paranoid Android'; 'Exit Music (For A Film)'; 'Fitter Happier'. See Allan Moore and Anwar Ibrahim, 'Sounds Like Teen Spirit: Identifying Radiohead's Idiolect', in Tate, p. 149.

[3] Pink Floyd's critical standing has waxed and waned. Dismissed by punks; briefly readmitted to respectability with the anti-establishment *The Wall*; went rubbish again in the 1980s; namechecked without irony in the early 90s by chillout performers such as the Orb; reclaimed as rock legends when they reformed for Live 8 in 2005. Of course, their earliest and greatest incarnation, when they were led by Syd Barrett, has always been critically sacrosanct, and Barrett's death in 2006 has only reinforced this status.

[4] Jim Irvin, interview, *Mojo*, July, 1997.

[5] 'OK Computer' was the original title for the song 'Palo Alto', which contains the line "I'm OK, how are you?" (see Chapters 2 and 18).

[6] Griffiths, *OK Computer*, p. 84. For example, *Music Of Quality And Distinction* by the British Electric Foundation, 1982; *Power, Corruption & Lies* by New Order, 1983.

[7] Interview, http://cokebabie.tripod.com/page31.html

[8] Brian Raftery, 'Bent out of Shape', *Spin*, August, 2006.

[9] David Adam, 'Rock tours damaging environment, says Radiohead singer', *The Guardian,* October 17, 2006.

[10] Clips from which were used in Queen's video for their 1984 hit 'Radio GaGa'.

[11] The line achieved more resonance a few years later, especially when the song was played in the United States; see Chapter 12.

[12] *OK Computer: A Classic Album Under Review.*

[13] See Irwin Chusid, Songs In The Key Of Z: The Curious Universe Of Outsider Music (London: Cherry Red, 2000)

[14] Chuck Klosterman, 'No More Knives', *Spin*, July, 2003.

[15] Thompson, p. 575.

[16] Phil Sutcliffe, 'Death Is All Around', *Q*, October, 1997.

[17] Lynne Truss holds sloppy teaching and the "ascendant medium" of e-mail and text messaging responsible for the decline in the correct use of English. See *Eats, Shoots & Leaves* (London: Profile, 2003), pp. 179-182. I blame the Eurythmics, for spelling "disappointment" with an extra "s" on the inner sleeve of their 1983 album *Sweet Dreams (Are Made Of This)*.

[18] My dad had held off from buying a CD player until The Beatles albums and the Ella Fitzgerald *Songbooks* were available on CD, as he refused to take the medium seriously until it accommodated these bedrocks of Western civilisation. Quite right too.

[19] Thus never recording the 'White Album'. See, these things *matter*.

[20] For more ideas along these lines, see Eric Steuer, 'The Infinite Album', *Wired*, September, 2006; also, Dylan Jones, *iPod, Therefore I Am* (London: Weidenfeld and Nicolson, 2005); and Chapter 25.

[21] Randall, pp. 162-163.

[22] Douglas Adams, *The Restaurant At The End Of The Universe* (London: Pan, 1980)

CHAPTER 17

**MAKES YOU LOOK PRETTY UGLY –
THE VIDEOS**

What are you looking at?
—Madonna, 'Vogue'

The use of moving pictures to promote musical performers and their recorded product goes back to the late 1920s, when jazz and blues artists made short films of their latest hits. This developed into Soundies, short, black-and-white films that were played on modified jukeboxes; Scopitones, shot on 16-millimetre colour film, were a French enhancement of the same idea, and were popular in Europe in the 1960s.

The increasing dominance of television, and the rise of youth-oriented pop shows, created a need for more filmed perform-ances, especially by performers who weren't present in the studio. Unsurprisingly, key innovations came from Bob Dylan ('Subterra-nean Homesick Blues', 1966) and The Beatles ('Strawberry Fields Forever', 1967). Queen's 'Bohemian Rhapsody' (1975) was one of the first promotional films to take advantage of the technical possi-bilities of videotape, but it was the launch of MTV, an all-video cable channel, in 1981, that created the situation whereby any band with a successful single was almost obliged to release a video. Landmark productions such as Michael Jackson's 'Thriller' (directed by John Landis, 1983), Robert Palmer's 'Addicted To Love' (Terence Do-novan, 1986) and 'Sledgehammer' (Stephen R. Johnson, 1986) by Peter Gabriel reached new levels of sophistication, innovation and (in many cases) budget. For consumers, the visuals became inextri-cably linked to the music; the releases of videos by performers such as Jackson and Madonna became news events in their own right, often overshadowing the music that they were supposedly intended to promote.

Many video directors (such as Spike Jonze, Michel Gondry and David Fincher) have gone onto successful Hollywood careers; and plenty of respected movie directors (for example, Landis and Martin Scorsese) have travelled in the opposite direction. However, the critical status of the promotional video in rock and pop is shaky. Of course, there's potential within the form for astounding artis-tic and technical achievement, but many critics hold the dismissive view that they're little more than advertisements, one more method to persuade the fans to part with their cash.[1] Part of this suspicion may come from the fact that the heyday of the video was in the materialist 1980s, and pioneers in the form (such as Duran Duran) were seen to be in thrall to the glossy, vacuous values of the time.

Radiohead, whose whole essence was in opposition to this kind of chocolate-box mentality, did not take to videos naturally, and many of their early promos are little more than filmed 'live' performances. It was only with Jamie Thraves' video for 'Just' (1995), the fourth single from *The Bends*, that they put their name to something particularly memorable.

In visual and narrative terms, it's relatively simple. A man in a suit half-collapses, half-lies down on a London pavement. People come to his assistance, but he refuses to say why he's there (all dialogue being conducted in subtitles). After he's reluctantly persuaded to offer up his secret (at this point the subtitles cut out, and we only see his lips moving) the people surrounding him are seen similarly slumped on the ground.

What makes the video oddly memorable is the core mystery – online speculation about the nature of the man's message is never-ending – and the overall look: the bright sunlight on the concrete; the drab browns and greys of the suits. There are two key points to note: the 'story' bears very little direct relation to the lyrics; and the members of Radiohead themselves play very little part in that story. They are seen 'performing' the song in a high-rise apartment (Thom in a particularly ill-advised leather-jacket-and-tie combo); and then they are pictured looking down at the spread-eagled bodies. They don't get involved.

'Lucky'

The band's physical involvement in the video for 'Lucky' is similarly minimal. The single – in fact, the first track on a multi-artist EP – was released only a few weeks after 'Just', as part of the promotion effort for the *Help* album, organised to raise money for the War Child charity (see Chapter 13). Radiohead are seen performing the song in the studio, but the band is of secondary importance. What sticks in the mind is the footage of children, injured, frightened, traumatised and dispossessed by the lunacy of war. Two images in particular stick out: a boy casually wielding an AK47 rifle; and a shot of a teddy bear that pans down to the scarred face of a little girl in a hospital bed.

Although the song's lyrics do not relate explicitly to the conflict in the Balkans, some clever juxtaposition of sound and image takes place; in particular with the refrain "pull me out of the air crash", which accompanies positive images of children being helped to safety, and the work that War Child was doing in Bosnia. There's also clever use of slogans (such as the words "DON'T FORGET", painted on a wall), prefiguring the Situationist-inspired use of found text on *OK Computer* tracks such as 'Fitter Happier'. Towards the end of the video, direct information linking the images to the work of War Child appears. It reinforces the message that, whatever its artistic qualities, the video is there to do a job, to raise awareness of, and cash for the charity. Viewers tend to tolerate such blatant 'selling' in the context of charity-related videos far more than they accept the explicit 'selling' of a band's material for profit. This process usually has to be conducted on a more subtle level.[2]

The 'Lucky' video raises awareness of the War Child charity, but is also intended to boost sales of the album from which it came (the function of most promo videos, since singles in recent years have tended to make very little, if any, profit for record companies). To this end, the last frames show scenes of other performers on the album, especially Noel Gallagher, Paul McCartney and Paul Weller, who had formed an ad-hoc supergroup, the Smokin' Mojo Filters. The matey, showbizzy, self-obsessed atmosphere is reinforced by shots of Stella (daughter of rock star) McCartney and Kate (serial girlfriend of rock stars) Moss.[3] The slightly sick-making imagery of rock millionaires chatting and joking in their own little bubble enforces (unintentionally, we presume) the notion that the benefit-rock explosion begun by Bob Geldof and Band Aid in 1984 may have done a lot of good for charities, but has been almost entirely disastrous for popular music.

Crucially, when the celebrity backslapping begins, the members of Radiohead are nowhere to be seen.

'Paranoid Android'

Radiohead had originally planned to film a video for each track on *OK Computer*, and the idea of a cinema release was even

159

bandied around for a while. The band soon realised they didn't have the time or the resources to do this, and a promo for 'Let Down' (an early idea for the lead single) was scrapped, leaving the band several thousand dollars to the bad.[4]

By this stage, Radiohead's videos were clearly moving to a point where the band members themselves were having less direct input; and the link between the 'content' of the songs and that of the visuals was all but completely severed. This was taken to the logical conclusion with the first video produced with a specific connection to *OK Computer*. The director, Magnus Carlsson, was a noted animator, which precluded band appearances (although more of that later); and he was not provided with a lyric sheet for 'Paranoid Android', so his visual ideas were a response to the overall sound of the track, rather than a depiction of Yorke's words.

Carlsson's visual style emphasises strong lines and bold colours, with superficially simple, childish draughtsmanship; there's a strong similarity to the work of the American animator Mike Judge (*Beavis and Butt-head*, *King of the Hill*). His central character, known as Robin, first appeared in a series of short films broadcast in 1993. He is apparently a young, casually dressed man whose defining characteristic is that things happen to him, rather than him consciously taking actions or making decisions on his own.

There is not so much a plot, more a series of loosely connected scenes. Robin is first seen in his bedroom. He showers, apparently rubbing soap into his eyes; then gets into a taxi with his friend Benjamin; they go out of town, and stop at a tree. A woman descends, and undresses for them; their lack of response angers her.

These antics are interconnected with images of a fat, balding man in a suit, who seems to be involved in intense negotiations at the United Nations, or some similar institution. His path intersects with that of Robin and Benjamin at a bar; in the background, a man with an extra head growing out of his midriff stands on a table, around which the members of Radiohead sit, looking bored. (In fact, the representation of the band is half-hearted; 'Thom' and 'Jonny' resemble the originals, but the others are as indistinguishable as the crew members you've never seen before who get beamed down to their doom in *Star Trek*. As Ed O'Brien put it: "If you freeze-frame

ADVANCE CD
RADIOHEAD
OK COMPUTER
PRIVATE & CONFIDENTIAL
155 OF 300

RADIO SOUND
HEAD GARDEN

ULTRAMEGA COMPUTER

RADIODREAD
EASY STAR ALL STARS

STAGE

RADIOHEAD
KARMA POLICE CD1

RADIOHEAD
KARMA POLICE CD2

RADIOHEAD
PARANOID ANDROID CD1

RADIOHEAD
PARANOID ANDROID CD2

RADIOHEAD
NO SURPRISES

CD1
FEATURES TWO
BONUS TRACKS
PALO ALTO
HOW I MADE
MY MILLIONS

RADIOHEAD
NO SURPRISES

CD2
FEATURES TWO
BONUS TRACKS
AIRBAG (LIVE)
LUCKY (LIVE)

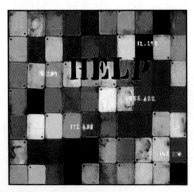

HELP

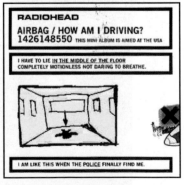

RADIOHEAD
AIRBAG / HOW AM I DRIVING?
1426148550 THIS MINI ALBUM IS AIMED AT THE USA

I HAVE TO LIE IN THE MIDDLE OF THE FLOOR
COMPLETELY MOTIONLESS NOT DARING TO BREATHE.

I AM LIKE THIS WHEN THE POLICE FINALLY FIND ME.

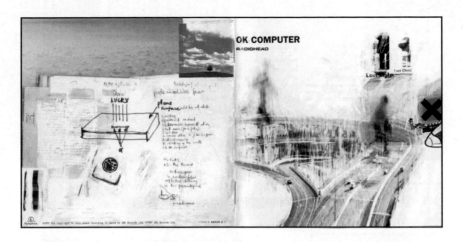

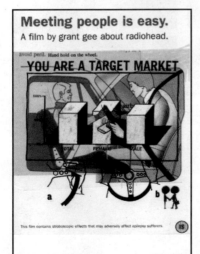

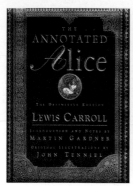

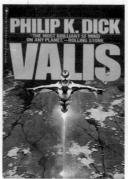

RADIOHEAD OK COMPUTER
A CLASSIC ALBUM UNDER REVIEW
– *AVAILABLE ON* **DVD** *NOW*

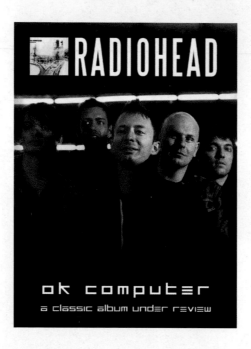

OK Computer: A Classic Album Under Review is a 60-minute documentary film which reassesses and offers new insight on what has become one of the seminal works of the rock age.

Includes comment, criticism and insight on every track from the album by; writer, journalist and author of *Radiohead; A Guide To Their Music* **Mark Paytress**; respected rock authority and ex-*Mojo* editor, **Barney Hoskyns**; Radiohead biographer **Alex Ogg**; musicologist and author of *Radiohead 33 1/3*, **Dai Griffiths**, legendary ex- *Melody Maker* and *Wire* contributor **David Stubbs** and *Record Collector* magazine's **Jake Kennedy**.

Extras include

'The Hardest Interactive Radiohead Quiz In The World Ever'
Full Contributor Biographies
'Beyond DVD' section.

it on video, the guy with the five strands of hair slicked back, that's Colin. It looks nothing like him."[5])

The three protagonists meet again on a bridge over a river. Robin elects to climb a lamp-post; the fat man removes his suit and, clad only in a studded jock-strap, tries to cut down the metal pole with an axe. Robin is rescued by an angel in a helicopter, who treats him to a game of table-tennis; the fat man cuts off his own limbs and tumbles into the river; mermaids rescue him, swaddle him like a baby, and place him in the tree from which the flashing woman descended earlier. A bird feeds him a worm. End.

It's an extraordinary video, and captures the demented turmoil of the music. Although there's no explicit link between the images and the lyrics of the song, there is a degree of conceptual crossover; the bar, for example, could well be the location of the "Gucci little piggy" incident; the angel a manifestation of "God loves his children". Moreover, Robin's pose on top of the lamp-post, and the fat man's descent into drunken self-destruction, correspond to the overall themes of the album: the feeble attempts to break away from the crushing monotony of modern society (see 'Subterranean Homesick Alien'); and the fact that such attempts are doomed to failure ('No Surprises').

It's also pretty disturbing, slotting in neatly to the trend of adult-oriented animation that developed in the 1990s. including the works of Mike Judge (see above), Matt Groening (*The Simpsons*, *Futurama*) and Trey Parker and Matt Stone (*South Park*). Despite the savagery of the fat man's auto-amputation, what particularly upset broadcasters was the number of breasts on display: Robin has a poster bearing the slogan "BIG TITS"; Benjamin fondles the nipple of a barmaid; the mermaids are topless – but then mermaids are meant to be topless. MTV insisted that the offending mammaries be shrouded in virtual bikinis, although the severed limbs were deemed suitable for family viewing.[6]

'Karma Police'
For the next promo, the band turned to Jonathan Glazer, who had directed the video for 'Street Spirit' in 1995. This had been an interesting concept that didn't quite come off. Shot in black-and-

white in a trailer park, it has the band members performing various stunts and moves, while the film slows down and speeds up. Part of the problem is that, Thom Yorke apart, the musicians seem awkward and self-conscious, too aware of the camera and the director. Moreover, Jonny Greenwood jumps like a girl and Phil Selway runs like a drummer.

For 'Karma Police', the only band member in shot is Yorke (who looks awkward, but awkward in a good, tortured, indie-rock-star way). He's in the back seat of a Chrysler New Yorker that's moving down a road despite the fact that there's no driver. He occasionally mimes the words of the song. A man appears in the headlights, running desperately away from the car, until he collapses with exhaustion. The car stops, and the man turns round to face his tormentor; interestingly, in this shot, one of his eyes seems to be half closed, mirroring Yorke's own face. He sees a trail of petrol coming from the car, and ignites it with his lighter; when the camera returns to the car's interior, Yorke has gone.

By contrast with Magnus Carlsson's promo for 'Paranoid Android', there's a clear link here between the video and the lyrics. Karma is at work: the car torments the man; the man responds and punishes the car. The facial similarity between Yorke and the actor being pursued may also reinforce the notion that our deeds come back to us, a key element of the notion of karma.

Additionally, there's a connection with the transport and industrial obsessions of the album as a whole (especially 'Airbag'); the driverless car symbolises the extent to which we have lost any sense of autonomy and self-determination in the face of mechanisation.

Under cover of this straightforward visualisation of the song's theme, Glazer is playing games with our expectations of the video form. When a performer plays a role in a music video, he's usually supposed to be the hero; here, however, Yorke seems to be complicit in an attempt to kill a man, although he seems to be playing no active part in the pursuit of the running man. As Greg Hainge puts it:

> …this video contravenes the conventions of the genre that it springs from, for we are unable to establish a good guy and a bad guy just as we are unable to comprehend why

Yorke is seen singing only occasionally while he is heard singing constantly.[7]

The audience is made complicit with the action: we're inside the car as it moves towards the man; we're back in there as the flames lick around it. But we also feel for the victim, and his desperate action in throwing the lighter seems understandable. Just as the songs of *OK Computer* force us into a state of empathy with deluded losers ('Subterranean Homesick Alien') and psychopaths ('Climbing Up The Walls'), so the videos allow us inside the heads of the people that Nietzsche called "the bungled and the botched"; although for most of us, that's not such a stretch of the imagination.

Glazer would return to a similar theme the following year, with the video for UNKLE's 'Rabbit in Your Headlights', on which Yorke provided vocals. In this film, a muttering man is seen walking in an underpass, where he is struck by several cars, but gets back on his feet. Finally a car strikes him and explodes. His final stance, stripped to the waist, arms outstretched, as autoparts fly in all directions, is defiantly Christlike (see 'Airbag'); alternatively, in a Nietzschean reading, a member of the bungled and the botched becomes a superman (see 'Lucky').

Glazer's evident fascination with themes of crime and revenge came to fruition in 2000, when he directed the gangster movie *Sexy Beast*, starring Ray Winstone and Ben Kingsley. The climactic death of the monstrous Don Logan (Kingsley), crushed by a television set, is an image that could easily have sprung from the technophobia that infests *OK Computer*.

'No Surprises'

The final single from *OK Computer* has a video that matches its downbeat subtext. Street lights, yet another transport motif, reflect on a dark background. Yorke's face appears, shrouded in shadow, strongly suggesting an iconic image of actor Keir Dullea as the astronaut Dave in Stanley Kubrick's *2001: A Space Odyssey* (2001). He's miming the words of 'No Surprises' which scroll up the screen in reverse. The effect is that of an autocue; effectively, we're seeing what he's reading, from behind. It also echoes the reversed Greek text on the album packaging.

At the line "I'll take a quiet life", the lighting becomes stronger, revealing not only Yorke's endearingly 'English' teeth, but water steadily rising up the screen. As it reaches his mouth, he stops miming, but the words continue. He appears to hold his breath for just under a minute[8], then the water subsides. After he gets his breath back, he rejoins the song.

The video is directed by Grant Gee, and its making is shown in Gee's documentary *Meeting People is Easy* (1998). Yorke is seen with his head inside an old-fashioned diving helmet, into which water is pumped ("full up like a landfill"?); when he can't take any more, he unseals the helmet, causing water to cascade into the container in which he stands.

Gee's use of his own video in his own documentary is elegantly postmodern. He adds to the metatextual effect by showing a clip from a daytime show on the British Sky TV station, where the 'No Surprises' promo is being shown. We immediately realise that this is not a sympathetic environment when the name of Radiohead's not entirely un-famous record label is misspelled as "Parlaphone". But this is nothing compared to the reaction from the studio presenters, who watch while munching the mid-morning pastries kindly provided by their employer, Rupert Murdoch. One of them describes the song as "music to cut your wrists to" and "the most miserable-sounding tune I've ever heard". "I can hear him, but I can't see his lips move," gasps one of her co-hosts, perhaps unaware that the bands on *Top Of The Pops* usually mime as well. "He's Roger DeCourcey's son," quips the in-house pop 'expert', compensating for his musical cluelessness with an encyclopaedic recall of notoriously undertalented British ventriloquists of the 1970s.

By the time 'No Surprises' was released in 1998, *OK Computer* had transcended its indie-rock roots, and was already being spoken of as a 'classic album' to rank with the landmarks of rock history. The reaction of the daytime drones suggests that Radiohead still hadn't entered the mainstream; that they still retained the power to confront and disturb.

Notes:

[1] Although making the fans part with cash is also a major component of releasing an album or staging a tour.

[2] There are, of course, exceptions. The use of Sting's track 'Desert Rose' in a TV commercial for Jaguar cars in 2000 reinforced the identity of the promo video as an advertisement, no more, no less. The commercial was prefaced with artist, track and album details, as if it were playing in rotation on VH1 or MTV. Not only did the commercial boost Jaguar's sales, it seemed to do no harm to Sting's profits or, crucially, his credibility. See Scott Donaton, *Madison & Vine: Why the Entertainment and Advertising Industries Must Converge to Survive* (New York: McGraw-Hill, 2004), pp. 137-143.

[3] Moss was present because her then-boyfriend Johnny Depp was on the album, playing guitar with Oasis. He was, of course, selected for his instrumental skills, not for his cheekbones.

[4] Clarke, p. 117.

[5] Randall, p. 168.

[6] A premonition of Janet Jackson and her 'wardrobe malfunction' at Super Bowl XXXVIII in 2004? In fact, Carlsson's apparent breast obsession is even more striking because Radiohead's music tends to be consciously asexual, at least by the standards of rock music. See Erin Harde, 'Radiohead and the Negation of Gender', Tate, pp. 52-61.

[7] Greg Hainge, 'To(rt)uring the Minotaur: Radiohead, Pop, Unnatural Couplings, and Mainstream Subversion', Tate, p. 69.

[8] It was actually a shorter time period; the film was slowed down in editing to make it fit the minute.

CHAPTER 18

ASBESTOS AND SKELETONS –
THE SONGS THEY LEFT BEHIND

They that observe lying vanities forsake their own mercy.
—Jonah, 2:8

The best indicator of the creativity and inspiration hovering around Radiohead in 1996-1997 is the quality of the tracks that never made it onto *OK Computer*. Of course, a successful album requires cohesion and coherency, and this isn't always the same thing as juggling the 12 songs that are individually the best. In qualitative terms, several of the also-ran tracks are probably better than the weakest songs on *OK Computer*, but that doesn't necessarily mean that the album would have been better if they had been there.

Although Radiohead worked on over 20 songs during the *OK Computer* sessions, only 14 were serious contenders for the final running order; the discarded pair were 'Pearly*' and 'Polyethylene (Parts 1 & 2)'. These two, along with most of the other rejected songs, were released as additional tracks on singles, and subsequently on the American and Japanese round-up EPs.

The demise of the 7-inch, 45-rprm vinyl single, and its replacement by CD, meant an increase in outlets for extra tracks (still generally known as B-sides, an echo of their previous status on singles). A CD single generally has three or four tracks. Moreover, to maximise sales, record companies generally issue CD singles in pairs, with exclusive tracks spread across the two versions; diehard fans and completists will buy both discs. Cassette and vinyl versions also turn up on an irregular basis. Welcome to the consumer society.

As an increasing proportion of single sales are conducted via online services such as iTunes, a model by which it finally makes economic sense to dispense music one track at a time, the need for a constant supply of B-sides is drying up. However, at the same time, the wonder of broadband means that any unreleased track is liable to be on the hard drive of a fan faster than it would have taken in analogue days to press and issue a single.

The tracks discussed here are the songs that didn't appear on the album in any form. The live recordings of 'Airbag' and 'Lucky' on the 'No Surprises' single, and the remixes of 'Climbing Up The Walls' on 'Karma Police', are discussed in their relevant chapters.

'A Reminder'

A classic on-the-road song, freighted with melancholy, 'A Reminder' was written during Radiohead's US tour, in August, 1996. It opens with background noise that was recorded at a railway station in Prague, an effect similar to the dinner-party chatter from which 'Re-make Re-model' (the first track on Roxy Music's eponymous debut album) emerges;[1] an organic variation on 'fridge buzz', maybe. The overall sound is similar to that of 'Let Down', with a Velvet Underground set-up of fuzz guitar and thumped drum offset by some *Bitches Brew*-influenced electric piano.

The core subject of the song, according to Thom, is memory: "I had this idea of someone writing a song, sending it to someone, and saying: 'If I ever lose it, you just pick up the phone and play this song back to remind me.'" With characteristic bleakness, the 27-year-old songwriter was already contemplating old age, although even that didn't seem inevitable: the first line is "If I get old", not "when". But there's real heart in among the misery, as the reference to "that night we kissed" nudges the lyric into that rare genre, the Radiohead love song. Don't get sentimental...

The back story suggests the way in which a patient is sometimes lured out of a coma or catatonic state with favourite music or other sounds. But the overall tone – especially the "Once I was free/ Once I was cool" couplet, also brings to mind *Krapp's Last Tape*, written in 1958 by Samuel Beckett (see Chapter 14). In the play, an old man listens to a tape of his own voice, made years before, and mourns his lost loves and missed opportunities.

'A Reminder' first appeared on the second 'Paranoid Android' CD, released in the UK in May, 1997; it subsequently turned up on the North American *Airbag/How Am I Driving?* EP, and the Japanese *No Surprises/Running From Demons* release.

'How I Made My Millions'

A track that Thom recorded straight to MiniDisc, and released without any subsequent production work, 'How I Made My Millions' is the only raw demo that Radiohead have released (on the first 'No Surprises' CD, in January, 1998, and the cassette version). The lyrics are simple to the point of banality, and thus open to numerous interpretations. They also bear no relation to the title, which may well be ironic; "*This* is how I made my millions – by playing the piano and mumbling."

Although it's a solo performance, background noise hints at the presence of Thom's girlfriend Rachel, who is doing the housework. From such a beacon of right-on causes and principles, this traditional division of domestic labours is somewhat disappointing; Rachel would be well within her rights to make a pointed reference to the *Bends*-era song 'You Never Wash Up After Yourself'.

In the summer of 2006, readers of the *NME* were asked to nominate the songs they wanted Radiohead to play at the V Festival in August that year. In among the obvious anthems, 'How I Made My Millions' appeared at number 12.[2]

They didn't play it.

'Last Flowers Till The Hospital' aka 'Cogs'

Colin Greenwood was particularly fond of this apparently Bowie-esque track, which the band worked on during the *OK Computer* sessions, but he seems to have been the only one. Thom claimed to be reworking it, under a new name, in 1999, but it failed to appear on *Kid A* or *Amnesiac*. In April 2005, while playing an impromptu set at the Trade Justice vigil in London, he introduced a song as 'Glass Flowers', with the characteristically technophobic opening line: "Appliances have gone berserk". Online fan consensus holds that this is in fact 'Last Flowers Till The Hospital', a title taken from a sign on the road approaching the John Radcliffe Hospital in Oxford.

'Lift'

If you want to spot a *serious* Radiohead fan, ask him (and it's usually a 'him') whether he thinks 'Lift' should have appeared on *OK Computer*. The song was written in 1996, and was a popular component of live sets at the time; many fans were surprised when it didn't even show up as a B-side. The band reintroduced it at a gig in Portugal, in 2002, but it also failed to appear on *Hail To The Thief* the following year. This may have been a case of band democracy in action: Ed O'Brien has been heard to dismiss the song as "a bogs-hite B-side".[3]

Its absence from *OK Computer* is particularly odd because it seems to fit the album's overall themes of paranoia and technophobia. As the title suggests, it's about someone stuck in a lift (for American readers, an elevator); although this seems to be an analogy, as he's also described as being in the belly of a whale, at the bottom of the ocean. This direct allusion to the Biblical story of Jonah[4], coupled with lines such as "today is the first day of the rest of your days", hints at some sort of religious overtone to the song; is he being helped out by angels, or some other celestial power? Is it really "time to go home" or are they "coming for to carry me home", like the angels of gospel tradition taking the faithful to the Promised Land, or even heaven? In this sense, 'Lift' can be considered as the third part of a trilogy of religion, redemption and resurrection, alongside 'Airbag' and 'Lucky'.

In its original form, 'Lift' was a mid-tempo song featuring an insistent acoustic guitar riff and soaring, Morricone-style synthesised strings (see Chapter 6); Thom's interjections (using his own name, and the sizeist pejorative "squirt") suggest that the man in the lift is the singer himself. In later versions, the song had slowed down, and the personalised lyrics had disappeared.

'Lull'

A chiming, Byrds-like guitar[5], coupled with a glockenspiel (more restrained than on 'No Surprises'), heralds this slight but interesting song, which lasts less than two and a half minutes.

Like 'A Reminder', its most obvious counterpart on *OK Computer* is 'Let Down', with which it shares a back-to-basics, C86 quality; the glockenspiel adds a certain primary-school tweeness to the whole experience.

It's a song about stress and anger, but Thom, being the nice young chap he is, apologises. The lull of the title is the calm after the psychological storm. 'Lull', which can be found on the first 'Karma Police' CD, has never been performed live by the band.

'Meeting In The Aisle'

'Meeting In The Aisle' is an early experiment with purely instrumental music that should have turned out rather better than it did. The melody is given a sinuous, slightly Middle Eastern feel, with lots of tasty echo and reverb; it sounds quite intriguing. But the whole thing is ruined by the sort of deeply irritating, programmed drum track that will be familiar to anyone who purchased one of the 'Stars on 45' cover-version medleys in the early 1980s. In many ways it's a blueprint for the much more successful 'Dollars and Cents', the anti-globalisation Krautrock tribute that appeared on *Amnesiac*. 'Meeting In The Aisle' was released on the first 'Karma Police' CD, and can also be found on both *Airbag/How Am I Driving?* and *No Surprises/Running From Demons*. In addition, Radiohead used it as entrance music for some 1998 gigs, but have never performed it live.

'Melatonin'

A more successful merger of synths and rhythms than 'Meeting In The Aisle', 'Melatonin' benefits from an intriguing lyric that sounds like a twisted lullaby, sung by excessively pushy parents. Melatonin is a naturally occurring hormone that regulates sleep cycles, and the synthetic version can protect international travellers from jet-lag. The body's ability to produce it reduces with age, so some regard it as an anti-ageing drug. In other words, someone dosed with the stuff can maintain a state of permanent youthfulness; a boon to the creepy parents who never want their little one to grow up.

There's more than a hint of the 'White Album' lullaby 'Good Night', although Ringo Starr's utterly sincere croon is replaced by a croaked threat of "Death to all who stand in your way." And The Beatles, of course, could afford real strings.

'Melatonin' is on the second 'Paranoid Android' CD, and on both standalone EPs.

'Palo Alto' aka 'OK Computer'

The song that, in a roundabout way, gave the album its title (see Chapter 2) has its origins in a visit the band made to Palo Alto, California, in 1996. This "city of the future" is home to many of the biggest American high-tech companies, including Apple and Xerox.

It's yet another song about capitalism and technology, and their incompatibility with a fulfilled personal life; the specific references to the symbolic heart of the IT revolution gives it an overtly political feel. Like the even more explicit 'Electioneering', it's a no-nonsense rocker, and a psychic link to the band's early influence, The Pixies. However, the finished version (on the first 'No Surprises' CD, as well as the cassette and 12"; also on the *Airbag/How Am I Driving?* EP) livens up the basic track with some spacey guitar effects. There's yet another Beatles nod, in the line "meet the wife" (see Lennon's 'Good Morning, Good Morning' on *Sgt Pepper*); the lyrics suggest the pop-psychology/self-help classic *I'm OK, You're OK*, Thomas Harris's 1969 best-seller about Transactional Analysis. Thom Yorke's tired drawl has something of Bob Dylan about it, and the transition into the "I'm OK" passage hints at 'The Headmaster Ritual' from The Smiths' 1984 album *Meat Is Murder*.

The bulk of the track was recorded while the band was touring to support *OK Computer*, in the latter half of 1997. The guitar and vocals were captured on the tour bus; only Phil Selway's drum part was the result of a studio session.[6]

'Pearly*'

More than any other track from the *OK Computer* sessions, 'Pearly*' (the asterisk has never been explained) sounds like a bid for a place in the hierarchy of classic rock. It opens with guitar feedback over a bed of busy drums, played by Phil Selway and Ed O'Brien, suggesting Ringo Starr's work on the Beatles' *Revolver* (1966); then the vocal track splits in two, the right channel commenting on the left, a trick that the Fabs played the following year on 'She's Leaving Home'. Jonny Greenwood's guitar line at 2:08 echoes Hilton Valentine's intro on 'House Of The Rising Sun' by The Animals (1964); the drums then leap forward to 1978, copying the stampeding intro to 'Another Girl, Another Planet' by The Only Ones; and the guitar finishes up at some point in the mid-1980s, plucking a few hints from a crumpled copy of *How To Play Like The Edge*.

If we accept such a pantheon of rock legends as being representative of Western culture over the previous 30-odd years, it provides an ironic setting for the lyrics. Thom lays into globalisation from a cultural, rather than specifically economic, angle. The need for Californian-style smiles and drinks from globally franchised restaurants are seen to mould the sexual preferences ("sweet tooth... for white boys") of a girl in the developing world. And the flabby, sweaty, Western males stepping off the plane at Bangkok Airport can't believe their luck. Thom has introduced the song in concert as "a dirty song for people who use sex for dirty things".

'Pearly*' was included on the first 'Paranoid Android' CD, and the *Airbag/How Am I Driving?* EP. A remixed version turned up on *No Surprises/Running From Demons*.

'Polyethylene Parts 1 & 2'

The multi-part song is a characteristic affectation of progressive rock, suggesting the movements of a classical symphony or concerto. Pink Floyd, inevitably, were particularly guilty of this, with examples occurring on *Ummagumma* (1969), *Wish You Were Here* (1975), *Animals* (1977) and *The Wall* (1979).

Radiohead, of course, were responsible for 'Paranoid Android', although their post-punk wariness of pretension dissuaded them from identifying it as a 'Suite for Rock Quintet in Three Movements'. 'Polyethylene', however, gets the treatment.

There's a 'realistic', metatextual edge to the first part, as we seem to hear a cue from the producer.[7] Thom begins singing wistfully, with only his own acoustic for accompaniment, but he trails off after about 40 seconds. A count-in heralds a Led Zep-style guitar and organ duel, after which the singer rejoins the fray, straining to be heard above the din.

The lyrics are wilfully obscure. There seems to be an element of sniping at the dreadful middle classes (see Chapter 12), and their desire to avoid illness and infection. "There is no significant risk to your health" could be one of the banal soundbites from 'Fitter Happier'.

The title 'Polyethylene' suggests the synthetic, plastic-wrapped sterility of modern bourgeois society, although James Doheny ingeniously suggests that it also refers to the song's structure. The acoustic first part is in regular, 4/4 time, before taking on a more complex irregular form; in the same way, polyethylene is created by the polymerisation of ethane into long chains of molecules.[8] While no member of Radiohead has yet confessed to an abiding fascination for molecular chemistry, it's as convincing as any other explanation.

'Polyethylene', in all its shrink-wrapped majesty, is on the first CD and 7" versions of 'Paranoid Android', and also on the *Airbag/How Am I Driving?* EP.

Notes:

[1] Thom and Jonny would go on to record three early Roxy songs for the *Velvet Goldmine* soundtrack, released in 1999.

[2] Stephen Dalton, 'The National Anthems', *NME*, 19 August, 2006.

[3] Randall, p. 141.

[4] Jonah 1:15-2:10. While on a boat to Tarshish, Jonah was blamed for causing a storm, and was cast into the sea, where he was swallowed by "a great fish" (not a whale); he prayed to God, who made the fish vomit Jonah onto dry land.

[5] Although to the ears of Mark Paytress (pp. 86-87) it suggests The Grateful Dead.

[6] Randall, p. 175.

[7] There was a vogue in the 1960s and 70s for studio chatter to appear on recordings; The Beach Boys were particularly fond of it. Other examples include 'Daydream Believer' (1967) by The Monkees, on which Davy Jones is heard talking back to the producer, and 'Black Country Woman', on Led Zeppelin's *Physical Graffiti* (1975), which includes the unplanned sound of a passing aeroplane, and it was the group's decision to keep it in.

[8] Doheny, p. 138.

CHAPTER 19

EVERY DAY IN EVERY WAY –
THE CRITICAL RESPONSE

Rock journalism is people who can't write, interviewing people who can't talk, for people who can't read.
—Frank Zappa

Journalists like it, which is always ominous.
—Jonny Greenwood, about *OK Computer*

Britain in mid-1997 was hopeful sort of place to be. In the General Election in early May, Tony Blair's Labour Party dismembered the Conservatives, who had held power for 18 years. A surge of optimism and enthusiasm seized the country, as we welcomed our first rock 'n' roll Prime Minister.

The excitement would wear off pretty soon, and Blair would prove himself to be yet another grinning shyster who would (as Thom sneered in 'Electioneering') "stop at nothing". But it's a fair bet that the Labour victory met with approval, however cautious, among most British musicians at the time: Blair, had, after all, aligned himself with the renewed spirit of cultural and creative optimism that was briefly saddled with the retch-making slogan, 'Cool Britannia'.

Cool Britannia supposedly encompassed British artists (Damien Hirst, Tracey Emin); designers (Alexander McQueen); writers (Irvine Welsh); film-makers (Danny Boyle, Guy Ritchie); but, above all, it was about music, in particular, the vibrant, ironic, self-referential brand of guitar music know as Britpop.[1] Conjured up by the music press in a slow news week, as a reaction against the plaid-shirted earnestness of American grunge, Britpop had been less a coherent musical genre, more a state of mind and a statement of intent. At first it was applied to bands like Suede, who tried to recapture some of the sleazy, early-70s glamour of Bowie and Roxy Music. Pretty soon, however, the term became shorthand for a sound and attitude influenced by the quintessentially British sounds of 1960s guitar pop (in particular The Kinks and The Small Faces, but also The Beatles, The Rolling Stones and The Who) with more than a tip of the hat to The Jam, Madness and/or The Smiths. The key bands were Oasis, Blur, Pulp, Elastica, Supergrass, The Boo Radleys and Menswear, although the label became attached to such unwilling participants as Manic Street Preachers and Radiohead; surely a sign of the extent to which it dominated the music scene at the time.

Britpop's glory days (in terms of mainstream media attention, if not musical quality) fell between the summers of 1995 (when Blur's 'Country House' and 'Roll With It' by Oasis tussled for the top spot in the UK singles charts) and 1996, when Oasis played to a quarter of a million people over two nights at Knebworth. (It might not be coincidental that this period of gutter-press fascination coincided with the gap between Robbie Williams leaving Take That, and the rise of The Spice Girls.) Unfortunately, by the time Tony Blair was moving his Fender Stratocaster into his official residence in Downing Street,[2] nearly a year after Knebworth, Britpop was falling to bits. Many of the bands had either failed to deliver on their initial promise or – far worse – become too successful, and had fallen prey to the predations of the tabloids and/or London's finest cocaine dealers. If there was a musical theme to 1997, it was *comedown*. Blur, having come off second-best in the duel with Oasis, went lo-fi and released their best album, simply called *Blur*. Oasis went lo-inspiration and came up with their lamest, the plodding *Be Here Now*; the disc described by the genre's smartest chronicler as "the record that would kill the Britpop dream stone dead."[3] Even the cheerful monkeyboys of Britpop, Supergrass, dimmed their chimpy grins a little when they released *In It For The Money*. Pulp, confirming their reputation for coming fashionably late to the party,[4] waited until early 1998 to release their anti-celebrity masterpiece, the mighty *This Is Hardcore*.

But the three key albums of 1997 were by bands that had for, various reasons, been hovering on the sidelines, and whose aura of melancholy wasn't a new thing. The Verve had been around since the late 1980s, and had suffered from disappointing sales, drug and health problems, and a temporary split after their second album. *Urban Hymns* maintained hints of their original blend of psychedelia and shoegazing, but fused it with strong tunes and heartfelt vocals that made frontman Richard Ashcroft an alt-rock sex symbol.

Spiritualized had formed at around the same time as The Verve started up, but frontman Jason Pierce had previously spent most of the 1980s with the pharmaceutically challenged trance-rockers Spacemen 3. For 1997's *Ladies And Gentlemen We Are Floating In Space*, he beefed up his band's spacey minimalism with gospel choirs, strings, horns, New Orleans piano from Dr John and a massive, Phil Spector approach to production that didn't disguise his persistent lyrical obsessions; loss and drugs. Pierce's dour mood wasn't enhanced when girlfriend and keyboardist Kate Radley dumped him in favour of Ashcroft, from The Verve.

Radiohead, of course, steered clear of such rock 'n' roll soap opera, and had even managed to avoid the drugs that seemed to be causing so many problems for their contemporaries. But *OK Computer* shares a number of traits with the albums by The Verve and Spiritualized. It's essentially downbeat in tone and content; it's varied in sound and texture, although still grounded in alternative guitar rock; it has moments of dizzying, epic grandeur; and the critics adored it.

The most influential voice on the British music scene was still that of the *New Musical Express*, in which James Oldham gave the album an all but unprecedented 10/10 rating. He praised its "towering lyrical ambition and musical exploration", described it as "both age-defining and one of the most startling albums ever made" and concluded with this:

> ...a spectacular success: a true articulation of the anxiety of late-20th century man backed with music not only of extraordinary grace and melody, but also of experimental clarity and vision. Truly, this is one of the greatest albums of

living memory - and the one that distances Radiohead from their peers by an interstellar mile.[5]

Taylor Parkes, in the rival weekly *Melody Maker*, was even more flowery, describing it as "crimson music, as grotesque and claustrophobic as those videos of internal organs filmed by a camera in a pipe shoved up inside the body" and comparing it to "a facsimile of unwanted feelings on wet weekday afternoons". His own summing-up was less assertive about the objective merits of the album, but he clearly shared Oldham's view that the release of *OK Computer* was a rare and special event:

> It's as pained and as slow-moving as the emotions that inspired it. I can't work out whether I like it, although I think I like it very much indeed. I definitely know it isn't good for me, and I'm certain it says more about my life than I'd like. In one way or another, Radiohead have excelled themselves. They've seen the future. It is murder. Who's going to join them there?[6]

This was a key question, and one that seemed to suggest that *OK Computer*'s importance was assured even before it had hit the shops. It was a marker to other bands, a sign that the bar had been raised and all the other acts that had been darlings of the music press for the previous three years had to contend with a redefinition of what a rock album could be.

The enthusiasm continued in the monthly magazines. *Q* called it a "a huge, mysterious album for the head and soul";[7] *Select* described it as "mould-breaking" and "a landslide victory".[8] A consistent message from the reviews was that the initial promise offered by *The Bends* had been fulfilled, or even exceeded.

In the United States, on the other hand, Radiohead's second album had performed only moderately, a situation not helped by the lack of a viable airplay hit. There at least, the band had still not transcended the fuggy aura of 'Creep'; so it was possibly a stroke of luck that *Rolling Stone* chose Mark Kemp, one of the few Stateside critics to have been unmoved by that breakout single, to review the new album. Kemp knew that many potential listeners would have been unaware of the massive musical developments that Radiohead had undergone in the previous four years, and warned that "*OK Computer* is not an easy listen"; however, with the zeal of the newly converted, he dubbed it "a stunning art-rock tour de force".[9] *Entertainment Weekly*, meanwhile, lauded its "poignant delicacy and breadth" and the band's ability to "take British pop [as distinct, maybe, from Britpop] to a heavenly new level".[10] In the *New Yorker*, Alex Ross praised Radiohead's willingness to take risks and mix unlikely influences, especially when compared with the plodding conservatism offered by Oasis:

> Throughout the album, contrasts of mood and style are extreme: a couple of the songs could almost have been sung by Sinatra (or so it's fun to imagine), while a couple of others, rescored for bass clarinets, might win appreciative shrugs from new music cognoscenti at The Knitting Factory. This band has pulled off one of the great art-pop balancing acts in the history of rock... Radiohead repeats the means but not the end of The Beatles' experiments; its fusion is original. I do not know how to describe what is an essentially indescribable sound, but I had one last idea while watching the very English spectacle of Princess Diana's funeral: the varieties of lament heard during the service – an Elgar elegy, an Elton John ballad, an other-worldly contemporary dirge by John Tavener – could have been telescoped into a fairly typical Radiohead song.[11]

Not only were the reviews almost unanimously positive, but they agreed on many specifics. Most warned that the album was a grower, and might need half a dozen listens to make full sense. Several spotted the Beatles and Pink Floyd connections, although most were keen to defend the band against accusations of "going

prog". But what was most significant was the way in which journalists – a notoriously insecure and needy species – felt confident
enough to vouch for the long-term, historical impact of the album.
Taylor Parkes, in *Melody Maker*, was not the only reviewer to
make a specific connection with the imminent end of the millennium, a looming inevitability that was obsessing style gurus, trend
analysts, IT managers and religious maniacs alike. There was an
overwhelming consensus that *OK Computer* was something above
and beyond a great record. It was a landmark, both for popular
music and for culture as a whole. Nick Kent, a music journalist
whose louche, rock 'n' roll reputation exceeded that of most of the
musicians he covered, declared in *Mojo*:

> In 20 years time I'm betting *OK Computer* will be seen as
> the key record of 1997, the one to take rock forward instead
> of artfully revamping images and song-structures from an
> earlier era.[12]

This practically unanimous acclaim was almost unprecedented. Not since 1967, with the release of *Sgt Pepper's Lonely
Hearts Club Band*, had so many major critics agreed immediately,
not only on an album's merits, but on its long-term significance,
and its ability to encapsulate a particular point in history. As Dai
Griffiths would later put it: "You want to know what 1997 felt
like? *OK Computer*: tracks six-eight."[13]

Bearing in mind that part of the critical and commercial success of *OK Computer* derived from its success in summing up
a particular historical moment, what is impressive and surprising
is the extent to which its status has endured since then. Of course,
some records maintain a position in the collective consciousness
because the era from which they come is bathed in a nostalgic,
often drug-addled glow: the psychedelic summer of 1967 for *Sgt
Pepper*; the loved-up, dancing-in-a-field daftness of 1989 for *The
Stone Roses*. But few people remember 1997 with sentimental

fondness, and even if you did, would you want a record as dark and unlovely as *OK Computer* to transport you there?

In short, *OK Computer* was that rarer-than-cellulite-on-a-supermodel commodity, an instant classic, that was simultaneously of its time, and able to transcend its time. To map its status, one only needs to track its performance in the various polls and lists that peppered the music media with increasing regularity in the next decade.[14]

Of course, it's important to view these lists with some level of scepticism. Although they are often presented with an aura of solemn objectivity, many are cobbled together in the pub, with the sole aim of raising the profile of the magazine or other medium in which they appear. On a slow day, news media will be delighted to run a new poll that announces Coldplay to be better than The Beatles, or Beyoncé Knowles to be the greatest female singer of all time; if only for the apoplectic response it will provoke. Polls that are based on votes from readers might have more value; however, more than occasionally, they can be tweaked by magazine staff to settle scores and give the 'right' results. The tendency of certain magazines to spin their lists into fully-fledged awards ceremonies also skews the statistics, as awards tend to be given to those artists whose attendance can be guaranteed by a fee within the publisher's budget.

On the other hand, however questionable an individual poll may be, considered en masse, they give an excellent perspective on the changing fortunes of musicians and their product. Oasis is a classic example. The band's second album, *(What's The Story) Morning Glory* was released to positive but hardly ecstatic reviews in 1995; it overcame this in subsequent years to secure a status in 'all-time' lists alongside The Beatles, Dylan, et al; and then, by the early 2000s, it began to fade.

OK Computer showed no such fragility. The initial promise of the reviews at the time of its release was confirmed in the various end-of-year polls. It placed second in both the *NME* (to *Ladies And Gentlemen...*) and *Melody Maker* (to *Urban Hymns*), a concentration of tuneful misery that seemed to contradict the elation and optimism that Blair's election had allegedly provoked. Second place was also recorded in *Rolling Stone*, *Village Voice* and *Uncut* (all to a resurgent Bob Dylan) and *Spin* (to the engaging Asian-dance-lo-fi hybrid that was Cornershop's *When I Was Born For The 7th Time*). The album topped the rankings in *Mojo*, *Vox*, *Select*, *Entertainment Weekly*, the Irish magazine *Hot Press*, the Dutch *OOR*, *Humo* (Belgium), *Eye Weekly* (Canada) and *Inpress* (Australia); and tied for the number one slot in *The Face* with *Homework*, by the French duo Daft Punk. It also placed in the un-ranked listings of *Q* and the French magazine *Les Inrockuptibles*. (In 1999, *Q* published a year-by-year retrospective of the past dec-ade, in which *OK Computer* topped the 1997 list.)

Two things are noticeable from studying these polls. One is that 1997 saw the last serious British challenge to the US rock's domination of its own back yard. If we take the liberty of count-ing the Icelandic Björk as an honorary Brit, 50% of the combined top 10 placings in the *Rolling Stone* and *Spin* lists were held by UK-based acts.

The other significant point is that, if a single sound from *OK Computer* signalled the way forward, it was Phil Selway's hacked-up drumming on 'Airbag'. The collision of rock and dance sounds had become the dominant genre in popular music, although the sounds ranged from frantic collisions of punk and hip-hop, to the chilly throb of trip-hop. Daft Punk, Cornershop and Björk's *Homogenic* were joined in the critical roundups by Prodigy (*Fat Of The Land*), The Chemical Brothers (*Dig Your Own Hole*), Beth Orton (*Trailer Park*) and Portishead's self-titled sophomore effort. Primal Scream, whose 1991 album *Screamadelica* was a key influ-ence on many of these bands, weighed in with *Vanishing Point*.

Rock music was clearly changing. However, this wasn't a scorched-earth, Year Zero revolution, like the punk putsch that had summarily guillotined rock's hairy old guard in 1977. Techno-logical developments, and a growing consumer taste for eclectic sounds from beyond the rock mainstream, had over the previous few years made the musical landscape more heterogeneous and diverse. *OK Computer* traced unlikely links between progressive rock and experimental techno, austere, atonal composition and jazz-rock improvisation, all bubbling up through a thin crust of indie guitar rock; it was like a compilation album of all the various strands that Radiohead's contemporaries were following, and a few that nobody else dared touch. Because of the multiple influences that were buzzing around in the ether of Canned Applause and St Catherine's Court, the album did not simply point a way forward; it also traced a path through the history of rock, creating a niche for itself alongside all the old warhorses whose names will forever be etched into the Great Rock Cenotaph.

The earliest appearance of *OK Computer* on an 'all-time' list actually came before the 1997 end-of-year rankings were compiled. Over August and September, customers of Virgin Megastores in the UK were asked for their submissions towards a 'Chart of the Century'. It was an eccentric selection, to say the least. It heavily favoured recent releases, and *OK Computer*'s number 16 slot, a mere three months after its release, seemed to be influenced by 'flavour of the month' syndrome: similar anomalies included *Spice* by The Spice Girls, which took sixth place; and solid showings by Britpop also-rans Ocean Colour Scene and Kula Shaker.

However, even as these passing fancies assumed the role of embarrassing, collection-tainting indiscretions, *OK Computer* hung in there. In early 1998, it topped a readers' poll in *Q*, to elect the greatest album of all time, and over the next few years placed high in lists published by *NME*, *Melody Maker*, *Spin*, *Alternative Press* and *Rolling Stone*. The latter magazine dealt the album an unexpected blow in 2003 when it slumped to 162nd place in a defiantly retrospective and conservative poll that placed it below such AOR titans as Billy Joel and Santana, and provided more Bruce Springsteen than is usually considered healthy.[15] But it saw a resurgence in 2006, with top 10 placings in *Q*, *Mojo* and *NME* polls, and a *Spin* endorsement as the best album of the previous 20 years. Even the brickbat offered by the BBC 6Music radio station in 2005, when *OK Computer* was named the sixth most overrated album of all time, was actually a backhanded compliment, reinforcing Radiohead's standing alongside The Beatles, U2, Nirvana and The Beach Boys.

Radiohead had achieved the uncomfortable status of living legends, a role that had been reinforced in 2000 by *NME*'s decision to label the band as second only to David Bowie in a list of the "most influential artists of all time".[16] It was a list that could have been based on the band's record collection; they were ranked just above The Beatles (third place) and Miles Davis (fifth); Aphex Twin, The Smiths and Kraftwerk also placed in the top 20.

Although *The Bends* and *Kid A* often placed respectably in these lists, it was clear that *OK Computer* had transcended the confused musical landscape of 1997 and now wore the millstone of Classic Album status round its skinny neck (see Chapter 25). With it, Radiohead had ceased to be defined as one-hit, alt-rock gloom-mongers. They were standing on the edge, gazing out over the urban landscape depicted on the album's cover; the rock world was laid out before them, waiting for their next move.

Notes:

[1] It's perhaps fitting that 'Cool Britannia' was originally a 1967 song by the Bonzo Dog Doo-Dah Band, whose sardonic brand of retro silliness surely influenced more than a few Britpop bands.

[2] The new Prime Minister was several steps ahead of Radiohead, having sung with an Oxford-based rock band (Ugly Rumours) when Jonny Greenwood was still in nappies.

[3] John Harris, *The Last Party: Britpop, Blair And The Demise Of English Rock* (London: Fourth Estate, 2003), p. 314.

[4] Pulp formed in 1978, and recorded their first John Peel session in 1981; it would be well over a decade until Britpop, and a fortuitous run-in with Michael Jackson, pitchforked Jarvis Cocker's misfits into the wider public gaze.

[5] James Oldham, album review, *NME*, June 14, 1997.

[6] Taylor Parkes, album review, *Melody Maker*, June 14, 1997.

[7] David Cavanagh, album review, *Q*, July 1997.

[8] John Harris, album review, *Select*, July 1997.

[9] Mark Kemp, album review, *Rolling Stone,* July 10-24, 1997.

[10] Album review, *Entertainment Weekly,* July 11, 1997.

[11] Alex Ross, 'Dadrock: Revisiting the Sixties with Oasis and Radiohead', *New Yorker*, September 29, 1997

[12] Nick Kent, album review, *Mojo*, July 1997.

[13] Griffiths, *OK Computer*, p. 114.

[14] Much of the data in the following paragraphs can be found on the superb, dangerously compulsive site, www.rocklist.net.

[15] 'The RS 500 Greatest Albums of All Time', *Rolling Stone*, December 2003.

[16] 'NME's 20 Most Influential Artists Of All Time', *NME*, December 2, 2000.

CHAPTER 20

LIKE A DETUNED RADIO –
THE COVER VERSIONS

Then there's the false authority in mass-producing a work, which gives it a false sense of significance. The thing of taking responsibility for your work is, to a high extent, bullshit because a big part of it is simply that yours is being mass-produced and someone else's isn't. Yours is getting marketed in ways that other people's isn't, and that's part of how people approach it, independent from the work itself.
—Thom Yorke, 1998

But you don't really care for music, do you?
—Leonard Cohen (and others), 'Hallelujah'

The role of the cover version has shifted over the years, in response to changes in the model of music production, and also the shifting concepts of authenticity and originality. Of course, before the mass availability of recorded music, the notion of 'covering' a song did not arise; songwriters would simply hope that as many people as possible performed their work. Even after the introduction of the 78-rpm shellac disc, sales of sheet music were, for many years, a core source of income for songwriters. Several performers might record a version of a popular tune, but few consumers would have a particular preference about who was singing when they bought a disc.

After World War II, the rise of singing superstars such as Frank Sinatra and Elvis Presley shifted the emphasis to the performer, although there were still episodes when songs held the upper hand: in 1953 and 1957, there were weeks when two separate versions of the same song ('Answer Me' and 'Singing the Blues', respectively) shared the top position in the British charts. But the stage had come when songs would become identified with particular singers; anyone else performing the same song was seen as something of a pale imitation,[1] and the phrase "cover version" began to acquire a derogatory air.

The arrival of The Beatles provided a new model. Their repertoire originally consisted of the same blend of rock 'n' roll, rhythm 'n' blues and show tunes offered by dozens of bands in Liverpool and Hamburg. But the songwriting prowess of Lennon and McCartney meant that, by 1964, the band existed as a self-contained writing and (with the inclusion of George Martin) production unit. Within a few years, any act that wished to retain any credibility with fans needed to be able to produce original material.

This did not mean that the cover version was dead. Now, though, there had to be a convincing artistic reason for one performer to attempt a song associated with another, and the cover should be as different as possible from the original. Examples included Otis Redding's versions of The Rolling Stones' 'Satisfaction' and The Beatles' 'Day Tripper', and Jimi Hendrix's take on Bob Dylan's 'All Along The Watchtower'.

This tradition was maintained by the first punk bands, whose ethos of self-sufficiency extended into writing their own material. When a cover version was attempted, there had to be a political or social subtext: The Clash's desire to bond with disaffected black youth by covering Junior Murvin's 'Police And Thieves' on their first album (1977); the Sex Pistols' ironic comment on their 'manufactured' status implicit in playing The Monkees' 'Stepping Stone'. As punk gave way to new wave and alternative rock, the ethos remained the same: a cover version could never be justified on the basis that it was a good song that people liked. There had to be context, meaning, maybe a sense of irony. With this last get-out clause, The Smiths could get away with covering a Cilla Black song; the Cocteau Twins could tackle 'Frosty the Snowman'; Sonic Youth could pledge allegiance to the ghost of Karen Carpenter, Oasis to the very-much-alive Burt Bacharach. And Radiohead were no exception, livening up their sets with the likes of Glen Campbell's 'Rhinestone Cowboy' and Carly Simon's Bond theme, 'Nobody Does It Better'. A sincere, credible rendition of a song that had been chosen on its own merits – for example,

Jeff Buckley's version of Leonard Cohen's 'Hallelujah' on *Grace* (1994) – became the exception.

It was a sign of the increased commercial success and mainstream respectability of alternative rock that, by the mid-1990s, older performers began seeing dollar signs in the back catalogues of Oasis, Nirvana and their ilk. Sometimes this was played exclusively for laughs (as with the Mike Flowers Pops version of Oasis' 'Wonderwall'), but the collective knowing smirk began to fade. The beauty of albums such as *Rock Swings* (2005), on which Paul Anka gives the big band treatment to the likes of 'Wonderwall', Nirvana's 'Smells Like Teen Spirit' and 'The Love Cats' by The Cure, is that the veteran performer plays things utterly straight, treating the songs with the respect he'd accord to George Gershwin or Cole Porter.

The first Radiohead song to be the subject of a cover frenzy was, inevitably, 'Creep'. Performers as diverse as Alanis Morisette, Beck, the Pretenders, Tears For Fears, Jeff Buckley, Moby, Eddie Vedder of Pearl Jam, Damien Rice, ex-Take That pin-up Mark Owen, Australian lounge singer Frank Bennett, Irish comedian Patrick Kielty and pseudo-operatic karaoke abomination G4 have all fallen prey to its tortured charms over the years. The motivation of the performers was many and varied: admiration of Radiohead's songwriting nous; desperation to recover a fading level of credibility; money; a laugh; in the case of G4, presumably, doing what they were told. But it was the unprecedented success of *OK Computer* that announced open season on the Radiohead songbook.

There seem to be three potential strategies when it comes to covering a Radiohead song. The first, and least interesting, is to think of Radiohead as an indie-rock band, first and foremost, and to treat their songs accordingly. The best thing that can be said about this tack is that it highlights how distinct Radiohead are from the mainstream of post-punk guitar bands. Listening to the overwrought live version of 'Karma Police' by Las Vegas emo-pop-punkers Panic! At The Disco,[2] or Shawn Lee's feel-my-pain

'No Surprises' (on the 2006 compilation *Exit Music: Songs With Radio Heads*) only makes the listener appreciate the subtlety and restraint of the originals. Silent Gray's 'Fitter Happier' (on the 2001 album, *Anyone Can Play Radiohead*) performs the unlikely stunt, of transforming one of the band's most radical sonic excursions into a buffed-up On A Friday demo. Miranda Sex Garden's 'Exit Music (For A Film)', on the same album, opens in a promisingly spooky manner, but soon dissolves into mainstream rock mundanity. True devotees of direness should, however, search out the EP *30 Seconds Of Silence* (2002) by Telepathy for a live version of 'Karma Police' that plumbs the depths of clichéd anguish (or, indeed, anguished cliché). You can hear the air being punched, see the tightness of the trousers.

Dai Griffiths identifies a second trend,[3] which is to treat the slower songs as if they're part of the classic American songbook repertoire, and to perform them as if the spirits of Ella Fitzgerald or Frank Sinatra were looking over your shoulder. This does at least add something new to the songs, but there seems to be an unspoken agenda, of making them palatable for an older, more affluent, non-rock audience. It's a similar effect to the Zero 7 remix of 'Climbing Up The Walls' (see Chapter 11). For example, something like Jacquie Barnaby's 'Karma Police' (from her *Washington Square* EP, released in 2005) may appeal to fans of early 70s Carole King; the British singer Ian Shaw's breathy high notes hover somewhere between Nat 'King' Cole and Jimmy Scott when he attempts 'The Tourist', on *A World Still Turning* (2003). Kate Rogers' take on 'Climbing Up The Walls' (on *Seconds*, 2005) has a more folktronica slant, but there's still a certain earnestness that rather misses the point. This is a song about a psychopath, after all. It's definitely an improvement on the neo-emo chest-beating of Shawn Lee, but the performers do give the impression that they're searching half-heartedly for some sort of psychic link to the hovering spirit of Sinatra.

If you're following the reinvention route, it's better to be whole-hearted about it, even if this means parting with some of the most cherished elements of the original. The words, for example. The American jazz performer Brad Mehldau has had great success applying his Bill Evans-inspired piano style to rock music. His take on 'Exit Music (For A Film)', on the 1998 album *The Art Of The Trio, Vol. 3: Songs*, is a clever, if restrained rearrangement, with drums standing in for the synthesised choir; the 9-minute-long 'Paranoid Android' (on 2002's *Largo*), pushes out beyond the piano trio format, with left-field percussive assistance from session legend Jim Keltner and Matt Chamberlain (ex-Smashing Pumpkins), and even a New Orleans-style funeral horn section. Mehldau's 19-minute version of the song (on *Live In Tokyo*, 2004) is perhaps too much of a good thing; but no-one can deny his inventiveness and technical bravura. Philadelphia jazz trio Ellipsis have a similar approach on the version of 'Karma Police' on their self-titled EP (2005), on which they also cover 'Morning Bell' from *Kid A* and 'Knives Out' from *Amnesiac*. Interestingly, both acts also have a penchant for late-period Beatles covers, although Ellipsis prefer *Abbey Road* – 'I Want You (She's So Heavy)' makes regular appearances in their sets – while Mehldau leans more towards the 'White Album' ('Blackbird', 'Martha My Dear'). The Bad Plus also take a trio version of 'Karma Police' into novel directions on the *Exit Music* album; the Cinematic Orchestra offer a more horn-based, Mingus-influenced slant on 'Exit Music (For A Film)', on the same compilation. The Brooklyn-based quartet Maroon reinstate vocals (and summon the ghost of Billie Holiday) for 'The Tourist', on *Who The Sky Betrays* (2003), alongside songs from Soundgarden, The Pretenders and John Lennon. The Dutch saxophonist Yuri Honing investigates the orchestral sweep of 'Paranoid Android' on *Symphonic* (2006); on the rest of the album, he maintains a distant thematic link with *OK Computer* when he selects tunes by Wayne Shorter and Joe Zawinul, both of whom played with Miles Davis on *Bitches Brew*.

Radiohead have acknowledged their debt of inspiration to modern classical composers such as Messiaen and Penderecki, and it's inevitable that serious classical musicians would wish to return the compliment. The sort of response that their music has received in the classical community gives some indication of how the band is generally perceived. Mainstream artists, such as Queen or Phil Collins, get the big, orchestral treatment; more credible, niche-oriented acts attract more credible, edgier classical interpreters and collaborators (and budget restraints tend to mean that the music is performed by soloists, or at best string quartets, rather than by full orchestras). Obvious examples include David Bowie, whose *Low* and *Heroes* were reworked by the minimalist composer Philip Glass; and the Kronos Quartet's rendition of 'Purple Haze' by Jimi Hendrix.

The London Philharmonic has yet to record a granny-friendly Tribute To Thom. More representative is the Section Quartet, a string quartet based in Los Angeles, that has covered the works of artists as diverse as Led Zeppelin, Enya, The Smiths, Nine Inch Nails, Coldplay, Björk and Tool. The group, led by violinist Eric Gorfain, has also released two albums consisting entirely of Radiohead tunes: *Strung Out On OK Computer* (2001); and 2003's *Enigmatic*, with tracks mainly drawn from *Kid A* and *Amnesiac*. The Section's arrangements sound like straightforward transpositions of the original recordings, without too much variation in pitch or tempo. What they do offer is a hint of how *OK Computer* might have sounded with a real string section (rather than Jonny's Mellotron) throughout.

Another classical musician whose interpretations have mined unexpected seams within Radiohead's back catalogue is Christopher O'Riley. Already noted for his interpretations of Stravinsky and Scriabin, the pianist released *True Love Waits* in 2003, and followed it two years later with *Hold Me To This*. His arrangements, for piano alone, are by definition more distinct from Radiohead's originals than those of the Section; a single instrument can't help to match the sheer instrumental density of something like 'Paranoid Android', and the arranger has to go back to the original melodies for inspiration.[4] Incidentally, O'Riley and the Section are among the few artists to have covered non-album

194

tracks by Radiohead: O'Riley tackled 'Polyethylene Part 2' and 'How I Made My Millions' on *Hold Me To This*; his later work *Enigmatic* includes a reworking of 'Palo Alto'.

Of course, a cover version doesn't have a concrete effect on the music of *OK Computer* itself, or the ones and zeroes that have been coming out of the speakers since 1997. However, the fact that trained musicians in areas of music generally identified as 'highbrow' – classical and jazz – have chosen to interpret the songs is bound to have an effect on how we listen to them. Is this no longer pop or rock music? Is it now art? Should we be studying Radiohead in conservatories, alongside Bach and Stravinsky? And, if not, why not?[5]

Some cover versions will not fit into any of these conceptual holes. Warren Haynes, sometime guitarist with Southern rock titans the Allman Brothers Band, released a surprising, rather moving take on 'Lucky', on his *Live At Bonnaroo* set in 2004. Dromedary, a folk duo comprising Rob McMaken and Andrew Reissiger, from Athens, Georgia (home of REM), included a lovely instrumental version of 'Airbag' on their album *Live From The Make Believe* (2003). Then, if you really want to hear how 'Exit Music (For A Film)' might have sounded with a choir of teenage Belgian girls, try to get a copy of the 2004 album *Dream On* by Scala and Kolacny Brothers. And if you want to take the school orchestra motif to its logical extreme, feel free to sample *Lullaby Renditions Of Radiohead* (2006), which is a bit like the glockenspiel part of 'No Surprises', extended to fill a whole album. (Other acts targeted in the series include The Pixies, Nirvana and Metallica. Sweet dreams.)

Sometimes the results of such genre-hopping are dreadful. The Bison Chips, a glee club based at Bucknell University, Pennsylvania, include an a cappella 'Karma Police' on their aptly-titled *Appalling And Ridiculous* (2004).[6] Corporate Love Breakdown's bluegrass instrumental reworking of 12 Radiohead songs (2005) is better, but still feels a little gimmicky. More satisfying – because you know, rather than hope, that they're taking the piss

– is the Los Angeles-based comedy duo Hard 'N Phirm, who, on their 2005 album *Horses And Grasses*, rework 'Fitter Happier' (now titled 'Fitter Clappier') into the divinely-inspired sales pitch of a televangelist; and follow it with a hysterical bluegrass medley, entitled, inevitably, 'Rodeohead'. Admit it, you've always wanted to hear 'Karma Police' sung by a banjo-player with ill-fitting dentures; or 'Paranoid Android' declaimed over a CB radio.[7] The radio DJs Mark Radcliffe and Marc 'Lard' Riley, in the guise of The Shirehorses, produced what might be seen as the British equivalent to Hard 'N Phirm's oeuvre, when they included the track 'No Big Sizes' (supposedly by 'Radioshed') on their 2001 masterpiece *Our Kid Eh*. It was the sequel to 1997's *The Worst Album In The World Ever... Ever!*, which clearly wasn't.

But the weirdest, bravest, yet perhaps most successful attempt to lure Radiohead into new sonic territories is *Radiodread*, a reggae version of *OK Computer* by the Easy Star All-Stars, released in 2006. At first, the conjunction of public-school indie-rock with the sounds of Trenchtown seems bizarre, almost tasteless. But there is a certain logic going on. One of the developments of *OK Computer* was a new focus on rhythms. Colin Greenwood's bass-playing had a new fluency, and was brought to the fore on tracks like 'Paranoid Android' and 'Exit Music'. Phil Selway's drums also had their spotlight moments, on 'Airbag' and 'Electioneering'. Above all, there's a new interest in space and silence, that echoes the dub innovations of the 1970s; on a track like the original 'Exit Music', the gaps, the stuff that's left unspoken, are as significant as the sounds. Listen to the bass solo at the end of the Easy Stars' 'Lucky' and join the dots. Meanwhile, the guitar riff of 'Paranoid Android' is transposed to a Skatalites-like horn section. At last! Radiohead do rocksteady!

Moreover, there's a thematic link between Radiohead's subject matter and the preoccupations of reggae. If *OK Computer* is 'about' anything, it's the crushing, draining, but superficially attractive impact of industrial, global capitalism at the turn of the Millennium; in the theology of Rastafarianism, the links with

Babylon, the Western hegemony that enslaves the black man, are clear. The religious overtones of 'Airbag' and 'Lucky' achieve a new sincerity. 'Electioneering' could be a pungent comment by Bob Marley about the warring political gangs of Jamaica in the 1970s; 'Fitter Happier' now sounds like a draconian sentence from Prince Buster's Judge Dread. Incidentally, three years earlier, the Easy Star crew had turned their attention to another album that combined sonic experimentation with a jaundiced look at modern society; *Dark Side Of The Moon*. Despite Jonny Greenwood's protestations (see Chapter 4), it seems that the Pink Floyd link is hardwired in too many minds to be dismissed.

Radiodread doesn't just succeed because it's a bright idea, of course. The album has an overall consistency, with the instrumental tracks performed by a core of musicians, and the vocals provided by a roster of top-level reggae stars, including the veterans Horace Andy, Frankie Paul and Toots Hibbert. It transcends its status as a 'novelty record', and does what only the best covers do – it helps us appreciate aspects of the original that we'd never noticed before.

That said, the original recordings still stand as the definitive article. No cover version of a Radiohead song has yet achieved the success of Buckley's 'Hallelujah', which became a radio-friendly simulacrum of the original, pushing poor Leonard Cohen into the margins (although he must be quite grateful for the enhanced pension plan).

Performers will continue to seek new angles on Radiohead's material. But the artistic success of the *Radiodread* project suggests that the long-term value of *OK Computer* is as an album – something greater than the sum of its parts.

Postscript:

Your Home May Be At Risk If You Do Not Collect Royalty Payments: Now That's What I Call The Best iPod-Compiled Radiohead Cover Version Album Ever
1. 'Airbag' – Dromedary
2. 'Paranoid Android' – Brad Mehldau
3. 'Subterranean Homesick Alien' – Rockabye Baby!
4. 'Exit Music (For A Film)' – Scala and Kolacny Brothers
5. 'Let Down' – Easy Star All-Stars, feat. Toots & The Maytals
6. 'Karma Police' – The Bad Plus
7. 'Fitter Happier' (aka 'Fitter Clappier') – Hard 'N Firm
8. 'Electioneering' – The Section
9. 'Climbing Up The Walls' – Kate Rogers
10. 'No Surprises' – Christopher O'Riley
11. 'Lucky' – Warren Haynes
12. 'The Tourist' – Maroon

Notes:

[1] Literally, in the case of the clean-cut American performer Pat Boone, whose speciality was producing successful and bad cover versions of songs by black artists such as Fats Domino and Little Richard.

[2] Who, by the end of 2006, had announced that they wished to have nothing more to do with emo, and wanted to be known as 'the new Radiohead'.

[3] Griffiths, *OK Computer*, p. 107.

[4] O'Riley seems to have a taste for gloom: his next project was reinterpreting the music of the doomed singer-songwriter Elliott Smith.

[5] In the sleevenotes to *True Love Waits*, O'Riley credits the compositions not to Thom Yorke, Jonny Greenwood, et al, but to Thomas, Jonathan, Edward... This shouldn't matter, but somehow it does. Does the use of the full, formal forms of the names somehow make the bearers more respectable? More middle-class, more Abingdon School? Older? Less rock 'n' roll? Do they become composers, rather than mere songwriters?

[6] College-based male harmony groups tackling rock classics is not a new idea, by any means. Zadie Smith's novel *On Beauty* (London: Hamish Hamilton, 2005) contains a hilarious, but utterly realistic depiction of what happens when young men in tuxedos confront the U2 songbook. See pp. 346-348.

[7] A slightly more straight-faced, but successful attempt to create a dialectic of Abingdon and Nashville came from the Albuquerque alt-country outfit Hazeldine, who covered 'Lucky' on their 1998 album *Orphans*, alongside songs by Peter Gabriel, Gram Parsons and Neutral Milk Hotel.

CHAPTER 21

PERFORMING MONKEY BOOKINGS– 1997-1998

Fat bloody fingers are sucking your soul away.
—UNKLE, 'Rabbit In Your Headlights'

Even before *OK Computer* was released, Thom Yorke was back in the studio, this time in San Francisco with the turntablist DJ Shadow, aka Josh Davis. *Endtroducing...*, Shadow's 1996 debut, was the first album entirely constructed from samples, and the fact that Thom was now working in this musical environment was further evidence of the distance he had travelled from the guitar-based orthodoxy of *Pablo Honey*. Yorke and Shadow came up with a moody track called 'Rabbit In Your Headlights', distinguished by a melancholy piano line that sounded like a composition by the French minimalist Erik Satie, recorded in a rainstorm. The track would have to wait over a year for its release, on the album *Psyence Fiction*, credited to the 'band' UNKLE (essentially Shadow and the Mo'Wax label boss James Lavelle). The other guest performers on the album gave some indication of the eclectic genre-bending that was going on: these included rapper Kool G Rap, head Beastie Boy Mike D, Metallica bassist Jason Newsted, Verve singer Richard Ashcroft and woolly-hatted troubador Badly Drawn Boy (Damon Gough).

Although Yorke was the only band member involved, the bleak soundscape of the track, as well as the lyrics and the video (similar in mood and content to Jonathan Glazer's 'Karma Police') had a distinctly Radiohead aura. If the line about being "scared of the spotlight" was autobiographical, the band would be living in fear for some time. In the course of the next year, they would spend very little time out of the gaze of baying crowds.

On returning from the States, Radiohead embarked on a number of open-air shows, including one in Dublin where the support bill (West Country trip-hop pioneers Massive Attack and Big Star-worshipping Scots Teenage Fanclub) seemed to sum up the twin poles of the headliners' new aesthetic. A week later, they played at the Glastonbury Festival.

In a world where it seems possible to attend a rock festival every week of the year, Glastonbury remains special. Founded in the early 1970s, and run pretty much annually since 1981, its main attraction is nominally music, but many people attend as much for the communal, moderately hippyish atmosphere as for the performers; in recent years, the festival has usually sold out even before the line-up is made public.

The problem for bands playing such events is that you can never guarantee the loyalty of the audience, or even their familiarity with your material. Radiohead had struggled with this ever since their breakout single had brought them to a new, more diverse group of listeners; only two weeks before, they had failed to wow the crowd at the KROQ Weenie Roast in Irvine Meadows, California. The event was billed as a UK vs US grudge match, for which Radiohead were lumped together with Oasis and Blur, two bands inescapably tagged with the Britpop label. Thom immediately hit a wrong note by announcing that his band had "come to show you how it's done", and baying members of the audience soon found themselves being described as "fucking mindless".[1] Not playing 'Creep' was possibly a dumb move as well.

Glastonbury also offered a diverse crowd, many of whom had not come to hear Radiohead; but this was, in theory, the band's core constituency, the fragmented followers of what still might be known, however loosely, as indie rock. Not that this necessarily raised the band's enthusiasm levels, of course; Thom had recently taken to introducing 'Creep' as "karaoke nonsense for the indie fans".[2]

The festival had suffered horrendous rain and flooding, and many people had already left before Radiohead played on Saturday night. The set began well enough, but after a few songs, Thom's monitor blew up, leaving him unable to hear anything. Then the lights began to malfunction, rendering the band effectively deaf and blind in front of 40,000 people. It was a public fuck-up of massive proportions. And then...

As 'Paranoid Android' began, Thom was dazzled by two white lights immediately in front of him. Rather than switch them off, the technician turned them round to shine on the audience; and the musicians saw, not a disgruntled, muddied mob of 'Creep' fans demanding compensation for the lousy sound, but an audience stretching to the horizon, hanging on their every word.

As described by journalist Paul Trynka, it was an event that challenged the critical vocabulary of many hardened music fans:

> Jonny's guitar playing was literally terrifying... As he hit the wrenching chords in 'Paranoid Android' that signal the full-blown riff, several people in the audience around me literally flipped, just spun into the mud with pleasure... Just after Radiohead went off-stage I bumped into a friend I'd been trying to find for hours. We were both in some kind of altered state; all we could say was, Did you see *that*? When I've talked to people since who witnessed that performance, it's been galling to hear the odd person describe it as merely 'a good gig'. It wasn't. It was something far more profound.[3]

In a way, it was entirely appropriate that this event should come in the wake of *OK Computer*. So much of their working process had consisted of stabs in the dark, attempting to find one sound and reaching another; Jonny Greenwood's "garbled version" (see Chapter 5) that somehow, against all the odds, rescues magnificence from calamity. As in 'Airbag' and 'Lucky', the band had confronted potential disaster, and yet, somehow, miraculously, they came through on the other side.

Surely this bizarre, transcendent moment (widely regarded, even by neutral observers, as one of the greatest performances in the history of Glastonbury), coupled with the superlatives that critics were hurling at the album, would shake Radiohead out of their collective grouch? July and August offered 20 dates across the States and Canada, and not a Weenie Roast among them; then it was back to Europe until mid-November. The film-maker Grant Gee was covering the band as they trekked through Europe, North America, Japan and Australasia. It's impossible to tell whether he was actually making matters worse, but his footage (released in 1998 as *Meeting People Is Easy*) records a band clearly suffering from a mixture of fatigue, boredom and frustration. At the same time, most of the members of Radiohead appeared to have developed coping mechanisms, and their impeccable manners held steady. Colin Greenwood is overheard on the film telling a radio journalist that he's "very flattered" for *OK Computer* to receive yet another best-of-1997 bauble, and that the record company has been kind enough to provide a LearJet to take the band to the awards ceremony. "We've never been on one of those before," he says sweetly. "It's very exciting."[4] Ed O'Brien, meanwhile, came perilously close to acknowledging that he was having a good time, telling Mac Randall about the band's dates in Japan, at the beginning of 1998:

> I came off stage last night going 'What a fucking great job to have, playing these great songs. And this is what I do for a living.' We basically play the songs that we like to play… We've done four gigs here, we've played 'Creep' once, and that's only because we wanted to. It's a lovely position to be in.[5]

Thom Yorke, inevitably, felt the pressure more deeply, and his bandmates became increasingly concerned for his mental equilibrium. His attitude seemed to be the diametric opposite of O'Brien's; although he had reacted angrily over the years to suggestions that he was another in the long line of self-inflicted rock casualties (Kurt Cobain and Richey Edwards being the most recent examples), he was clearly deeply sensitive and thin-skinned, even by the standards of his genre. As Colin Greenwood described:

> The worst point was playing shows in the UK right after *OK Computer* came out. There is nothing worse than having to play in front of 20,000 people when someone – when Thom – absolutely does not want to be there, and you can see that hundred-yard stare in his eyes. You hate having to

put your friend through that experience. You find yourself wondering how you got there.[6]

For all Yorke's avoidance of rock 'n' roll excess, he maintained one self-destructive habit: he thought too much. His contempt for the honours and awards that *OK Computer* was attracting (the Grammy for 'Best Alternative Album'; two Ivor Novello awards; a platinum disc for selling one million copies in the United States) overspilled several times while Gee's cameras were rolling. Rather than admit to being "flattered", as his bass-playing colleague had done, Yorke dismissed all the plaudits as "bollocks", and complained to Dean Kuipers of *Raygun* about the privileged role that his own rock star status gave him, especially when he was asked his opinion on political matters:

> I don't think it's a legitimate role, I think it's fucking ridiculous that we're the only people allowed to do it. I think it's a fucking farce, man, because we're not that informed, you have to make such a huge effort. Surely you would think someone who gets paid to be a politician would be better informed than you. But it's in their interest to keep you uninformed. That's fucked, man. I mean, it's great to talk about records and stuff, but when we were at home for three weeks you have the old Kyoto environmental conference going on, and the double-think going on there was just fucking mind-blowing, man.[7]

The tension was still visible four years later, when Alex Ross of the *New Yorker* described an exchange between Yorke and Radiohead's co-manager, Chris Hufford:

> "This is reality, Thom," he said. "This is the marketplace we're in."
> "No," Yorke replied, "the marketplace is where we sell records. This isn't the marketplace. It's an area of, I don't know, oversight."

"Come on," Hufford said, "it's capitalism, it's what we have to work with."

"Bollocks!"

"Capitalism!"

"Bollocks!" Yorke yelled.[8]

By 2006, Yorke seemed to have come to terms with the inconsistencies and imperfections of his own lifestyle, or at least refused to be beaten down with excessive guilt. As he told Craig McLean of *The Observer*:

> I'm not doing enough! None of us are… No one's going to come out of this dirt-free; I don't come out of it dirt-free. It's basically about having to make a decision whether to do nothing or try to engage with it in some way, knowing that it's flawed. It's convenient to project that back on to someone personally and say they're a hypocrite. It's a lot easier to do that than actually do anything else. And yeah, that stresses me out, because I am a hypocrite. As we all are.[9]

If journalists were going to ask for Yorke's views, from now on he was going to have something worthwhile to say to them. Up to this point, he had demonstrated his support for a number of good causes (such as the Free Tibet campaign) without thinking of the underlying reasons for the world's problems. *OK Computer* was dotted with jibes against the crushing power of capitalism and technology, without providing any sense of a coherent alternative. But the band's apparently never-ending globetrotting had not only allowed Yorke to see how cultures and economies interacted and influenced each other, it also gave him a chance to read. And as he travelled and read and thought, he began to see what was going on around him. In the mid-1990s, a series of financial disasters struck developing nations, most notably the Mexican peso crisis of 1994, and the meltdown that afflicted Southeast Asia in 1997.[10] In the latter case, Western investors withdrew their funds, bringing a sudden halt to the economic growth that the so-called 'tiger economies' had experienced since the 1980s. The "voodoo economics" of 'Electioneering' had done their worst.

Thom began to be convinced that such collapses of vulnerable economies, which might burn the fingers of global investors, but throw millions of ordinary people into poverty, were a symptom of the onward march of globalisation, and its supranational gatekeepers, the World Bank and the International Monetary Fund. Through reading the works of thinkers such as Eric Hobsbawm, Noam Chomsky and Will Hutton, and later Naomi Klein's anti-brand manifesto *No Logo*, Thom was developing a cohesive, articulate view of the way concentrations of money and power conspire to keep people poor and to ruin the environment. At one point in Grant Gee's film, he can be seen brooding about the after-effects of the Asian crash to journalists who probably only wanted to know why the band didn't play that 'Creep' song so much these days. He accuses the west of acting as "a huge loan shark" and says that the arguments for globalisation as self-serving and facile. "This is justified as 'this is how the world economy works'," he sneers.[11]

Thom's reading began to permeate the lyrics he was writing as the band moved around the planet, although few of these ever made it to performance or recording. Radiohead had always been 'serious', but this was a new, focused seriousness, the required radical rethinking about not just politics and economics, but also about music itself.

Following the Asia tour, the band rested for most of February and March, then embarked on yet another traipse around the United States and Canada, this time supported by Spiritualized. The tour culminated in Washington, DC on June 13, where Radiohead were scheduled to play another show in support of the people of Tibet, just as they had at Randall's Island the previous year.

However, a freak electric storm struck the RFK Stadium, injuring a number of spectators and forcing the postponement of the concert. Undeterred, Radiohead went to a nearby nightclub and staged an impromptu show, supported by Pulp and featuring a surprise appearance by Michael Stipe. Stipe also joined the band for a rescheduled show the following day, and Thom returned the compliment for REM. Finally, on the 15th, Thom played an acoustic version of 'Street Spirit' at a rally on the West Capitol Lawn.

There was a certain symmetry going on. At Glastonbury, and then in Washington a year later, Radiohead had faced down technical nightmares to provide scintillating sets. Whatever the onstage equivalent of a jacknifing juggernaut or an air crash might be, they had survived it twice over, and experienced redemption and resurrection. It was almost as if life was imitating art.

It had been an extraordinary 12 months. As Phil Selway later recalled:

> At a certain point, around 1997, we were simply over-whelmed and had to vanish for a bit. This was our honest reaction to the situation we were in. But some people thought we were playing a game, or had started taking ourselves too seriously.[12]

It certainly wasn't a game. Radiohead, despite all the high points since the release of *OK Computer*, now realised that they had to step off the treadmill; it was the only way they could hold the band together. Following the rally, they went back to Oxford, and for nearly 18 months, with the exception of an Amnesty International benefit in France at the end 1998, Radiohead would disappear almost completely.

Notes:

[1] Keith Cameron, 'Notorious Pig', *NME*, June 28, 1997.
[2] Clarke, p. 129.
[3] Jim Irvin, 'We Have Lift-Off', *Mojo*, September 1997.
[4] *Meeting People Is Easy*. There is, of course, the possibility that the Greenwood tongue may be in the Greenwood cheek.
[5] Randall, pp. 177-178.
[6] Chuck Klosterman, 'No More Knives', *Spin*, September, 2003.
[7] Dean Kuipers, interview, *Raygun*, March, 1998.
[8] Alex Ross, 'The Searchers: Radiohead's unquiet revolution', *The New Yorker*, August 20-27, 2001.
[9] Craig McLean, 'All Messed Up', *Observer Music Monthly*, June, 2006.
[10] The devaluation of the Thai baht, which triggered the crisis throughout Southeast Asia, took place on July 2, 1997, the day after *OK Computer* was released. No direct link between the two events has ever been established.
[11] *Meeting People Is Easy*.
[12] Alex Ross, 'The Searchers: Radiohead's unquiet revolution'.

CHAPTER 22

LABYRINTHINE CATACOMBS –
1999-?

Really, we don't want people twiddling their goatees over our stuff. What we do is pure escapism.
—Phil Selway

Most bands start going rubbish around their fourth album, don't they?
—Jonny Greenwood

Radiohead biographer Mac Randall has neatly characterised the band's recording methodology thus: "1) Band enters studio, 2) Band falls apart, 3) Band takes stock of itself and shifts gear, 4) Band finishes album, 5) Band says it's learned its lesson and this will never happen again."[1] *The Bends* certainly followed this pattern; and the sessions for *OK Computer* had also become aimless and tetchy until the band settled into St Catherine's Court. But for sheer, drawn-out misery, tension and lack of direction, the work that began in Paris in February, 1999 would take some beating.

The first problem was that Thom Yorke, still emotionally fragile from the constant media attention he'd endured in the wake of *OK Computer*, had very little to offer in the way of new songs. What he had instead were a renewed enthusiasm for dance music (in particular, the weird and wonderful products of the Sheffield-based Warp label) and a dogmatic insistence that the next album was going to be, in some unspecified way, utterly different from the last. His bandmates were with him on the last point, but distinctly divided on the first. His main opponent was Ed O'Brien, who sought a return to guitar-based pop; his closest ally, but still slightly sceptical, was Jonny Greenwood.

A change of venue to a studio in Copenhagen didn't break the deadlock, and it was only when Nigel Godrich moved the band to a mansion in Gloucestershire, Batsford Park,[2] that the work rate improved, although the product of their labours still seemed messy and unfocussed. Unusually, the band's progress, or lack thereof, took place in the public eye; Ed O'Brien maintained an online journal (the word 'blog' was not then in common usage) on the band's official website, detailing his and the band's frustrating, I-go-for-wards-you-go-backwards journey towards album number four.

At the beginning of September, the band moved into a new, state-of-the-art recording space at their base in the village of Sutton Courtenay. By the end of the year, they still had just half a dozen tracks in anything like a finished state.

When they regrouped at the beginning of 2000, Nigel Godrich realised that what Radiohead needed was a kick in the fashionably distressed cargo pants. Just as his predecessor John Leckie had done during the sessions for *The Bends*, Godrich took the band even further out of their comfort zone, by separating them. One group would create beats and sound loops in the pro-gramming room; the other would develop melodies to go over the top. No guitars, though; no drum kits; none of the basic tools that Radiohead/On A Friday had been using for the past decade and a half. Godrich was forcing the band down the route that Kraftwerk had begun 25 years before; to make music without instruments; to cease to be musicians, in the ordinary sense of the word.

It sounds like a task set in a particularly arty-farty manage-ment training session; what next, paintball? However, it appears to have worked. The Luddites were won over by this new (to them), counterintuitive way of making music; O'Brien, for the moment at least, laid down his Rickenbacker. Suddenly, the previously glacial pace of music-making accelerated until it seemed out of control. Within a matter of weeks, the number of tracks ready for release had gone from six to 24.

This left the band with a new problem; what to do with all this stuff? The obvious step would be to release a double album but, possibly stung by the prog allegations that were hurled at *OK Computer*, they resisted. Instead, they took 10 tracks from the sessions, and set the others aside for future use.

What sort of noises, then, were bouncing off the stu-dio walls in Sutton Courtenay as the new millennium stumbled into existence? Thom's beloved Warp artists were clearly in the conceptual gumbo, as were old favourites Can and Talking Heads. At the same time, Jonny Greenwood had rekindled a passion for one of his teenage heroes, the French composer Olivier Messiaen (1908-1992). Messiaen's most famous work was the Turangilîla Symphony, which featured the ondes martenot, an early analogue synthesiser. Jonny set himself the task of mastering this unwieldy instrument, and it replaced the Mellotron of *OK Computer* as his anachronistic keyboard of choice. Yorke, meanwhile, was exploring the work of the jazz bassist and bandleader Charles Mingus, who coupled caustic social comment with raucous, big-band-style horn arrangements.

These were all credible reference points, but did they actually combine to make coherent music? In this case, the fans were able to make a few educated guesses. The band had already been organising occasional webcasts since December, 1999, to showcase their work in progress, although none of the songs performed would make it to the next album.[3] In June and July they toured some of the more interesting venues of Europe and Israel, with setlists stacked in favour of as-yet unreleased material. Even when playing at London's Royal Festival Hall, as part of the Meltdown event curated by Scott Walker, they avoided the temptation to play a greatest-hits set; the main performance ended with 'Everything In Its Right Place', from the as-yet unreleased album, and three out of the five encores were also new tracks.

Thanks to the increasing availability of digital recording technology, and constantly improving bandwidth on the internet, Radiohead obsessives across the planet began to form their own ideas about what the new album would be like. These, of course, were live versions, with guitars, drums and Thom's pretty-much-unadulterated voice to the fore. And then, three weeks before the scheduled release of *Kid A*, the whole album appeared online.

In normal circumstances, this would herald a major commercial disaster. Why should consumers shell out their cash for a product they could get for free on Napster? Radiohead, however, seemed oddly unconcerned by the whole situation, which in turn led to rumours (still neither confirmed nor denied to this day) that they were behind the leak.

If such a thing were true, it would tie in with the somewhat eccentric marketing campaign. There were no singles, no videos, and few promotional copies of the album were sent to the media. Press interviews were kept to the bare minimum. The closest thing to advertising was a series of viral blips that fans eagerly disseminated across the planet.

The fans didn't seem unduly bothered by these unorthodox methods; despite the fact that many of them had already heard the album, they still bought it in sufficient numbers to see it top the charts on both sides of the Atlantic. But music journalists, possibly aggrieved by the band's approach, took a different view. For the first time since the release of 'Pop Is Dead', seven years before, the initial critical response to Radiohead product was negative; most of the reviews patrolled the territory between incomprehension and outright savagery. The latter tendency was most creatively expressed by the on-its-last-legs *Melody Maker*, in which Mark Beaumont dismissed the album as "tubby, ostentatious, self-congratulatory, look-ma-I-can-suck-my-own-cock whiny old rubbish". In particular, 'The National Anthem' came in for a good kicking; according to Beaumont, it "utterly redefines the notion of 'unlistenability', propels us to a whole new sphere of self-indulgence, invents – if you will – post-bollocks."[4]

In retrospect, it's hard to see what riled the hacks quite so much. *Kid A* certainly takes the Radiohead sound further along the move away from conventional rock dynamics that *OK Computer* had started. But, at the same time, there's little on it that's weirder or more post-bollocksy than, for example, 'Fitter Happier'. For example, on the opening track, 'Everything In Its Right Place', Thom Yorke's voice is distorted beyond recognition, but it is still possible to discern a clear melody line. 'How To Disappear Completely' (originally planned as a collaboration with Montreal post-rockers Godspeed You Black Emperor!), 'Optimistic' and the soaring 'Motion Picture Soundtrack' could all have found a home on *OK Com-*

puter, or even *The Bends*, although maybe the latter track would have had to lose its deeply conceptual two-minute silence. Even 'The National Anthem', the most obvious manifestation of Thom's Mingus infatuation (and the song that upset Mark Beaumont so much) is only disorienting to the ears of a conventional rock fan because it's propelled by atonal horns rather than distorted guitars. (Thom, still obsessed with transport hell, told them to play as if they were cars stuck in a traffic jam.) It's another few steps into the jazz/rock dialectic previously explored on 'Subterranean Home-sick Alien'; if it has a precursor, it may be Ornette Coleman's collaboration with Yoko Ono on her *Plastic Ono Band* album (1971).

There are, of course, tracks that challenge those who have trouble thinking outside the 12-bar box; the "Toytown ethnicity"[5] of the title track, and the collision between Warp-style electronica and the avant-garde composition of Paul Lansky[6] on 'Idioteque' represent the sort of risk-taking that distinguishes Radiohead from, to pick a name at random, Oasis. After the initial critical wobble and/or fit of pique, the music press apparently came to terms with *Kid A*, and it placed respectably in end-of-year polls (*NME*, no. 11; *Melody Maker*, no. 5). In February 2001, the album gave the band another Grammy, again for Best Alternative Album.

And there was more where that came from, although for the first time, Radiohead seemed to have taken half a step backwards. *Amnesiac*, consisting of songs recorded at the same sessions that produced *Kid A*, was released in June, 2001, just eight months after the previous album. It's probably unfair to dismiss the collection as 'Kid B', the songs that weren't quite good enough to make the cut the year before, but the simple fact that the reviews for *Amnesiac* weren't nearly as vitriolic seems to point towards a mood of equilibrium and consolidation. In some ways, rather than a progression from *Kid A*, the next album seems like a mirror image of its predecessor. There's the Mingus-influenced track ('Pyramid Song'); the unlikely collision of influences ('Packt Like Sardines In A Crushd Tin Box', described by James Doheny as "Kraftwerk go on a field trip to India with George Harrison");[7] even a second attempt at a song that the band had already recorded ('Morning Bell/Amnesiac'). There are surprises: the doleful Dixieland jazz of Humphrey Lyttelton (whose band Colin Greenwood had booked when he was in charge of entertainments at his Cambridge college) adds a tongue-in-cheek feel to 'Life In A Glasshouse'; and 'You And Whose Army', with harmonies influenced by Greenwood family favourites The Ink Spots, shows a resurgence of Yorke's political side, with a savage assault on the Britpop Prime Minister, the Right Honourable Anthony Charles Lynton Blair, MP.

The singer's involvement in confrontational politics had been growing since the release of *OK Computer*. He was particularly interested in the side-effects of globalisation on the developing world, and had been present in Cologne in June, 1999, when protesters attempted to persuade world leaders attending the G8 summit to relieve poorer countries of their debt obligations. The experience inspired the song 'Dollars and Cents' on *Amnesiac*, in which the big currencies boast that "we're gonna crack your little soul". Yorke was also enthused by the criticisms of branding outlined by the Canadian writer Naomi Klein in her bestseller *No Logo* (2000). The fact that Radiohead's concerts at the end of that year took place in tents rather than conventional venues, and succeeded without the help of corporate sponsorship, was a small step towards putting Klein's theories into action.

Klein faced a paradox when *No Logo* became a success. Not only had the book been published by a major conglomerate, the sort of multi-tentacled capitalist entity that she criticised so eloquently; but the title itself quickly became a fashionable buzzword, casually applied to anything or anyone that appeared to be vaguely anti-consumerist. Effectively, it had become a brand, just like the Nikes and the Coca-Colas upon which Klein poured her scorn.

Radiohead were in much the same boat. First, they had bellowed against technology and transport while making full use of those things to record and promote *OK Computer*; now they placed themselves in the vanguard of anti-capitalist thought and action, while relying on EMI, Capitol and Toshiba to shift their product.

The accusations of hypocrisy were, if not justifiable, at least under-standable; the band's activities in the second half of 2001 appear to express a sense of confusion. In July, they played in Oxford's South Park, in an effort to reconnect with their oldest fans, and also to raise funds for local causes. The roster of support acts hint-ed that it was a gig that wouldn't play by the rules: Beck; Super-grass; Icelandic experimentalists Sigur Rós; 'Glasshouse' veteran Humphrey Lyttelton; local unknowns Rock of Travolta. 40,000 people braved the exquisitely English drizzle, and were rewarded with a storming combination of old and new tracks, culminating in a rare rendition of 'Creep'. (Also that year, they made an appear-ance in the *other* South Park, the Colorado home of Cartman, Ken-ny and their chums. In the episode 'Scott Tenorman Must Die', Thom stole the show with his moving rendition of the timeless line, "He has cancer… in his ass.")

When the band released their third LP in little more than a year, it almost seemed as if they were trying to squeeze every last cent from a devoted audience, especially as a) it was a live album and b) it included that tired old marketing standby, the previously unreleased song.

As it turned out, *I Might Be Wrong*, released in November, was a different proposition from the standard live album (essential-ly, a collection of greatest hits with added bum notes, and maybe an unlikely cover version). It consisted almost entirely of songs from the previous two albums, and offered an interesting perspective on how they sounded without studio treatments or laptop-gener-ated glitches. The new song, 'True Love Waits', had been popping in and out of Radiohead's set lists for nearly six years, and went back to one of Thom's early lyrical preoccupations, the self-loath-ing lover; the new 'Creep', possibly.

2002 began quietly for Radiohead, but July and August saw a series of concerts in Portugal and Spain, including an appearance at the Benicassim Festival. In October, Thom played two solo sets at the Bridge School Benefit, an event organised by Neil Young to help children with disabilities.

A highlight of these charity gigs was Thom's rendition of Young's 'After The Goldrush', a choice that might have hinted at a shift in Radiohead's musical direction, back towards more accessible, conventional song structures. The beginning of the band's next album, released in 2003, seemed to support this instinct; Jonny plugs in his guitar, and Thom says, "That's a nice way to start". It's a back-to-basics, stripped-down, metatextual nudge that has antecedents as diverse as Elvis Presley ('Milkcow Blues Boogie') and The Sweet ('Ballroom Blitz'). However, it was (deliberately?) misleading. Although *Hail To The Thief* lacks the sheer, avant-garde bloody-mindedness of *Kid A*, it's a mighty long road from bog-standard rock 'n' roll.

For a start, the album and every song on it is provided with an alternative title, none of which seem to have any bearing on the finished product. A few of the tracks bear some relation to orthodox rock forms, especially the Beatlesy opener '2+2=5 (The Lukewarm)'; 'Where I End And You Begin (The Sky Is Falling In)', which wouldn't have been out of place on the first Stone Roses album. But the Warp-inflected bleeps on 'Sit Down. Stand Up (Snakes & Ladders)', the Brecht/Weill decadence of 'We Suck Young Blood (Your Time Is Up)' and the monumental Latin jazz percussion that kicks off 'There There (The Boney King Of Nowhere)' are all well beyond the boundaries of rock orthodoxy. The subject matter is often starkly political: 'Sit Down. Stand Up' was inspired by the Rwanda genocide of 1994; 'I Will (No Man's Land)' by the first Gulf War; the flan-throwing reference in 'A Wolf At The Door (It Girl. Rag Doll)' is about a patisserie-related assault on British government minister Clare Short, as part of a globalisation protest.[8] The album's title was a reference to the chants and banners of protesters against George W Bush's somewhat unorthodox victory in the 2000 Presidential election, although the band denied that it was a specific dig at the man who had sent troops into Iraq a few months before the album's release. [9]

Listeners had become used to the band's political outbursts, but a more surprising aspect was the theme of childhood running through the lyrics and titles; 'The Sky Is Falling In' and 'The Boney King Of Nowhere' refer to Chicken Licken and Bagpuss, iconic figures from Thom Yorke's childhood. The album credits are oozing with thanks to wives, partners and an increasing number of children (by this stage, one each to Thom and Jonny, and three to the prolific Phil Selway).

So, despite Nigel Godrich's decision to record the album in the hair-metal Babylon that is Los Angeles, and Ed O'Brien's belief that Radiohead had replicated the swagger of The Rolling Stones circa 1968-73,[10] *Hail To The Thief* was hardly a reawakening of the band's inner Bon Jovi. It had some interesting, quirky moments, but it didn't have the instant classic status of *OK Computer*, or the "what-the-fuck?" weirdness of *Kid A* or *Amnesiac*. Reviews were, on the whole, positive but not ecstatic. Alexis Petridis pinpointed the core problem in *The Guardian*, noting that the new album was superficially similar to *Amnesiac*, but that "it seems slightly less impressive than *Amnesiac*, because the sound is strangely familiar"[11]. Yorke would later concur, sticking up for 'There There' and '2+2=5' but deciding that, overall, "I wish [I'd] had another go at that one."[12] In October 2003, they partially redeemed themselves in the eyes of fans who wanted more envelope-pushing strangeness, when they provided music for the Merce Cunningham dance piece, at the Brooklyn Academy of Music.[13]

Hail To The Thief may have sounded familiar, not because Radiohead had run out of ideas, but because the success of *OK Computer* had provoked an explosion of Radiohead Lite bands such as Coldplay and Travis (the latter produced by Nigel Godrich) who were replicating the moody sound, but missing the original's sonic inventiveness, not to mention the lyrical substance.

It was time to take stock, perhaps. *Hail To The Thief* was Radiohead's last album under their contract with EMI: following the release of the video compilation *The Most Gigantic Lying Mouth Of All Time* in 2004, they were free agents. A final spasm of touring in April/May, 2004 (later described by Thom Yorke as "three or four weeks of constant sleep deprivation... just shite")[14] reminded them all of the downsides of the rock 'n' roll lifestyle, and Radiohead was pushed to the back of the closet for a while, although they did reunite in September 2005 to record the track 'I Want None Of This' for the War Child album *A Day In The Life*.

The parting of the ways gave the individual members a new feeling of freedom. In recent years, most of them had broken away from the constrictions of the group, contributing to recordings by artists including Björk, PJ Harvey, Pavement, Sparklehorse, Neil Finn and Asian Dub Foundation. Thom and Jonny also played on the 2004 version of Band Aid's 'Do They Know It's Christmas?';[15] Jonny and Phil joined Pulp's Jarvis Cocker to perform three songs in the 2005 movie *Harry Potter and the Goblet of Fire*.

But these guest spots were just teasers for the main event. It was time for the dreaded solo projects to come out of the box. Jonny Greenwood was first with *Bodysong* (2003), the (mostly guitar-free) soundtrack to a documentary by film-maker Simon Pummell. (Ed O'Brien had also contributed to the soundtrack of the 1999 TV series *Eureka Street*, based on the novel by Robert McLiam Wilson, but this was never released as an album.) Jonny then took up a post as composer in residence for the BBC Concert Orchestra: his debut composition was, not surprisingly, heavily influenced by Krzysztof Penderecki (see Chapter 11).[16]

Inevitably, though, the punters were really interested in *The Eraser*, the first solo outing by Thom Yorke. Made in collaboration with Nigel Godrich, and released in 2006, it's a sparse, techno-influenced affair, although it does represent rather more than a batch of demos for an as-yet-unmade Radiohead album. True, there are moments where you wonder what certain tracks would sound like with Colin's dubby bass, Phil's busy drums, Ed's swagger or Jonny's mad-professor antics. (The younger Greenwood does provide some crackly piano samples on the title track.) But it remains an interesting piece in its own right, offering such delights as Thom the human beatbox (on 'The Clock'), Thom as funk guitar hero (on the single 'Harrowdown Hill', about David Kelly, allegedly a victim of the British government's policy in Iraq),[17] and even Thom as early

80s synth-pop star (on 'And It Rained All Night', which owes more than a little to 'Cars' by Gary Numan – see Chapter 3).

The Eraser, contrary to the shit-stirring of the music press, wasn't just a surreptitious way for Yorke to back out of Radiohead and launch a fully-fledged solo career. 2006 also saw the band touring North America and Europe, including two sold-out appearances at New York's Madison Square Garden, and festival appearances in the UK, the USA, France, Switzerland, Belgium and Hungary. Highlights of the concerts included new songs, such as the mellow, bluesy 'House Of Cards', the beats-driven '15 Step' (apparently influenced by Peaches' 'Fuck The Pain Away'), 'All I Need', 'Down Is The New Up', 'Bodysnatchers', 'Videotape', '4-Minute Warning' and 'Bangers 'n' Mash'; there were also old live favourites, including 'Nude'/'Don't Get Any Big Ideas', that had never made it to release. Thom was also keen to cover Björk's 'Unravel', from her album *Homogenic* (1997). Perhaps these will all end up on the next group album, due in 2007, and described by Yorke as "like *OK Computer*, but even more terrifying".[18] Perhaps not, although it's interesting that it's the third album that the frontman still identifies as the benchmark against which all future development must be measured.

The Radiohead juggernaut ploughs on. A decade after delivering their magnum opus, and more than 20 years after they began their Friday rehearsals, it seemed that they were fitter, healthier and more productive than ever.

Notes:

[1] Randall, p. 187.

[2] For people who profess to be uncomfortable with their privileged backgrounds, these boys just love the stately homes of England.

[3] 'Knives Out' (webcast on December 9, 1999) would appear on *Amnesiac*; 'There There' (played on February 10, 2000) eventually resurfaced in 2003, on *Hail To The Thief*.

[4] Mark Beaumont, album review, *Melody Maker*, September 20, 2000.

[5] Paytress, p. 54.

[6] Lansky wrote about how his 28-year-old composition, *mild und liese*, came to be sampled by Radiohead, in 'My Radiohead Adventure', Tate, pp. 168-176.

[7] Doheny, p. 112.

[8] Flanning, or *entartage*, became a popular tactic of anti-globalisation activists in the early 2000s, thanks to the influence of the Belgian provocateur Noël Godin, aka Georges Le Gloupier. Godin's victims include Microsoft boss Bill Gates.

[9] Randall, pp. 214-215.

[10] Paytress, p. 70.

[11] Alexis Petridis, album review, *The Guardian*, June 6, 2003.

[12] Brian Raftery, 'Bent out of Shape', *Spin*, August, 2006.

[13] Most aspects of the performance, including choreography, costumes, décor and even running order (Radiohead played before Sigur Rós) was decided on the basis of dice rolled by Cunningham and modern art legends Robert Rauschenberg and Jasper Johns.

[14] Nick Kent, 'Ghost in the Machine', *Mojo*, August, 2006.

[15] However, the band didn't play at the Live8 concert the following year: Thom described the event as "a form of distraction… A convenient political sideshow to what was probably the most important G8 meeting." Craig McLean, 'All Messed Up', *Observer Music Monthly*, June 2006.

[16] Robert Sandall, 'Pop pioneer in love with the classics', *Daily Telegraph*, March 22, 2005.

[17] Kelly was a weapons expert, employed by the Ministry of Defence, who was indirectly involved in a controversial radio broadcast about the British government's dossier on Iraqi weapons of mass destruction. Days after he appeared in front of a Parliamentary committee investigating the affair, he was found dead on Harrowdown Hill, near his Oxfordshire home; coincidentally, only a few miles from Abingdon School. The coroner's verdict was suicide, but there are conspiracy theories that contradict this, many drawing attention to the lack of blood at the death scene. As Yorke sings: "Did I fall or was I pushed? And where's the blood?"

[18] 'Word!', *Q*, June, 2006. The progress of Album Seven appears to be following the stop-start methodology of its predecessors. On October 15, 2006, Thom posted the following message on the band's website: "weve started the record properly now. starting to get somewhere i think. finally."

CHAPTER 23

**EVERYTHING'S GONE GREEN –
OK COMPUTER
AS AN AMBIVALENT ECO-MANIFESTO**

I'm not afraid of being taken over by computers though, because the thing is, computers cannot resist. You can always smash 'em up, and they're totally defenceless. All we need are more people with hammers.
—Thom Yorke

A decade after the release of *OK Computer*, one subject has outstripped most observers' expectations and has become a central preoccupation for humanity. The environment, and the future of the planet that we share, has moved from the political periphery to the core of public policy. The UN's Kyoto Agreement on carbon emissions was made open for signatures six months after *OK Computer* was released; nine years later, the Stern Report suggested that Kyoto's guidelines were still only scratching the surface.

In recent years, Thom Yorke and Radiohead as a whole have been highly vocal in their commitment to minimising carbon emissions, and associated campaigns. The singer even suggested that international tours by the band might become unsustainable on environmental grounds (see Chapter 16). In fact, by 2006, Yorke's public support for the protection of the environment appeared to have become more pressing than his battles against globalisation and international capitalism, although the two are inevitably interconnected.

Because of these developments, it's tempting to apply a retrospectively 'green' agenda to *OK Computer*. After all, its dominant theme is the impact of technology, which is at the heart of the urgent warnings about global warming that occupy our news bulletins.

However, consciously or otherwise, Yorke's lyrics tend to evade any such interpretation, at least on at explicit level. Ten years on, air travel sparks earnest debates about carbon footprints and rising ocean levels, but the aeroplanes in 'Let Down' and 'Lucky', and the ones on the album's artwork, have no such associations. The lyrics in the slow movement of 'Paranoid Android' might just hint at acid rain, but that's possibly an interpretation too far. Even the abused moths, ants, cats and pigs of 'Fitter Happier' are there as metaphors for the misery of humanity, rather than as examples of people's unthinking cruelty to animals.

The only track that raises the concerns of a conventional green agenda – essentially, the need to protect nature from the ravages of industrialisation and pollution – is 'Subterranean Homesick Alien'. "The smell of the warm summer air" is a rare hint of the authentic and the natural in a word-landscape that's almost entirely artificial. If the narrator keeps his eye on "the cracks in the pavement", he might even see a rogue patch of greenery poking through.

OK Computer does have green credentials, but they owe their provenance to a slightly different tradition from Al Gore-style campaigning. In the 1970s, a trend developed for people in the developed, Western world to reject the material benefits of modern life, and opt for a simpler, more natural existence. Books such as Henry David Thoreau's *Walden* (1854), *Living the Good Life*, by Helen and Scott Nearing (1954) and *Small Is Beautiful*, by the economist E.F. Schumacher (1973) became alternative Bibles for people who aspired to reject the conveniences that industrialisation brought. Some moved into self-sufficient communes; many more rediscovered the delights of growing and rearing food, while still retaining some contact with their old lifestyles.

Although there were clear ecological and environmental benefits to such changes in lifestyle, the prime motivation was to escape from the effects that scientific development had had on individuals, and to gain spiritual or mental wellbeing by stepping off the work-centred treadmill. And it's this strain of environmental thinking, that focuses on the way people cope with the industrial world, that appears to preoccupy Yorke as a lyricist. His concern is not so much for melting ice caps or a ravaged ozone layer: it's more for the traumatised survivors of the crashes in 'Airbag' and 'Lucky'; the psychopath and his/her victims in 'Climbing Up The Walls'; the deflated, defeated salaryman in 'No Surprises' (who succumbs to carbon monoxide, not the dioxide of global warming notoriety).

And yet there's a heavy dose of ambiguity mixed up with Yorke's concerns. As noted before, there's a central contradiction in using technology to tell us all how bad technology is. His focus on the human aspect of industrialisation and modernity reinforces the idea that it's not machines or computers or transport that cause the problem, but people's response to them, and over-reliance on them. And he's well aware of the accusations of hypocrisy when a successful rock star complains about the damage that *homo sapiens* is inflicting on the environment.[1]

This complex response to the dangers of technology was a running theme through British popular culture while the members of Radiohead were growing up. In 1975, three different television series began on the BBC, all of them dealing with situations where the protagonists find themselves existing without the supposed benefits of the modern world, by choice or by circumstance. *The Good Life* (known as *Good Neighbors* in the United States) was a comedy about a man resigning from his job and, with his wife, turning their suburban home and garden into a self-sufficient farmstead; *Survivors* concerned a plague caused by a laboratory mishap in China, that kills 95% of the world's population, forcing the remainder to return to a pre-industrial society; and *The Changes*, a drama for children, envisaged a near future when people in Britain suddenly and irrationally destroy all their machinery and electrical equipment (those "people with hammers"), again returning to an agricultural past.[2]

What united all of these programmes was that, rather than coming out as wholeheartedly pro-self-sufficiency, pro-back-to-nature tracts, they focused on the difficulties that modern humans would encounter if they were suddenly deprived of all their gadgets and amenities. All three shows end with the characters finding a way out of the pre-industrial state, to a greater or lesser extent. Tom and Barbara, in *The Good Life*, give up the effort gracefully, with the encouragement of their more conventional neighbours, and return to the rat race; the *Survivors* eventually begin to rebuild a modern infrastructure; and Nicky, the central character in *The Changes*, discovers and tames the supernatural source of the madness that has afflicted the country, and everything returns to normal.

Similarly, Yorke hates the effects of development, but he can't help hinting at the gleaming beauty of man's incessant desire to build and to move. From the "intastella burst" to the "sparks a-flowin'", he's drawn to technology as much as he's repelled by it.

Just as the crash survivors get a perverse rush from their brushes with death, Yorke often finds himself celebrating the destruction that he sees around him, sometimes in almost religious terms (for example, "it's gonna be a glorious day", from 'Lucky').[3]

It's this ambivalence about technology that ties Yorke to the characters in the TV shows from the 1970s. Like them, he can appreciate the damage that 'progress' does; and yet he has no clear idea what he could do, what he might be without it. This confusion and fear is expressed by his characters, many of whom feel that they can't step off the industrial merry-go-round without something dreadful happening to them: social rejection ('Subterranean Homesick Alien'); madness ('Climbing Up The Walls'); failure ('No Surprises'). A potential compromise ("slow down", rather than "stop") is offered to the protagonist in 'The Tourist', but we come to the end of the album without ever knowing whether he took it up.

This, then, is the green politics of *OK Computer*. It's not so much a manifesto, more a snapshot of people responding to their environment. Yorke does not judge, or offer any explicit argument; not until the end of the album does he even hint at any possible way out of the situation he depicts. There's a very clear division between Yorke the artist and Yorke the activist. In his music, he tends to allusion, implication, a policy of "no comment"; in the face of the news media he is more focused and issue-specific. (Although it's interesting to compare his nervous, sometimes inarticulate 'performances' in this context with the flamboyant, fluent speechifying of Bono or Bob Geldof when they discuss poverty and debt relief.)

Environmental campaigners might be frustrated that such an intelligent and committed supporter of their causes seems to shy away from explicit engagement with the big issues that run through his own work. On the other hand, in a world where ordinary people are repelled by political grandstanding, it may be that Yorke's "human, all too human" approach (see Chapter 6) is a more effective recruiting call for the environmental cause than any big, scripted gesture, and certainly more than yet another speech by yet another middle-aged man in a suit. When Yorke places a political or environmental message on the band's Dead Air Space site, he usually caps it with a self-deprecating comment such as "sermon over".

He hates cars, but understands how difficult it is to live without them. He hates the damage that air travel does, but he's a rock star, and he needs to tour. He doesn't claim to have all the answers, but at least he asks one or two of the right questions.

OK Computer, if it's considered in literary terms, as a narrative text, is vague when it comes to characterisation. Voices appear, disembodied, without names or other identifiers, and then die away again. Yorke's repeated "I"[4] seems to apply to a constantly shifting cast of individuals, none of whom feel 'real' in the sense that we normally understand characters. But we hear their voices. For all its association with big themes and difficult ideas, at its core – like most of the best art – the album is in many ways less about ideas, let alone politics. It's more about *people*.

Notes:

[1] Leo Hickman, 'Are rock tours bad for the environment?', *The Guardian*, October 18, 2006; see also David Adam, 'Radiohead singer snubs Blair climate talks', *The Guardian*, March 22, 2006.

[2] The orgy of appliance-smashing in *The Changes* was triggered by a mysterious, unbearable electronic noise, that made everyone loathe and fear machines – a precursor to the "fridge buzz" of 'Karma Police', perhaps?

[3] In 2004, in an interview with a Christian magazine, Yorke was forced to reject repeated insinuations that his lyrics might be expressing some kind of submerged Christian theology. See Brian Draper, 'Chipping Away', *Third Way*, December 2004.

[4] The pronoun appears in the lyrics of 11 tracks on the album, all of them except 'Fitter Happier'.

CHAPTER 24

THE EMPTIEST OF FEELINGS –
OK COMPUTER
AND THE DEATH OF INDIE MUSIC

...and, gazing up at the dark sky spangled with its signs and stars, for the first time, the first, I laid my heart open to the benign indifference of the universe.
—Albert Camus, *The Outsider* (1942)

And your blues keep getting bluer with each song.
—Johnnie Ray, 'Cry' (1951)

But don't forget the songs that made you smile
And the songs that made you cry.
—The Smiths, 'Rubber Ring' (1985)

Teenage angst has paid off well,
Now I'm bored and old.
—Nirvana, 'Serve The Servants' (1993)

You know, everyone has problems; it doesn't mean you have to be a little crybaby about it.
—Thom Yorke on *South Park* (2001)

That unimpeachable music resource allmusic.com classifies the musical styles of Radiohead under the following headings:

Alternative Pop/Rock
Britpop[1]
Experimental Rock
Indie Electronic

In the 'Moods' column (based on the suggestions of the site's users), we have the following:

Distraught
Insular
Cold
Epic

Suffocating
Sprawling
Austere
Atmospheric
Brooding
Melancholy
Eerie
Theatrical
Cathartic
Angst-Ridden
Aggressive
Poignant
Wintry
Gloomy
Paranoid
Wistful
Plaintive

Clearly, these adjectives are no more objective or scientific than the votes that give *OK Computer* a particular ranking in a magazine poll. But they do seem to suggest a certain consistency in the way in which Radiohead have been perceived over the years.

From the moment 'Creep' began to whine its way around the world, Radiohead have been categorised as an indie/alternative band. They have an entry in *The Virgin Encylopedia of Indie and New Wave* (1998); another in Dave Thompson's *Alternative Rock* (2000). They play at festivals such as Glastonbury, Coachella, Benicàssim and Bonnaroo. When touring, they are unlikely to utter phrases such as "Woo! Hello, Düsseldorf!" without at least a suggestion of irony.

But does this categorisation and classification actually have a meaning? Colin Larkin, compiler of *The Virgin Encyclopedia Of Indie And New Wave*, makes a valiant effort at identifying a common musical identity for indie/alternative musicians with "Post Sex Pistols Music Sometimes Lo-Fi Or Grungy Played By Creative On The Edge Artists Who Are Often Influenced By The Byrds, Velvet Underground and Blondie."[2] It's as good an attempt as any, if now slightly outdated; bands that find themselves in the indie camp today tend to be influenced by those bands that were influenced by The Byrds, Velvets, et al.

To confuse the issue even further, "indie" was originally a reference to the business model of certain record labels: specifically, those that operated outside the control of the major music companies. Such independent operations have existed for as long as recorded music, and the word 'indie' was first applied to a record label as long ago as 1945, in *Billboard* magazine.[3] However, they first became a significant force in Britain in the mid-late 1970s. Their importance was confirmed in January, 1980, when the now-defunct trade paper *Record Business* published the first Indie Chart. The criteria for inclusion were that a record was not released by a major record company, and that no major was involved in its manufacturing, distribution or promotion. The most important labels in the 1980s included Rough Trade, Factory, Mute, 4AD and Creation, with the likes of Postcard and Cherry Red having a significance that outstripped their sales figures. Key bands were Joy Division/New Order, The Smiths, Cocteau Twins and Depeche Mode.

Fairly soon, a definition of indie music began to coalesce that was not so much about the technical details of its journey to the consumer, but more about a sound, an attitude and an image, all of which were shared by performers and fans. This is where those adjectives ('melancholy', 'angst-ridden' and so on) come in: indie kids read Camus and Oscar Wilde; wore their hair over their eyes and their grandads' cardigans; and worried equally about nuclear war and their own hapless love lives. Although mainstream British radio tended to ignore indie music, the maverick Radio One DJ John Peel provided a late-night refuge for fans. The *NME* identified closely with the movement, and attempted to commemorate it with the *C-86* compilation (see Chapter 7); some purists have identified this as the death of the whole indie scene. By the end of the decade, nominally 'indie' bands had jumped ship to the majors, and a number of labels were doing the same thing, maintaining their left-field identities while quietly contracting out business arrangements to the likes of EMI and Polygram. At the same time, their places were taken by companies that had no time for spotty, shy kids with Rickenbackers. By 1989, grinning, gleaming soap stars such as Kylie Minogue and Jason Donovan were topping the Indie Chart; former Smiths frontman Morrissey, whose sardonic demeanour personified the indie concept for many fans, was now signed to a major, and thus ineligible.

In North America, fans tended to be less precious about the moral purity of record labels, and the preferred term for the music was 'alternative'. Acts such as Beat Happening demonstrated kinship with the introverted, sometimes androgynous strain of British indie, but more representative of the scene were punk- and metal-influenced bands like Black Flag and Sonic Youth. These in turn were among the influences on a group of bands based in the Pacific Northwest, many of them with connections to the Sub Pop label. So-called grunge bands such as Mudhoney and Soundgarden coupled alt-rock existentialism with hard rock dynamics; it was Nirvana's move to the more mainstream Geffen organisation, and the release of *Nevermind* (1991) that finally dragged the music into the mainstream, and forced performers, journalists and fans to ask a couple of pointed questions: alternative to what?; independent of whom?

It was against this background, an explosion of success that also prompted a crisis of identity in a whole genre, that Radiohead signed with the massive EMI organisation. It was a move that some observers might have seen as a contradiction of what the band stood for, but Thom Yorke was exasperated by such attitudes, grumbling that "the British hate success... we're not an indie band. We write pop songs, but some people can't see that."[4] And, moreover, indie-label purism meant that any political or social comment that a band might make through its music would be a case of preaching to the converted. Most major punk acts of the late 1970s signed to major labels, many of them without even a preliminary gestation period in the land of the hand-printed record label. As Andy Gill of the virulently political Leeds quartet Gang of Four put it: "We could have hidden away on Rough Trade, say, but we wanted people to hear our music."[5]

What nobody could have predicted in 1993, when Yorke made that comment to an Oxford journalist, was that Radiohead would become partly responsible for a situation in which the idea of a separate 'alternative' genre became pretty much academic. The release of *OK Computer* was the concluding part of a step-by-step process that had begun with the global success of *Nevermind*, along with REM's *Out Of Time* (1991) and *Automatic For The People* (1992). Of course, Kurt Cobain was not the first angst-ridden, dysfunctional singer to achieve stardom, and Michael Stipe wasn't the first to make a virtue of ambivalent sexuality. In the 1940s, much was made of the young Frank Sinatra's frailty and shyness; in the following decade, a deaf, alcoholic, bisexual called Johnnie Ray had women swooning as he burst into tears on stage. But Nirvana repackaged alienation and existentialism with knowing nods to the arena-rock riffs hardwired into youthful brains around the world, and sold it to the MTV generation. It did help that, under the lank hair and grubby plaid shirts, Cobain was very, very beautiful. REM managed the trick by creating records that resonated with the big themes in people's lives, from celebration ('Shiny Happy People') to commiseration ('Everybody Hurts'). The fact that the original meaning of the songs probably had very little to do with the meaning that the listener perceived was neither here nor there; this was the stuff of TV sports round-ups.

The second stage, although it was less visible in North America, was the rise of Britpop. Although the genre owed a debt to punk and post-punk acts, its evident lineage from The Beatles and The Kinks made it palatable to a wider audience; the surviving hardcore of indie purists sneered at the credentials of the major bands. (Blur's label, Food, was owned by EMI; Creation, which released Oasis' records, was in partnership with Sony.)

At the same time, there was a faintly disreputable air about some of the performers that enabled Tony Blair to maintain a vicarious sense of danger and excitement through his association with the phenomenon. His political role model, President Bill Clinton, had played the saxophone on network TV, and used Fleetwood Mac's 'Don't Stop' as his campaign song. Blair went one better, proudly displaying his electric guitar as he moved into the Prime Minister's residence in Downing Street, and inviting Noel Gallagher to an official reception. But the superficial sheen of cool this gave to the new Prime Minister's reputation was short-lived; the long-term damage inflicted in Gallagher's credibility was more severe, although it's probably reading too much into events to note that this period in the middle of 1997 signals the beginning of his and his band's inexorable creative decline.[6]

Ed O'Brien noticed the demographic change in Radiohead's audience profile in 1995, and he seemed to be in two minds about welcoming the 'wrong' sort of people to his band's gigs. He characterised the most visible newcomers as:

...those people from college that you detested, the sports jocks. The ones who normally stayed away from so-called alternative shows, and who were seen at a Van Halen or Bon Jovi show, and now think that alternative music is their thing. And that's fine, I'm very much for winning those people over, but don't bring your fucking bullying instincts to one of our gigs... Maybe we should have a cage at stage right, like Metallica. We could throw them meat during the show.[7]

There's a distinct whiff of snobbery about O'Brien's attitude, as if these are the 'wrong' sort of people to be coming to his band's gigs. The rise of Oasis had provoked similar instincts in the indie community: when the band played their Knebworth concerts in the summer of 1996, 250,000 people shattered once and for all the notion that this was the music of outsiders, of sensitive souls, of the *other*.

Another example came in the aftermath of the death of Diana, Princess of Wales, in a car crash in Paris. The following day, September 1, 1997, saw the official launch of Xfm, London's first legitimate 'alternative' station. Rather than genuinely offering an alternative to the sentimental drivel that was paralysing the rest of the media in Britain and beyond, the station dutifully blacklisted any records that might cause offence, including Radiohead's 'Airbag'; announcers made all the same dutiful expressions of regret that were being parroted on mainstream media outlets. Oasis, meanwhile, dedicated a performance of 'Live Forever' to the late princess. The taboo-busting vitriol that the Sex Pistols had offered in 'Anarchy In The UK' and 'God Save The Queen', just two decades before, had been replaced by lame gestures of deference.

In between came *OK Computer*. Despite all Thom's protestations about Radiohead not being an indie band, their whole public persona was based on all those qualities (see the allmusic list above) that get attributed to purveyors of alternative rock. And yet it topped the British charts; the singles were played on daytime radio and the videos were put on heavy rotation on MTV. This had, of course, happened to Blur and Oasis, but *OK Computer* wasn't packed with half-remembered singalong tunes that harked back to the togethery vibes of '67 and '77. The Beatles were in the mix, but the pervasive influence was the sprawling experimentalism of the 'White Album', recorded when the myth of Swinging London had started to seem as embarrassing as Cool Britannia did in 1997. There were weird, uncomfortable bits of jazz-rock, avant-garde strings, Mellotrons and feedback, songs about murder and suicide and plane crashes, and one track that sounded as if it was being squawked by a robot. And yet, as the year went on, you could hear the album playing in shops and coffee bars around the world; it was becoming hip muzak. In early 1998, *OK Computer* was awarded a Grammy for 'Best Alternative Rock Performance', which threw up a whole new set of conundrums. The category upheld Radiohead's alternative status, their essential 'other'-ness; but the simple fact that such an honour was bestowed at all (it had first been awarded in 1991, to Sinéad O'Connor) indicates the extent to which alternative music had been absorbed into the belly of the corporate beast.

However, the cultural impact of *OK Computer* spawned a new slew of bands whose claims to not be Radiohead were met by hollow laughter all round. What is worrying is that most of these groups, which include Coldplay (who won the 2002 Grammy for Best Alternative Album), Travis, Keane and Snow Patrol, seem to have grasped only the radio-friendly dynamics of the album, without daring to confront the depths of pain and despair contained within;

let alone the levels of innovation that Radiohead explored on subsequent albums. The band's contempt for such wannabes is clear:

> [MTV VJ] Yago got them all to laugh when he introduced a question from a so-called 'Stanley from Coney Island', which read, "How do you guys feel about the fact that bands like Travis, Coldplay, and Muse are making a career sounding exactly like your records did in 1997?" Yorke cupped his hand around his mouth and called out, "Good luck with *Kid A*!"[8]

Bands such as Coldplay found themselves in a similar position to the many bands and musicians that tried to respond to the conceptual perfection of The Beatles' output between 1965 and 1968. One or two went insane in the attempt, like Brian Wilson; many others, ELO being the most egregious examples, made lots of money from vacuous simulacra of *Sgt Pepper*, replacing the restless invention of Lennon, McCartney and Martin with cellists in silver trousers.

But the likes of Coldplay and Snow Patrol are ultimately too dull, too safe for any kind of psychological torment, or even ludicrous stagewear. They're too amenable, too eager to please. Compare the views of Coldplay frontman Chris Martin with those of Thom Yorke on the subject of Tony Blair:

> Do you read *Harry Potter*? It's just sad that the world is run by Muggles. It always had been and always will be. Being a leader of a country is incredibly difficult. You're never going to please everybody – or, indeed, anybody. I've got great respect for anybody who wants to do it, but the type of person you have to be to be a politician is different from the type of person that you really want a person to be.[9]

> Blair is finished. The British people finally had enough after seeing him time and time again on the telly trying to explain his dodgy politics and just coming across as a smug cunt. Which is all he is.[10]

Of course, Radiohead can't be held responsible for the lack of convincing opposition (something they share with Bush and Blair). Nor can they be blamed for the commercial success that albums such as *OK Computer* and *Kid A* have enjoyed, or the favoured place they have achieved in the industry as a result. They haven't become champagne-swilling bastions of the rock aristocracy, and they don't play polo. They don't even take cocaine, as far as anyone knows. The fanbase remains loyal, and accepts that they are entitled to all the gongs and gold discs, provided they take them with a sort of glum indifference, as an example of the bullshit they have to put up with. Thom and Jonny were smart enough to avoid picking up the Grammy for *Kid A*, passing the buck to their three embarrassed-looking bandmates.[11]

This is what alternative rock has come to, in the years after Nirvana, REM, Oasis and Radiohead made it big business. Alternative bands can be successful, but not too successful, as that would scuff the outsider status that remains their defining characteristic. This is a point that was entirely missed by Gary Gersh, the president of Radiohead's US label Capitol in 1997, when *OK Computer* was released:

> There's nothing I've seen in any country in the world that's excited me as much… Our job is just to take them as a left-of-center band and bring the center to them. That's our focus, and we won't let up until they're the biggest band in the world.[12]

But in attempting to make Radiohead "the biggest band in the world", executives such as Gersh risk alienating the group's core constituency – people who will stop loving them the moment they threaten to become that big. They're allowed to shift 23 million units worldwide, but they've got to behave as if they'd have difficulty shifting 23. Here's an online post about Thom's solo appearance at the Bridge School benefit concert in 2002:

> The idea of Thom Yorke playing solo, brought a very dedicated, distinctive crowd, but this also means that Thom's fans

were distributed vaguely among the thousands of people. It was interesting to see the reaction of the people who weren't use to Thom's creepiness. It makes you wonder what sense Leanne Rhymes (she played the same day) fans made of the music. Maybe it made Thom happy to know he was really only playing for a few us, because it seems he played comfortably to an unfamiliar crowd. It was a wonderful show full of suprises (sic!) that no one will ever see again!haha[13]

Haha, indeed. The sense of moral and aesthetic superiority over admirers of Leanne Rhymes (sic!) is what keeps fans like this going. The feeling that, in a mainstream audience, Thom is "only playing for a few us" (sic!) is utterly essential to Radiohead's ethos, and there is only a certain level of success that the band can enjoy before a credibility gap opens up. This is a genre that's defined by its fanbase as much as by its musicians: "Radiohead," as one admirer put it, "is music for miserable people who were dropped on the floor when they were little."[14] There's no need to keep artists poor in order to keep them pure;[15] but when a genre is founded on concepts of alienation and rebellion, bringing "the center" to alternative bands will just result in giving increased coverage to a stream of bland Coldplay clones. Or worse: I've just seen the front of a British men's magazine (the sort in which the women keep most of their underwear on, just about) directing the reader to a photo feature depicting "THE SEXIEST GIRLS OF INDIE MUSIC".[16] The purists of the *C-86* era would have choked on their lollipops.

And all the time that Radiohead fans are feeling a nice glow in their tummies over being further from "the center" than fans of Coldplay or indeed LeAnn Rimes, there remain purists for whom there's little or no difference between any of them:

When critics talk about independent pop music, usually they mean mainstream music dressed up in slightly different clothes and with a sneer (or smile, or sniffle) on its lips. If you're still excited by the thrill of the new, you don't like to imagine that what you're hearing has been heard a million times before,

and that's kind of implicit in the very word "mainstream"…
If you enjoy the music of Coldplay and Radiohead and The
Strokes then you enjoy the music of the mainstream, or at least
mainstream independent pop. I never liked it when independent became codified into a description. Sometimes in the mid/
late Eighties (and I personally blame Alan McGee and *NME*'s
Danny Kelly for this) indie grew to mean "white middle-class
boys playing jangling guitars who own every Smiths album
and a couple of early Creation singles."[17]

Under this aesthetic, even being on an authentically indie label
isn't enough. The London indie Domino achieved major success in
2005/6 with acts such as Franz Ferdinand and Arctic Monkeys, who
follow the Coldplay route of throwing post-punk shapes with a radio-friendly coating. When bands like this are selling more records
than anyone else, surely it's time to come up with a few more defini-
tions?

Of course, *OK Computer* didn't really kill alternative music.
But the cumulative effect of the leftfield successes of the 1990s may
have reinforced the idea that the genre is nothing but a package of
attitudes and poses. There's always been a tendency to resort to this
reductive level of criticism, especially in music: opera is fat people
holding the high notes; heavy metal is tight trousers and interminable guitar solos; reggae is ganja and/or homophobia, with the bass
turned up. But these have been the views of the outsiders, the haters.
Now alternative rock is reduced to a catch-all description of 'mid-
tempo guitar rock sung in a slightly sad way'. The only difference is
that it's the self-styled fans who believe this, and provided they see
themselves as ever so slightly distinct from "the center", that suits
them just fine. They see nothing odd in an exquisitely damaged alt-
rock star such as Pete Doherty proclaiming his psychic link to the
Sex Pistols and William Blake, while at the same time copping off
with a supermodel. Similarly, it only seems natural that Chris Martin
or even Fab Moretti of The Strokes should be shacking up with Hollywood stars. Although, according to the Legend!'s analysis (above),
if you're a fan of Coldplay, maybe Kate Moss and Gwyneth Paltrow

and Drew Barrymore will seem pretty edgy, leftfield and alternative. The music writer and indie club promoter Ian Watson, taking a tip from the fragmentation of heavy metal into multiple genres, has dubbed this commercially viable wing of alternative rock as "hair indie";[18] the indie equivalent, presumably, of Bon Jovi and Mötley Crüe.

No member of Radiohead has yet snuggled up to a starlet. But where does this situation leave the band? *OK Computer* showed that they could play with the big boys; *Kid A* demonstrated that they had the guts to walk away from a winning formula; *Hail To The Thief* showed that they weren't scared of losing some of their new, avant-garde friends.[19] They do their own thing, which was, in theory at least, the whole point of the indie and post-punk culture that arose in the late 1970s. As I type this, they're in a state of perfect indie grace, having been free from any recording contract whatsoever since 2004. They don't care about their credibility, and as a result it remains intact. In addition to the indie cred this may give them, of course, it does tie in with Thom Yorke's increasing involvement in the struggles against corporate globalisation. The downside is that if Radiohead do bother to release another album, they'll need to tangle with the big bad record industry somehow.

Maybe they should stay in that label-free limbo. Malcolm McLaren, situationist provocateur and punk pioneer, recently declared:

> If I'd had my way, the Sex Pistols would never have released any records at all – I wanted them to remain enigmatic. I loved the idea of managing a group who never went into the studio but became more popular than the groups who were actual recording artists. But the Pistols decided that they wanted to release records that would compete in the charts with Cliff Richard.[20]

Maybe this is the indie ideal, and if On A Friday had stayed in the Jericho Tavern doing Pixies impressions, they would have lived up to it; but if that had been the case, you wouldn't be reading this.

It's a genre that will forever be defined by its smallness, its outsiderdom.

It's a little like Jonny Greenwood's explanation of the effect that the music of Miles Davis had on the recording of *OK Computer*, where the original is a crucial piece of inspiration, but the finished article sounds nothing like it (see Chapter 5). Without the whole concept of post-punk/indie/alternative music, the album would not have been made; but the end result sounds nothing like The Pixies or Magazine or Joy Division or any of the bands that shaped the band; moreover, the ideology of the genre also went missing in action some time after The Smiths left Rough Trade. Once Nirvana and the Manics and Radiohead went stratospheric, they somehow tainted those alternative bands that remained small and perfect into the new millennium: to pluck a handful at random, The Gossip; Pants Yell!; Electrelane; Maher Shalal Hash Baz; Comets On Fire; Aberfeldy. They must *want* to be at least as big as, say, Pearl Jam, we presume. And when they don't, we feel sorry for them, and when they do, we get snotty, and say we preferred the early stuff that only got released on mauve vinyl.

On the other hand, in the wider world, beyond fanzinedom, the success of *OK Computer* has been so great, its cultural impact so pervasive, that such discussions of purity and credibility aren't that relevant. Sure, as Alex Ross put it, Radiohead are "the poster boys for a certain kind of knowing alienation – as Talking Heads and REM had been before... a magnet for misfits everywhere."[21] But they've transcended that misfit constituency. It's not Coldplay or Keane that Radiohead have to contend with now. It's the Beatles and the Stones and Springsteen and U2 (all of whom were 'alternative' once, of course). This is historical. Radiohead are now, officially, allowed to play with the big boys.

Notes:

[1] A slightly bizarre classification (see Chapter 19). The site also claims that the band formed at Oxford University in 1988.

[2] Colin Larkin (ed.), *The Virgin Encyclopedia of Indie & New Wave* (London: Virgin, 1998), p. 3.

[3] Andrew Collins, 'Wan Love', *The Word*, October 2006.

[4] Ronan Munro, 'Radiohead', *Curfew*, February 1993; quoted in Randall, p. 49.

[5] Irvin & McLear, p. 428.

[6] Gallagher's, I mean, not Blair's. Although... The Oasis leader's bitter rival Damon Albarn refused an invitation to the same event, claiming to have become a communist. See Harris, *The Last Party*, pp. 344-345.

[7] William Stone, *Radiohead: Green Plastic Wateringcan* (London: UFO, 1996), p. 50.

[8] Alex Ross, 'The Searchers: Radiohead's unquiet revolution', *The New Yorker*, August 20-27, 2001. To be fair, one of the bands often labelled as Radiohead clones, Muse, finally released something that approached the eclectic weirdness of their predecessors (without sounding much like them) in 2006, with the deranged, pretentious and excellent *Black Holes & Revelations*. However, the fact that they only got to that point nine years after the release of *OK Computer* is not insignificant.

[9] Alan Light, '20 Years of *Spin*: Chris Martin', *Spin*, October, 2005.

[10] Nick Kent, 'Ghost In The Machine', *Mojo*, August, 2006.

[11] Clarke, pp. 150-152.

[12] Barney Hoskyns, 'Exit Music: Can Radiohead save rock music as we (don't) know it?', *GQ*, Oct 2000.

[13] Anonymous review, http://www.greenplastic.com/gigography/showDetails.php?showID=721

[14] Ross, 'The Searchers: Radiohead's unquiet revolution'.

[15] Interestingly, fans of hip-hop, an anti-establishment genre that has achieved commercial success over roughly the same period as alternative rock, see no contradiction in their idols enjoying a high-end

lifestyle. Perhaps this is because, thanks to the economic inequality endemic in American and Western culture, the image of a rich black man still packs a subversive punch of its own.

[16] Matt Hill and Ian Davies, 'Girls Girls Girls', *Arena*, October, 2006.

[17] The Legend!, sleevenotes, *Rough Trade Shops Indiepop 1* (Mute, 2004). The reference to early Creation singles is particularly poignant because the Legend! (aka Jerry Thackray, aka Everett True) was actually the first performer to release a single on Alan McGee's label.

[18] Collins, 'Wan Love'.

[19] Griffiths, *OK Computer*, p. 114. The theorists and chin-strokers of *The Wire*, it seems, can be as unforgiving of apostates as any member of the indie Taliban.

[20] Jon Wilde, 'An Audience With Malcolm McLaren', *Uncut*, September 2006, p. 44.

[21] Ross, 'The Searchers: Radiohead's unquiet revolution.'

CHAPTER 25

A SONG TO KEEP US WARM –
OK COMPUTER
AND THE DEATH OF
THE CLASSIC ROCK ALBUM

A significant melody which says a great deal soon makes its way round the entire earth, while a poor one in meaning which says nothing straightaway fades and dies.
—Arthur Schopenhauer, 1851

I have heard the mermaids singing, each to each.
—T.S. Eliot, 1917

Awopbopaloobopawopbamboo.
—Little Richard, 1955

We now know that a text is not a line of words releasing a single 'theological' meaning (the 'message' of the Author-God) but a multi-dimensional space in which a variety of writings, none of them original, blend and clash. The text is a tissue of quotations drawn from the innumerable centres of culture.
—Roland Barthes, 1968

We write pop songs, As time has gone on, we've gotten more into pushing our material as far as it can go. But there was no intention of it being 'art'.
—Thom Yorke, 1997

I know someone who started to create a soundtrack to his life, a song for whatever situation he was in, there at the roll of his thumb.
—Dylan Jones, 2005

I don't know anybody who's made a record that sounds decent in the past 20 years.
—Bob Dylan, 2006

There's a lot of impending doom about at the moment.
—Thom Yorke, 2006

Several of the original reviews of *OK Computer* considered it in the context of millenarianism, the belief that the imminent Year 2000 would bring with it unspecified social and spiritual changes. It's difficult to recall now exactly how significant 'Y2K' seemed to everyone at the time, whether we were concerned about the moment when (as the *Melody Maker* put it) "Jesus Christ Almighty turns up on Holloway Road wearing knuckledusters and murder in his eye",[1] or our computers going insane and telling us that Queen Victoria was still alive. Those who lived in London as the 1990s counted down to oblivion may also recall the bulbous embarrassment that went by the name of the Millennium Dome. (Those lucky enough to have avoided it might care to imagine the scribbly structure on the cover of the 'Paranoid Android' single, although it wasn't that much fun once you got inside. This was proof, if any is still needed, that God ceased to love his children a long time ago.)

Whether or not the palpable feeling of dread and despondency that oozes from *OK Computer* was in fact provoked by this sort of end-of-the-century angst, there's no doubt that it is redolent of a specific historical moment. The 1990s were an in-between decade that saw many people thrashing around for some kind of moral and political certainty. The balance of power between the United States and the Soviet Union, that had defined global politics since the end of World War II, was no more. Even South African apartheid, the definitive evil against which liberals of all flavours could shake their fists, was dead by the middle of the decade. There were occasional intimations of the face-off between the Western and Islamic worlds that would characterise the beginning of the 21st century, but few people at the time realised how significant this clash of cultures would become.[2]

Of course, there were hideous things going on during the 1990s, in Rwanda, in Bosnia and elsewhere. But professional malcontents such as Thom Yorke had trouble finding any Big Idea on which they could focus their anger. Radiohead's first two albums were, for the most part, packed with internalised rage. The 'characters' that Yorke played in his lyrics were depressive self-loathers, unworthy lovers, the creeps and weirdos that occupy the films of Jim Jarmusch and the fiction of Albert Camus. By the time of *Kid A*,

Yorke had seen the light (or, perhaps, the darkness) and had identified the Bad Wolf of the coming century as global capitalism and its political, social and cultural bedfellows.

OK Computer exists at the cusp of these two points of view. The gauche, droop-eyed misfit still finds himself grotesquely out of place in yuppie bars; but there's a growing realisation that this sense of dislocation is more than just student angst. Why are there yuppie bars? Why are there yuppies? Why are they networking? Why is there Gucci, and why does everyone, piggy or otherwise, lust after it? *OK Computer* marks Yorke's realisation that his whole personality is, in part, crafted by vast political forces, of which we're only vaguely aware. The album confronts the personal and the political at one and the same time. It is very much of its own time and yet, a decade on, it speaks to us clearly. This – coupled, of course, with great tunes and imaginative production and a weird cover and the potential to provoke arguments about whether or not it's prog rock into the wee small hours – is why it is a classic album.

And that classification brings with it another hundred or so further questions and qualifications, and the depressing likelihood of another history lesson. But it's important. What is (and isn't) a classic album? Why do we need them? Who decides?

The idea of The Classic Rock Album – essentially, that some albums have a more lasting significance than others – began to take hold in the mid-1960s, when a few critics offered the (to many people at the time) laughable suggestion that pop music ought to be taken seriously. A number of factors coincided to make this position feasible: the post-war baby boom ensured that teenagers began to outnumber other age bands, so their tastes became more significant; an increasing number of pop performers wrote their own material; record companies began to focus on albums by rock acts as self-contained products, rather than simply attempts to squeeze more cash from the release of 7-inch singles. Musicologists identified the "Aeolian cadences" in the music of The Beatles; literary academics compared Bob Dylan favourably with Keats.

The start of *Rolling Stone* magazine in 1967, and *Creem* two years later, established a model of rock criticism distinct from the breathless, PR-influenced hype that had dominated up to that point.

Rock music was more than just a bunch of fun tunes to dance to; it was *important*. And the most important vehicle for this importance was the 33 rpm, 12-inch album (although the significance of live performance was always acknowledged, and the concise, precise impact of a single never quite went away either). This attitude soon moved across the Atlantic, most notably to the *New Musical Express*, where critics such as Nick Kent and Charles Shaar Murray became cultural icons almost as significant as (and invariably much more intelligent than) the musicians about whom they wrote.

Because rock music was now considered to be culturally important, it was inevitable that some traits from other schools of cultural appreciation should crop up in the midst of rock critics' meanderings. The academics of serious literature and classical music had built up canons; lists of key artists and works that were considered fundamental to any understanding of their respective fields. Literature students needed to know about Chaucer, Shakespeare, Milton and Dickens; music students about Bach, Mozart, Beethoven and Wagner. Although rock 'n' roll had only been in existence since the early 1950s, a set of definitive works became must-haves in the collection of anyone who aspired to be knowledgeable about music. These included the major albums by The Beatles and Dylan, alongside such leftfield masterpieces as *The Velvet Underground and Nico* (1967) and Captain Beefheart's *Trout Mask Replica* (1969). As the 1970s progressed, artists such as Pink Floyd, Led Zeppelin and Bruce Springsteen were admitted to the inner sanctum. The rock canon was updated on a regular basis, in end-of-year polls, and occasional all-time lists (see Chapter 19). The punk revolution rattled a few teeth, especially as a combination of low budgets and amphetamine sulphate (with its attendant short attention spans) made the 7-inch single the medium of choice for many of the new bands. But pretty soon, the likes of Elvis Costello, The Clash and Talking Heads had produced long-playing records that took their place in the canon.

As the 1980s progressed, the introduction of compact disc reissues meant that new generations became acquainted with the music to which their parents had danced in an embarrassing manner. New albums, as well as previously forgotten gems, were added to the canon. But some things remained unchangeable. The top album was almost always by The Beatles (*Revolver* or *Sgt Pepper*); *Born To Run* and *Pet Sounds* would be in there; and there would be a token offering by a black artist, usually either something by Stevie Wonder, Bob Marley, or Marvin Gaye's *What's Going On* (1971).

There were attempts to breathe new life into this canon. Publications would attempt to demonstrate kinship with their readership demographic by asking them to vote for the best album of the previous 10 years, or the best in the lifetime of the magazine itself. In 1999, *The Guardian* proposed an alternative list, excluding anything by The Beatles or Dylan, the most obvious 'classics' by Pink Floyd and The Beach Boys (and, of course, Radiohead), and so on;[3] what emerged, inevitably, was a list of the sort of albums that tend to occupy positions 101-200 in these lists. (Nick Drake's *Bryter Later* came top.) The paper then asked readers which albums had been missed off *this* list... An infinite number of canons, all firing in different directions.

When publications have thrown off all their quirks and conditions and simply listed the Best Albums Of All Time, two things become clear. One is that the old guard, the Bachs and Shakespeares of rock, is staying put; the other is that the rate at which new albums are admitted to the canon is slowing down to an imperceptible dribble. When *Rolling Stone* published their all-time Top 500 in 2003, only one album in the top 50 (Nirvana's *Nevermind*) had been released since the end of the 1980s.[4]

If we can define a classic rock album based on the content of these lists (a definition similarly ham-fisted to the notion that something is art simply because it's in an art gallery), then *OK Computer* is a classic album. It can be mentioned in the same sentence as *Revolver* and no-one will snicker; as Alex Ross puts it, "this band is taken as seriously as any since The Beatles."[5] The important word here is 'seriously': once an album becomes a classic, pure pleasure slips well down the list of priorities.

So, *OK Computer* makes the cut. But its inclusion may also signal the point at which the slow-down identified on the *Rolling Stone* list became a complete drought. Albums become classics not because they sell in huge quantities (although many of them do), but because they achieve a special emotional connection with a critical mass of listeners; in most cases, that connection is above and beyond the music itself. An album becomes a Proustian trigger for specific responses and memories; a badge of recognition for fellow fans; in the language of the marketing imbeciles that Naomi Klein and Thom Yorke came to despise, it exists as a means of branding oneself. By definition, it has staying power; but it will also probably sum up a time and a place related to its conception and recording. *OK Computer* was a key component of London's soundtrack in the summer of 1997, its keening melancholy easing from Walkman headphones (there was life before iPods!) and through open windows; it played as you sipped an espresso or tried on a new pair of jeans; making a strange soup of noise as it battled with its only real competitor, *The Buena Vista Social Club*.

The following summer brought a different flavour of soup; it consisted of *Moon Safari* by Air, with a healthy splash of Fatboy Slim's maddening 'Rockafeller Skank'. 1999 was all about Moby's *Play*, and if the album itself didn't get you, the individual tracks seemed to soundtrack every other commercial on your TV. The only things that offered any respite from the hyperactive Christian vegan were Groove Armada's *Vertigo* and *Remedy* by Basement Jaxx (featuring Thom Yorke's old DJ partner, Felix Buxton).

All of a sudden, it seemed as if all the rock bands had packed up their guitars and checked out of the zeitgeist. Dance music – in the sense of the synthetic, beat-driven sounds that owe their inspiration to the house, techno and garage sounds that came from Chicago, Detroit and New York in the 1980s – had been a major presence throughout the 1990s, but it was essentially a single-based genre. Now, by taking the bpm down a notch or two, and adding a few hip samples, dance acts were reaching out to audiences that had never been clubbing, or were too old for it.

There's nothing, of course, to stop dance artists from taking a place in the Classic Album Canon, but there remains a tendency for rock critics to operate within fairly strictly defined parameters, based on knowing what they like:[6] is it any coincidence that the two albums that won critical respectability for hip-hop (*Raising Hell* by Run DMC and *Licensed To Ill* by the Beastie Boys, both 1986) featured big, fat raawwk guitars? Moreover, dance music as a genre downplays the two aspects of music that critics find it easiest to talk about: instrumental technique and lyrical inventiveness.

Play and *Moon Safari* were classic albums, in their own way, but they felt like albums to be heard, rather than listened to. And they sure as hell weren't rock. Of course, major rock artists released major rock records in the years immediately following 1997; Beck and the Flaming Lips, to name two, produced some of their most satisfying work. The real innovation seemed to be going on in a strange zone that used rock instrumentation, but incorporated elements of jazz, techno, ambient, minimalist and other musics. Bands as diverse as Tortoise, Mogwai, Sigur Rós and Stereolab had the 'post-rock' label bestowed upon them, as did Radiohead after *Kid A* and *Amnesiac*, but few of them seemed keen to be part of a common scene. In any case, this was music never likely to capture the popular imagination. It seemed as if the new millennium would be seen out to a soundtrack created with computers and sequencers rather than guitars and drums.

Some observers saw this shift as a seismic change in the history of music, one that only occurs every few decades. *Sgt Pepper's Lonely Hearts Club Band* might be seen as the last great Pop album, in that The Beatles were all about well-crafted songs and the human voice; the next 30 years, the years of Rock, were ruled, to a greater or lesser extent by the guitar, and *OK Computer* was the final statement of the hegemony enjoyed by Messrs Fender, Gibson and Rickenbacker. After that, we were due for the decades of Dance, a long reign by that all-pervading component of modern music, the beat. This ascendancy of music that was smart, imaginative and engaging, but essentially content-free, coincided with the rise of a debate about dumbing down and the collapse of cultural standards. As Barney Hoskyns mused, with an apparent millennium of dunces looming:

> For all the hosannas heaped upon Radiohead's magnificent *OK Computer* (1997) – an album precisely about the soullessness of our techno-numbed culture – there were just as many people who derided it as wanky 'progressive' rock. In a world

where we're expected to take Chris Evans seriously, is it any wonder that Radiohead are deemed to be po-faced?[7]

On similar lines, the occasion of *OK Computer*'s triumph in a 'Best Album of the 1990s' poll on the Pitchfork site provoked a gloomy sense of nostalgia:

> The resurgence, and arguable final entrenchment, of manufactured Pop Stars by their handlers over supposedly more artistic fare – and more importantly the acceptance of such common pleasures by critics – razed the significance of the complete album. Which is why *OK Computer*, and its Best Albums Ever companion [My Bloody Valentine's] *Loveless*, eternally top these polls: somehow we doubt we'll ever see their like again.[8]

These depressing visions of a populace too dim and superficial to cope with anything more challenging than New Kids On The Block were perhaps a little premature. Within a few years, the new dance/pop hegemony had checked into rehab. Maybe teenage boys just realised that a lowslung Strat pulled the girls better than a pair of top-of-the-range headphones. In any event, when guitar rock did crash back into the public eye, it was a very different beast from the ambitious experimentation seen on *OK Computer*, or *The Soft Bulletin* by the Flaming Lips. Bands such as The White Stripes, The Strokes, The Vines and The Hives offered a stripped-down, no-bullshit sound that was influenced by 70s punk, 60s garage rock and, in the case of The White Stripes, country blues music. It was exciting, it was immediate, and it was, in some instances, bloody superb, but it was hardly original or thought-provoking. It had an element of abrasive shock value, but punk rock had been and gone, and wouldn't shock us in the same way again.

As the 2000s progressed, it seemed as if every week heralded a new band that owed its sound and image to an act from 25 years before. It was, of course, a good thing that teenagers might rediscover Joy Division or Magazine as the result of a mention by Franz Ferdinand or Interpol. Radiohead had done the same thing. But Radiohead were able to take diverse and unlikely influences so far down the experimental route that they ended up sounding nothing like the original, once more following Jonny Greenwood's "garbled version" aesthetic (see Chapter 5). By contrast, most of the hip young guitar-slingers that appeared in the post-Strokes guitar boom were little more than efficient karaoke acts. They were unlikely to add to the list of classic albums; the only effect they might have on the rock canon would be to remind people of the merits of, say, Television's *Marquee Moon* (1977) or *Entertainment!* by the Gang of Four (1979), and shift them a few notches upwards in the critical pecking order.

In any case, even if rock were able to pull itself up from a rut of derivative soundalikes, there was a more immediate threat to the idea of the classic rock album; indeed, of the rock album itself. The internet had made it possible for fans to exchange sound files, often before an album's official release. Radiohead, of course, had experienced this (indeed, might even have sanctioned it) shortly before *Kid A* came out (see Chapter 22). By the time the music industry shifted its complacent ass to confront the issue, potential consumers had become accustomed to getting hold of music how and when they wanted it; and any legitimate delivery mechanism would need to have that flexibility built in. As a result, when services such as iTunes were launched, the user was able to pick and choose individual tracks from an album, rather than purchasing the whole package. Within months, it seemed as if the whole notion of The Album itself was in peril.

People had been able to play around with the contents of an album before iTunes came into our lives. The appearance of compact discs gave us the option to shuffle running order, or skip tracks entirely. Before that, the laborious process of compiling customised tape compilations was a rite of passage for music fans in the 1970s and 80s. And, of course, DJ culture and sampling broke music down to components even smaller than individual tracks, with or without the permission of the artist. In any case, the precise content of albums often changed from territory to territory. Each of The Beatles' albums before *Sgt Pepper's Lonely Hearts Club Band* had different track listings on the UK and US versions; *OK Computer* was the first Radiohead album where the Japanese content matched the UK original precisely.

Now, however, an album's release onto iTunes, allowing you to pick and choose the tracks you want, for 99 cents or 79 pence, feels like an act of surrender on the part of the record companies.[9] "We know you bastards are doing this anyway," they seem to be saying. "At least throw us some small change when you do it."

Artists still cling to the notion of an album, with a fixed running order, a beginning middle and end: tracks are listed in a particular order and there is usually an effective discount if a whole album is downloaded in one transaction, rather than as piecemeal tracks. But even this desperate adherence to a 60-year-old format seems threatened.[10]

Beck Hansen, one of the few major artists to rival Radiohead in their ability to combine musical reinvention and commercial success, was interviewed by *Wired* magazine in 2006. He discussed his album of the previous year, *Guero*, which has appeared in a number of different forms, some official, some less so. An unfinished mix was leaked at the end of 2004 (although the ambiguous nature of that leak has parallels with the similar episode surrounding the on-line appearance of *Kid A*); then came the 'proper' album, released as a CD, in boring old record shops; there was a DVD edition, with interactive visuals and surround sound; then *Guerolito*, a collection of remixes; and parallel to all these, a series of unofficial fan-authored mashups. Asked if this heralded "the end of the album as we know it", Beck replied:

> There are so many dimensions to what a record can be these days. Artists can and should approach making an album as an opportunity to do a series of releases – one that's visual, one that has alternate versions, and one that's something the listener can participate in or arrange and change. It's time for the album to embrace the technology... In an ideal world, I'd find a way to let people truly interact with the records I put out – not just remix the songs, but maybe play them like a videogame.

As to whether he still yearned for the glory days of gatefold sleeves bearing strands of tobacco and coffee-mug stains, the tousle-haired maverick continued:

I'm something of a traditionalist, so I have a soft spot for a record with just a standard side A and side B. But there's simply more room for information with digital media, and it would be ridiculous not to take advantage of that. It's sort of like the difference between a wire recording and a piano roll and a cassette tape. They're different formats, and they inspire different approaches.[11]

According to Beck's analysis then, the album is not dead; but the sense of an album being a discrete collection of songs, in a predetermined order (even if that order can subsequently be abandoned) is about to fade away. The next album released by Radiohead might be so interactive, so flexible in form and content, that no two versions are exactly the same. You don't like the bassline on track two? You want a different video for track five (which you actually want to play first)? You want to throw in a bit of 50 Cent, or Britney? Or Coldplay? You're the boss. Of course, by the time you read this, the new album might have been released, and it might only be available in a boring old record shop, as a boring old CD. Or an eight-track cartridge. Or it may never appear at all.

The idea of variable content isn't entirely new, of course. In 1973, the Monty Python team released their *Matching Tie and Handkerchief* album, on which the second side had two parallel grooves; it was a matter of chance which route the stylus followed. Later, the 1985 movie *Clue* (based on the murder mystery board game, also known as Cluedo) had three different endings, of which cinemas would be allocated one at random. On a similar basis, Blink-182's album *Take Off Your Pants and Jacket* (2001) was initially released in three versions, each with a different pair of bonus tracks. And cinematic blockbusters such as the original *Star Wars* trilogy (1977-1983), *Close Encounters Of The Third Kind* (1977) and *Blade Runner* (1982) have all reappeared in new forms, provoking intense debate over which is the 'best' and most 'authentic' (and, of course, squeezing extra revenue from the original property).

In these cases, the listener or viewer is pretty much passive, with no input into the changes that might occur. Fiction writers, on the other hand, have tended to give their readers a little more input into the artistic experience: Georges Perec's novel *Life: A User's Manual* (1978) is constructed so that the individual chapters can be read in various different orders; B.S. Johnson's *The Unfortunates* (1969) was published as 27 separate sections in a box, which could be juggled into any order the reader chose.[12]

But these are anomalies, unusual enough for the perversity of the concept to be the most memorable thing about them. Also, there is a finite number of variations available in each case; the artist/producer has decided the options from which the consumer can choose. Beck is talking about consumers being able to take an album (or book, or film) into areas that the artist never contemplated; moreover, this level of interactivity could become the normal state in which we consume music (and, presumably, any other work of art). One practical effect of this would be that the classic rock canon would be sealed up for good. *OK Computer* ended up as a classic rock album because a critical mass of people responded to it, and continue to respond to it, intellectually and emotionally. It *matters* to people. If it had emerged in the multiple forms and formats that Beck predicted, people would still have responded to it, but this would have been a case of different people reacting to different entities. If each listener's *OK Computer* experience were hand-tooled to fit that listener's tastes, the idea of *OK Computer* at number four on a list of the Greatest Albums Of All Time would be meaningless. When *OK Computer* was admitted to the canon, it began with *that* guitar, and ended with *that* triangle, and had *that* weird computer voice in the middle. Whenever critics or fans discussed it, they were singing off the same hymn sheet; maybe the one used by the Mellotron angels from 'Exit Music (For A Film)'. If every album from now on is going to exist in multiple different forms, the common, agreed idea of what that album *is* will cease to exist. And if we can't agree what an album is, how can we compare it with other albums? Technology, that evil, suffocating beast that stalks *OK Computer*, helps to ensure that *OK Computer* is the last entry into the Rock Album Hall of Fame.

Way back in the Introduction, I suggested that you should take a look at Roland Barthes's essay 'The Death of the Author'.[13] Barthes rejects the critical tradition that ascribes the meaning and worth of a work to the author: he argues that the work only makes sense when it is read: "a text's unity lies not in its origin but in its destination." If we accept Beck's predictions, then Barthes seems to have won his argument, although not quite in the way he imagined. The reader (a word that can encompass viewers, listeners, and so on) has not only become more important than the author (musician, film-maker, etc); he or she has become the author. And if everyone's an author, and everyone gets a place in the canon, what's the point of a canon?

Roland Barthes died in 1980, after he was run over, not by a jacknifed juggernaut, but by a laundry van.

Still, I think he would have appreciated *OK Computer*.

I wrote this book in Bangkok, the capital of Thailand, City of Angels, Village of the Wild Hog Plum. It's a location that seems to have leaked onto these pages more than once, and more than I expected when I began writing. To defend myself against allegations of self-indulgence, I can only say that anyone involved in creating something will be influenced by his or her surroundings; not simply in the sense of a physical environment, but by the pervasive vibe that we still call the Zeitgeist, because nobody's come up with a better word, despite the fact we're all sick of this one. *OK Computer* is as much a product of St Catherine's Court and 1996 as it is of five or six blokes with guitars and imaginations (or, according to Barthes, of everyone who listens to it).

In some ways, Bangkok brings to life the worst nightmares described in *OK Computer*, except that they're now in garish Technicolor. The traffic, for a start, is renowned throughout the world for its dreadfulness. Roads are narrow, potholed and frequently flooded during the rainy season; most licences are bought, rather than earned; the *tuk-tuks* (motorised rickshaws, beloved of tourists) are noisy, smelly and dangerous; taxi drivers often have a somewhat sketchy grasp of the city's geography, and many routes seem to take you to their cousins' jewellery shops; buses stop in the middle of a three-lane street to let people on and off. The whole mess is regularly enlivened by a collision between a speeding motorcyclist and an oblivious trucker, the former protected by a sacred amulet under his foreskin, the latter by pictures of Al Pacino (in *Serpico*) on his mudflaps, both protagonists out of their gourds on Red Bull and the hardcore amphetamine known as *yaa-baa*. Encircling the city is a noose-like network of freeways, and when the rain comes down, you could be looking at the cover of *OK Computer* itself. The whole thing creates a soundscape that resembles a mash-up of the slogans from 'Fitter Happier', the insects from 'Climbing Up The Walls', the horns from 'The National Anthem' and the drums from 'Airbag'.

This, of course, is where the Asian financial crisis of 1997 really began, confirming all of Thom Yorke's suspicions about the impact of global capitalism. But middle-class Bangkokians picked themselves up, and within three or four years they were celebrating the return of the good times with an orgy of never-never spending on cars and condos, phones and laptops. Today, a teenage girl eats KFC and drink Starbucks, in preference to the *khao man kai* and *kafae tung* that her parents enjoyed. She doesn't necessarily like the taste, but these are the places in which to be seen, and what's more important than that?[14] She paces the air-conditioned opulence of the new shopping malls, maybe hoping for a *farang* boyfriend who'll turn her into a Gucci little piggy, or Armani, or Versace; preferably the real thing, although the real thing and the knock-off might well be made in the same place. (Ah, the wonders of globalisation!) And yes, as Yorke suggested in 'Pearly*', half the adverts seem to be selling the delusion of "dewdrop dentures, whitewashed faces".

It's still possible to walk down a *soi* (side-street) and discern what Raymond Chandler called the "individual bony structure under the muck" that distinguishes great cities: food vendors and fortune tellers; blind musicians and baby elephants; spirit houses and garlanded trees; the pervasive stench of the drains and the *khlongs* (canals). At the same time, though, it seems as if Bangkok just wants to become the new Singapore, a city more American than America (except that, in Singapore, the kids speak better English).

In 2005, I interviewed one of Bangkok's leading branding consultants. He'd never even heard of Naomi Klein, and he didn't seem too threatened about what she might have to say. I didn't ask him if he'd heard of Radiohead. Here, they prefer the Black Eyed Peas.

And yet... and yet. Bangkok, not Palo Alto, is the "city of the future". Well, Bangkok and Shanghai and Ho Chi Minh City and Bangalore and several dozen other places. This is where the motorways and tramlines of capitalism and globalisation are heading. This is the Asian century and then some. Forget what you heard about America being the most powerful nation in the history of the world; they're just keeping the seat warm for China. This is what you get when you mess with us.

I wrote, a few thousand words ago – don't go back and check, just trust me – that a classic album attains its status because it sums up the time and place in which it was created, and at the same time, speaks to future generations. *OK Computer* expresses the aimless confusion that characterised the mid-90s, and also hints at the soulless consumption culture that continues to bubble its way across the globe ten years later.

In 'Lucky', Thom Yorke claimed to be "standing on the edge". Now we know what he could see from there.

Notes:

[1] Taylor Parkes, album review, *Melody Maker*, June 14, 1997.
[2] It's possible to argue that the 1990s actually extended backwards and forwards beyond its strict chronological boundaries, beginning on November 9, 1989, with the fall of the Berlin Wall, and only ending on September 11, 2001. See also John Robb, *The Nineties: What the F—k Was That All About?* (London: Ebury, 1999).
[3] Tom Cox, 'Uncharted Waters', *The Guardian*, January 29, 1999.

[4] 'The RS 500 Greatest Albums of All Time', *Rolling Stone*, December 2003. Radiohead did unusually badly on this list, but this appears to have been a blip (see Chapter 19).

[5] Alex Ross, 'The Searchers: Radiohead's unquiet revolution', *The New Yorker*, August 20-27, 2001.

[6] As David Lee Roth is alleged to have said: "Rock critics like Elvis Costello because rock critics look like Elvis Costello."

[7] Barney Hoskyns, 'The day the music died', *The Independent*, March 5, 1999. Chris Evans, for those unacquainted with his work, is a British radio DJ and TV presenter whose inane schtick became hugely popular in the mid-to-late 1990s, and a key component of the social phenomenon known as 'laddism'.

[8] Brent DiCrescenzo, 'Top 100 Albums Of The 1990s', http://www.pitchforkmedia.com/article/feature/36737/Staff_List_Top_100_Albums_of_the_1990s/page_10

[9] Interestingly, despite their fascination with technology, and their ambivalence about bootlegging and other copyright violations, Radiohead have yet to make their albums available on iTunes.

[10] Of course, the idea of 'the album' predates vinyl records by several decades. The original albums were cardboard books, which the listener could use to store a number of 78 rpm shellac discs. As a result, people could pick and choose the order in which they listened to an 'album', leave some tracks out, add new ones. In many ways, iTunes is simply returning to the days when music was only available in three-minute portions, and gramophones (your great-grandmother's iPod) had to be cranked by hand. See Griffiths, *OK Computer*, p.5.

[11] Eric Steuer, 'The Infinite Album', *Wired*, September, 2006.

[12] A cinematic variation on audience interactivity was the 2006 movie *Snakes on a Plane*, in the course of making which the writers and directors gradually ceded creative control to Internet obsessives: for example, Samuel L Jackson's key line, "I have had it with these motherfucking snakes on this motherfucking plane" originated in an Internet spoof of the (then unreleased) movie, and was added after principal filming wrapped. By the time the film made it to cinemas, there were so many spoofs bouncing around the Web that the finished product was something of an anti-climax, and

a box-office disappointment. If cinema can be driven by such ad hoc focus groups, why not music?

[13] In *Image-Music-Text* (tr. Stephen Heath, New York: Hill and Wang, 1977), pp. 142-148.

[14] To add to the equation of coffee with cool, a new radio station has just launched in Bangkok: it's called Radio Latte 106. Its incessant jingle is "All Moods, All Good", and it's as bad as it sounds.

CHAPTER 26

SPINE DAMAGED –
DISCOGRAPHY, BIBLIOGRAPHY, ETC.

It died an ugly death by back catalogue.
—Radiohead, 'Pop Is Dead'

For those of you with a tape-recorder, that was 'In Limbo'.
I wouldn't want you to get it wrong.
—Thom Yorke, onstage in Arles, France, 2000

This is an overview of the most important Radiohead releases: the fullest list of Radiohead recordings that I know is at www.rhdiscog.com. The chapter also includes details of the most important books, films and recordings to which I've referred in the preceding chapters.

DISCOGRAPHY

Radiohead material until 2004 was released on Parlophone in the UK; Capitol in the United States; Toshiba in Japan. Non-UK releases are included when they differ substantially from UK versions, or include material unavailable elsewhere.

Pre-Radiohead material

Hometown Atrocities EP: *I Don't Want To Go To Woodstock (Headless Chickens, feat. Thom Yorke, guitar and backing vocals). Also tracks by Beaver Patrol, Jackson Penis, Mad At The Sun.*
7" vinyl – Hometown Atrocities, 1989. Re-released on the compilation *Year Zero: The Exeter Punk Scene 1977-2000* (Hometown Atrocities, 2000).

On A Friday: *What Is That You Say? / Stop Whispering / Give It Up*
Cassette, 1991

Manic Hedgehog: *I Can't / Nothing Touches Me / Thinking About You / Phillipa Chicken / You*
Cassette, 1991. The inlay lists tracks 2 and 3 in the wrong order.

Albums

Pablo Honey: *You / Creep / How Do You? / Stop Whispering / Thinking About You / Anyone Can Play Guitar / Ripcord / Vegetable / Prove Yourself / I Can't / Lurgee / Blow Out*
US version added: *Creep (radio edit)*
Japanese version added: *Pop Is Dead / Inside My Head / Million Dollar Question / Creep (live) / Ripcord (live)*
CD, LP, cassette – Parlophone 1993

The Bends: *Planet Telex / The Bends / High And Dry / Fake Plastic Trees / Bones / (Nice Dream) / Just / My Iron Lung / Bullet Proof... I Wish I Was / Black Star / Sulk / Street Spirit (Fade Out).*
Japanese version added: *How Can You Be Sure? / Killer Cars*
CD, LP, cassette, MiniDisc – Parlophone 1995

OK Computer: *Airbag / Paranoid Android / Subterranean Homesick Alien / Exit Music (For A Film) / Let Down / Karma Police / Fitter Happier / Electioneering / Climbing Up The Walls / No Surprises / Lucky / The Tourist*
CD, double LP, cassette, MiniDisc – Parlophone 1997

Kid A: *Everything In Its Right Place / Kid A / The National Anthem / How To Disappear Completely / Treefingers / Optimistic / In Limbo / Idioteque / Morning Bell / Motion Picture Soundtrack*
CD, LP, cassette, MiniDisc – Parlophone 2000

Amnesiac: *Packt Like Sardines In A Crushd Tin Box / Pyramid Song / Pulk/Pull Revolving Doors / You And Whose Army? / I Might Be Wrong / Knives Out / Morning Bell / Amnesiac / Dollars And Cents / Hunting Bears / Like Spinning Plates / Life In A Glasshouse*
CD, LP, cassette – Parlophone 2001

Hail To The Thief: *2+2=5 (The Lukewarm) / Sit Down. Stand Up (Snakes & Ladders) / Sail To The Moon (Brush The Cobwebs Out Of The Sky) / Backdrifts (Honeymoon Is Over) / Go To Sleep (Little Man Being Erased) / Where I End And You Begin (The Sky Is Falling In) / We Suck Young Blood (Your Time Is Up) / The Gloaming*

(Softly Open Our Mouths In The Cold) / There There (The Boney King Of Nowhere) / I Will (No Man's Land) / A Punchup At A Wedding (No No No No No No No) / Myxomatosis (Judge, Jury & Executioner) / Scatterbrain (As Dead As Leaves) / A Wolf At The Door (It Girl. Rag Doll)
CD, LP, cassette – Parlophone 2003

EPs/mini-albums

Drill: *Prove Yourself / Stupid Car / You / Thinking About You*
CD, 12", cassette – Parlophone 1992

Itch: *Stop Whispering (US version) / Thinking About You / Faithless, The Wonder Boy / Banana Co. / Killer Cars (live) / Vegetable (live) / Creep (live)*
CD – Toshiba (Japan) 1994

Live Au Forum: *Just / Bones (live) / Planet Telex (live) / Anyone Can Play Guitar (live)*
CD – Parlophone (France) 1995. Bundled with some copies of *The Bends*.

The Bends Live EP: *Fake Plastic Trees / Blow Out / Bones / You / High And Dry*
CD – EMI (Belgium) 1996

No Surprises/Running From Demons: *No Surprises / Pearly* (remix) / Melatonin / Meeting In The Aisle / Bishop's Robes / A Reminder*
CD – Toshiba (Japan) 1997

My Iron Lung: *My Iron Lung / The Trickster / Lewis (mistreated) / Punchdrunk Lovesick Singalong / Permanent Daylight / Lozenge Of Love / You Never Wash Up After Yourself / Creep (acoustic)*
CD, 12", cassette – EMI (Australia) 1998. Bundled with some copies of *OK Computer*.

Airbag/How Am I Driving: *Airbag / Melatonin / Pearly* / A Reminder / Polyethylene (Parts 1 & 2) / Palo Alto / Meeting In The Aisle*
CD – Capitol (US) 1998

I Might Be Wrong: Live Recordings: *The National Anthem / I Might Be Wrong / Morning Bell / Like Spinning Plates / Idioteque / Everything In Its Right Place / Dollars And Cents / True Love Waits*
CD, 12", cassette – Parlophone 2001

COM LAG (2plus2isfive): *2+2=5 (live at Earl's Court) / Remyxomatosis (Christian Vogel remix) / Paperbag Writer / Sktterbrain (Four Tet remix) / I Will (Los Angeles version) / I Am Citizen Insane / Fog (Again) (live) / Where Bluebirds Fly / I Am A Wicked Child / Gagging Order*
CD – Toshiba (Japan) 2004

Singles

Creep / Lurgee / Inside My Head / Million $ Question
CD, 12", cassette – Parlophone 1992

Anyone Can Play Guitar / Faithless, The Wonder Boy / Coke Babies
CD, 12", cassette – Parlophone 1993

Pop Is Dead / Banana Co. (acoustic) / Creep (live) / Ripcord (live)
CD, 12", cassette – Parlophone 1993

Creep / Faithless, The Wonder Boy
Cassette – Capitol 1993
Creep / Yes I Am / Blow Out (remix) / Inside My Head (live)
CD, 7", cassette – Parlophone 1993

Creep (acoustic) / You (live) / Vegetable (live) / Killer Cars (live)
12" – Parlophone 1993

Stop Whispering (US version) / Creep (acoustic) / Pop Is Dead / Inside My Head (live)
CD – Capitol 1993

Stop Whispering (original version) / Prove Yourself / Lurgee
CD – Capitol 1993
*My Iron Lung / The Trickster / Punchdrunk Lovesick Singalong
/ Lozenge Of Love*
CD – Parlophone 1994

*My Iron Lung / Lewis (mistreated) / Permanent Daylight / You
Never Wash Up After Yourself*
CD – Parlophone 1994

*My Iron Lung / Punchdrunk Lovesick Singalong / The Trickster
/ Lewis (mistreated)*
12" – Parlophone 1994

*My Iron Lung / The Trickster / Lewis (mistreated) / Punchdrunk
Lovesick Singalong*
Cassette – Parlophone 1994

*High And Dry / Planet Telex / Maquiladora / Planet Telex (Hexa-
decimal mix)*
CD – Parlophone 1995

*Planet Telex / High And Dry / Killer Cars / Planet Telex (LFO JD
mix)*
CD – Parlophone 1995

*Planet Telex (Hexadecimal mix) / Planet Telex (LFO JD mix)
/ Planet Telex (Hexadecimal dub) / High And Dry*
12"– Parlophone 1995

*Fake Plastic Trees / Planet Telex (Hexadecimal mix) / Killer Cars
/ Fake Plastic Trees (acoustic)*
CD – Capitol 1995

Fake Plastic Trees / India Rubber / How Can You Be Sure?
CD, cassette – Parlophone 1995

*Fake Plastic Trees / Fake Plastic Trees (acoustic) / Bulletproof...
I Wish I Was (acoustic) / Street Spirit (Fade Out) (acoustic)*
CD – Parlophone 1995

Just / Planet Telex (Karma Sunra mix by UNKLE) / Killer Cars (Mogadon version)
CD, cassette – Parlophone 1995

Just / Bones (live) / Anyone Can Play Guitar (live)
CD – Parlophone 1995

Street Spirit (Fade Out) / Bishop's Robes / Talk Show Host
CD – Parlophone 1996

Street Spirit (Fade Out) / Banana Co. / Molasses
CD – Parlophone 1996

Paranoid Android / Polyethylene (Parts 1 & 2) / Pearly*
CD – Parlophone 1997

Paranoid Android / A Reminder / Melatonin
CD – Parlophone 1997

Paranoid Android / Polyethylene (Parts 1 & 2)
7" – Parlophone 1997

Karma Police / Meeting In The Aisle / Lull
CD – Parlophone 1997

Karma Police / Climbing Up The Walls (Zero 7 mix) / Climbing Up The Walls (Fila Brazillia mix)
CD – Parlophone 1997

Lucky / Meeting In The Aisle / Climbing Up The Walls (Fila Brazillia mix)
CD – Parlophone (France) 1997

No Surprises / Palo Alto / How I Made My Millions
CD, cassette – Parlophone 1998

No Surprises / Airbag (live) / Lucky (live)
CD – Parlophone 1998

No Surprises / Palo Alto
12" – Parlophone 1998

Pyramid Song / The Amazing Sounds Of Orgy / Trans-Atlantic Drawl
CD – Parlophone 2001

Pyramid Song / Fast-Track / Kinetic
CD – Parlophone 2001

Pyramid Song / Fast-Track / The Amazing Sounds Of Orgy
12" – Parlophone 2001

Knives Out / Cuttooth / Life In A Glasshouse (full-length version) / Knives Out (video)
CD – Parlophone 2001

Knives Out / Worrywort / Fog / Life In A Glasshouse (full-length version)
CD – Parlophone 2001

Knives Out / Cuttooth / Life In A Glasshouse (full-length version)
12" – Parlophone 2001

There There / Paperbag Writer / Where Bluebirds Fly
CD, 12" – Parlophone 2003

Go To Sleep / I Am Citizen Insane / Fog (Again) (live)
CD – Parlophone 2003

Go To Sleep / Gagging Order / I Am A Wicked Child
CD – Parlophone 2003

Go To Sleep / I Am Citizen Insane / I Am A Wicked Child
12" – Parlophone 2003

2+2=5 / Remyxomatosis (Christian Vogel remix) / There There (demo)
CD – Parlophone 2003

2+2=5 / Skttrbrain (Four Tet remix) / I Will (Los Angeles version)
CD – Parlophone 2003

Compilations and Soundtracks

Volume 7: *Stupid Car (Tinnitus mix)*
CD, cassette – Volume 1993

Volume 13: *(Nice Dream) (demo)*
CD, cassette – Volume 1995

Help: *Lucky*
CD – Go! Discs 1995

Clueless OST: *Fake Plastic Trees (acoustic)*
CD – Capitol 1996

William Shakespeare's Romeo And Juliet: *Talk Show Host (Nellee Hooper mix)*
CD – Premier 1996

Evening Session Priority Tunes: *Just (session)*
CD – Virgin 1996

Help:A Day in the Life: *I Want None Of This*
CD – Independiente, 2005

Solo albums

Jonny Greenwood, **Bodysong:** *Moon Trills / Moon Mall / Trench / Iron Swallow / Clockwork Tin Soldiers / Convergence / Nudnik Headache /Peartree / Splitter / Bode Radio-Glass Light-Broken Hearts / 24 Hour Charleston / Milky Drops From Heaven / Tehellet*
CD, LP – Parlophone 2003

Thom Yorke, **The Eraser:** *The Eraser / Analyse / The Clock / Black Swan / Skip Divided / Atoms For Peace / And It Rained All Night / Harrowdown Hill / Cymbal Rush*
CD – XL 2006

Guest appearances

Various Artists, **Come Again:** *Wish You Were Here* (Sparklehorse with Thom Yorke)
CD – EMI, 1997

Drugstore, **White Magic For Lovers:** *El President* (Thom Yorke)
CD – Roadrunner, 1998

UNKLE, **Psyence Fiction:** *Rabbit In Your Headlights* (Thom Yorke)
CD – Mo'Wax, 1998

Various Artists, **Velvet Goldmine OST:** *2HB / Ladytron / Baby's On Fire / Bitter-Sweet / Tumbling Down* (as Venus In Furs, with Thom Yorke and Jonny Greenwood)
CD – London, 1999

Pavement, **Terror Twilight:** *Platform Blues / Billie* (Jonny Greenwood)
CD - Matador, 1999

PJ Harvey, **Stories From The City, Stories From The Sea:** *One Line / Beautiful Feeling / This Mess We're In* (Thom Yorke)
CD – Island, 2000

Björk, **Selmasongs: Music From The Motion Picture Soundtrack Dancer In The Dark:** *I've Seen It All* (Thom Yorke)
CD – Elektra, 2000

Neil Finn & Friends, **7 Worlds Collide:** *Paradise* (Ed O'Brien, Phil Selway)
CD, DVD – Parlophone, 2001

Asian Dub Foundation, **Enemy Of The Enemy:** *1,000 Mirrors / Blowback / Enemy Of The Enemy* (Ed O'Brien)
CD – Ffrr, 2003

Band Aid 2004, **Do They Know It's Christmas?** (Thom Yorke, Jonny Greenwood)
CD – Mercury, 2004

Patrick Doyle, **Harry Potter And The Goblet Of Fire, OST:** *Do The Hippogriff / This Is The Night / Magic Works* (Jonny Greenwood, Phil Selway)
CD – Warner/Sunset, 2005

Video / DVD

Live At The Astoria: *You / Bones / Ripcord / Black Star / Creep / The Bends / My Iron Lung / Prove Yourself / Maquiladora / Vegetable / Fake Plastic Trees / Just / Stop Whispering / Anyone Can Play Guitar / Street Spirit (Fade Out) / Pop Is Dead / Blow Out* (Parlophone 1995)

Radiohead: 7 Television Commercials: *Paranoid Android / Street Spirit / No Surprises / Just / High And Dry (US version) / Karma Police / Fake Plastic Trees* (Parlophone 1998)

Meeting People is Easy: A Film by Grant Gee About Radiohead (Parlophone 1998)

The Most Gigantic Lying Mouth Of All Time: *The Cat Girl / The Slave / When An Angel Tries To Sell You Something / Skyscape / Sit Down. Stand Up. / Lament / The Big Switch / The Scream / Inside Of My Head / De Tripas Y Corazon / Listen To Me Wandsworth Road / Hypnogoga / And Murders Of Crows / Freak Juice Commercial / "Running" / Push Pulk / Spinning Plates / Dog Interface / HYTTE / Momentum / Chickenbomb / Welcome To My Lupine Hell / The Homeland Hodown / I Might Be Wrong / The National Anthem* (Parlophone, 2004)

Websites

There are hundreds of sites wholly or partly devoted to Radiohead; this is just a selection of the ones I've accessed while writing this book.

www.radiohead.com The official site: includes Dead Air Space, Radiohead's chief means of contact with their fans.

www.waste.uk.com The band's official merchandise site: takes its name from a renegade postal service in Thomas Pynchon's 1966 novel, *The Crying Of Lot 49*, sometimes considered to be a fictional precursor of the Internet.

www.slowlydownward.com The official site of Stanley Donwood/ Dan Rickwood, Radiohead's design guru.

www.ateaseweb.com,
www.followmearound.com
www.greenplastic.com
www.treefingers.com All-encompassing fan sites.

www.nepasevaler.net Radiohead en français. Title taken from a T-shirt worn by Thom Yorke.

www.rhdiscog.com The fullest Radiohead discography on the Web.

www.pulk-pull.org Site run by Joseph Tate, editor of *The Music And Art Of Radiohead*.

www.edquarters.net "A site dedicated to Ed O'Brien". Does what it says on the tin.

I've also referred to *www.allmusic.com*, *www.imdb.com*, *www.nme.com*, *www.pitchforkmedia.com*, *www.rocklist.net*, *www.rocksbackpages.com*, *www.tangents.co.uk*. And, yes, I've used Wikipedia, and any writer who says he hasn't is a damned liar.

Radiohead bibliography

Black, Susan, *Radiohead: In Their Own Words* (London: Omnibus, 2002)

Clarke, Martin, *Radiohead: Hysterical And Useless* (London: Plexus, 2003)

Doheny, James, *Radiohead: Karma Police; Stories Behind Every Song* (London: Carlton, 2002)

Footman, Tim, *Radiohead: A Visual Documentary* (New Malden, UK: Chrome Dreams, 2003)

Griffiths, Dai, *OK Computer* (New York/London: Continuum, 2004)

Hale, Jonathan, *Radiohead: From A Great Height* (Toronto: ECW, 1999)

Johnstone, Nick, *Radiohead: An Illustrated Biography* (London: Omnibus, 1995)

Malins, Steve, *Radiohead: Coming Up For Air* (London: Virgin, 1997)

Ogg, Alex, *Radiohead: Standing On The Edge* (London: Boxtree, 2000)

Paytress, Mark, *Radiohead: The Complete Guide to their Music* (London: Omnibus, 2005)

Randall, Mac, *Exit Music: The Radiohead Story* (London: Omnibus, 2004)

Stone, William, *Radiohead: Green Plastic Wateringcan* (London: UFO, 1996)

Tate, Joseph (ed.), *The Music and Art Of Radiohead* (Aldershot, UK: Ashgate, 2005)

Cover versions of Radiohead songs (see Chapter 20)

Jacquie Barnaby, *Washington Square* (Pie Lady, 2005)

Corporate Love Breakdown, *The Bluegrass Tribute To Radiohead* (CMH, 2005)

Dromedary, *Live From The Make Believe* (Dromedary, 2003)

Easy Star All-Stars, *Radiodread* (Easy Star, 2006)

Ellipsis, *Ellipsis* (Lo-FI, 2005)

Hard 'N Phirm, *Horses And Grasses* (Hard 'N Phirm, 2005)

Warren Haynes, *Live At Bonnaroo* (ATO, 2004)

Hazeldine, *Orphans* (E Squared, 1998)

Yuri Honing, *Symphonic* (Challenge, 2006)

Maroon, *Who The Sky Betrays* (Head Fulla Brains, 2003)

Brad Mehldau, *Largo* (Warner, 2002)

Brad Mehldau, *Songs: The Art Of the Trio, Vol. 3* (Warner, 1998)

Christopher O'Riley, *Hold Me To This* (Harmonia Mundi, 2005)
Christopher O'Riley, *True Love Waits* (Odyssey, 2003)
Rockabye Baby, *Lullabye Renditions Of Radiohead* (Baby Rock, 2006)
Kate Rogers, *Seconds* (Grand Central, 2005)
Scala and Kolacny Brothers, *Dream On* (Bvba Fratelli, 2004)
The Section, *Strung Out On OK Computer* (Vitamin, 2001)
Ian Shaw, *A World Still Turning* (441, 2003)
The Shirehorses, *Our Kid Eh* (Columbia, 2001)
Telepathy, *30 Seconds Of Silence* (Kufala, 2004)
Various Artists, *Anyone Can Play Radiohead* (Vitamin, 2001)
Various Artists, *Exit Music: Songs With Radio Heads* (BBE, 2006)
Various Artists, *Plastic Mutations: The Electronic Tribute To Radiohead* (Vitamin, 2001)

General discography

AC/DC, *Back In Black* (Atlantic, 1980)
Air, *Moon Safari* (Astralwerks, 1998)
Paul Anka, *Rock Swings* (Verve, 2005)
Basement Jaxx, *Remedy* (XL, 1999)
The Beach Boys, *Pet Sounds* (Capitol, 1966)
The Beatles, *The Beatles* (Apple, 1968)
The Beatles, *Sgt Pepper's Lonely Hearts Club Band* (Parlophone, 1967)
Beck, *Guero* (Interscope, 2005)
Björk, *Homogenic* (One Little Indian, 1997)
Blur, *Blur* (Food, 1997)
David Bowie, *Low* (RCA, 1977)
Jeff Buckley, *Grace* (Columbia, 1994)
Johnny Cash, *At San Quentin* (Columbia, 1969)
Elvis Costello and the Attractions, *Blood and Chocolate* (F-Beat, 1986)
Miles Davis, *Bitches Brew* (Columbia, 1970)
DJ Shadow, *Endtroducing...* (Mo' Wax, 1996)
Emerson, Lake & Palmer, *Brain Salad Surgery* (Manticore, 1973)
The Flaming Lips, *The Soft Bulletin* (Warner Bros, 1999)

Genesis, *Selling England By The Pound* (Charisma, 1973)

Groove Armada, *Vertigo* (Columbia, 1999)

Jesus and Mary Chain, *Psychocandy* (Blanco y Negro, 1985)

Joy Division, *Closer* (Factory, 1980)

King Crimson, *In The Court Of the Crimson King* (Island, 1969)

Kraftwerk, *Autobahn* (Philips, 1974)

Led Zeppelin, *Physical Graffiti* (Swan Song, 1975)

Manic Street Preachers, *The Holy Bible* (Epic, 1994)

Olivier Messiaen, *Turangilîla Symphony*, Andre Previn, LSO (EMI, 1978)

Moby, *Play* (Mute, 1999)

Monty Python, *The Monty Python Matching Tie and Handkerchief* (Charisma, 1973)

Muse, *Black Holes And Revelations* (Atlantic, 2006)

Nirvana, *In Utero* (DGC, 1993)

Nirvana, *Nevermind* (DGC, 1991)

Oasis, *Be Here Now* (Creation, 1997)

Yoko Ono, *Plastic Ono Band* (Apple, 1970)

Lucia Pamela, *Into Outer Space With Lucia Pamela* (Gulfstream, 1969)

Krzysztof Penderecki, *Threnos – Als jakon erwachte – 2 Capriccios*, Bernhard Glaetzner, Dresdner Philharmonie, etc (Berlin Classics, 2003)

Pink Floyd, *Wish You Were Here* (EMI, 1975)

Pulp, *This is Hardcore* (Island, 1998)

REM, *Automatic For The People* (Warner Bros, 1992)

The Smiths, *The Queen Is Dead* (Rough Trade, 1986)

Smog, *Wild Love* (Drag City, 1995)

Sparklehorse, *Vivadixiesubmarinetransmissionplot* (Capitol, 1995)

Spiritualized, *Ladies and Gentlemen, We Are Floating In Space* (Dedicated, 1997)

Supergrass, *In It For The Money* (Parlophone, 1997)

Talking Heads, *True Stories* (Sire, 1986)

U2, *Achtung Baby* (Island, 1991)

Van Der Graaf Generator, *Pawn Hearts* (Charisma, 1971)

Various Artists, *NME-C86* (NME, 1986)

Various Artists, *Rough Trade Shops Indiepop 1* (Mute, 2004)

The Verve, *Urban Hymns* (Virgin, 1997)
The Who, *Sell Out* (Track, 1967)

General bibliography

Adams, Douglas, *The Hitchhiker's Guide To The Galaxy* (London: Pan, 1979)

Bage, Thomas, *Hermsprong* (1796; London: Penguin, 1985)

Ballard, J.G., *Crash* (1973; London: Vintage, 1995)

Barthes, Roland, *Image-Music-Text* (tr. Stephen Heath, New York: Hill and Wang, 1977).

Baudrillard, Jean, *The Intelligence Of Evil Or The Lucidity Pact* (tr. Chris Turner, Oxford: Berg, 2005)

Beckett, Samuel, *Waiting For Godot* (New York: Grove, 1954)

Blake, William, *Songs Of Innocence And Experience* (1789, 1794; Oxford: OUP, 1990)

Butler, Samuel, *Erewhon* (1872; London: Penguin, 1974)

Carroll, Lewis, *The Annotated Alice* (ed. Martin Gardner, New York: Clarkson N. Potter, 1960)

Chusid, Irwin, *Songs In The Key Of Z: The Curious Universe Of Outsider Music* (London: Cherry Red, 2000)

Conrad, Joseph, *Heart of Darkness* (1902; London: Penguin, 1973)

Coupland, Douglas, *Generation X* (New York: St Martin's, 1991)

Dick, Philip K, *VALIS* (New York: Doubleday, 1981)

Donaton, Scott, *Madison & Vine: Why The Entertainment & Advertising Industries Must Converge To Survive* (New York: McGraw-Hill, 2005)

Donne, John, *The Major Works* (ed. John Carey, Oxford: OUP, 1990)

Dostoevsky, Fyodor, *Notes From Underground* (1864; London: Everyman, 2004)

Eliot, T.S., *Collected Poems, 1909-1962* (London: Faber and Faber, 1963)

Ellis, Bret Easton, *Lunar Park* (New York: Knopf, 2005)

Fitchett, Alistair, *Young And Foolish* (Exeter, UK: Stride, 1998)

Gray, Thomas, *Selected Poems* (London: Bloomsbury, 1997)

Haddon, Mark, *The Curious Incident Of The Dog In the Night Time* (London: Jonathan Cape, 2003)

Harris, John, *The Last Party: Britpop, Blair And The Demise of English Rock* (London: Fourth Estate, 2003)

Hobsbawm, Eric, *Age Of Extremes: The Short Twentieth Century, 1914-1991* (London: Michael Joseph, 1994)

Hutton, Will, *The State We're In* (London: Vintage, 1996)

Irvin, Jim & Colin McLear (eds), *The Mojo Collection* (Edinburgh: Canongate, 2000)

Jones, Dylan, *iPod, Therefore I Am* (London: Weidenfeld and Nicolson, 2005)

Kafka, Franz, *Metamorphosis* (1915; London: Penguin, 2006)

Klein, Naomi, *No Logo* (New York: Knopf, 2000)

Kosinski, Jerzy, *Being There* (New York: Harcourt, 1971)

Larkin, Colin, *The Virgin Encyclopedia Of Indie And New Wave* (London: Virgin, 1998)

Lloyd Parry, Richard, *In The Time Of Madness* (London: Jonathan Cape, 2005)

MacDonald, Ian, *Revolution In The Head: The Beatles' Records And The Sixties* (London: Pimlico, 1995)

McLuhan, Marshall, *Understanding Media* (London: Routledge and Kegan Paul, 1964)

Marcus, Greil, *Lipstick Traces* (Cambridge, Massachusetts: Harvard University Press, 1989)

More, Thomas, *Utopia* (1516; London: Penguin, 2003)

Morley, Paul, *Words And Music: A History Of Pop In The Shape Of A City* (London: Bloomsbury, 2003)

Murakami, Haruki (ed.), *Birthday Stories* (London, Harvill, 2004)

Quantick, David, *Revolution: The Making Of The Beatles' White Album* (London: Unanimous, 2002)

Raine, Craig, *A Martian Sends A Postcard Home* (Oxford: OUP, 1979)

Rinpoche, Sogyal, *The Tibetan Book Of Living And Dying: Revised Edition* (San Francisco: HarperCollins, 2002)

Robb, John, *The Nineties: What the F—k Was That All About?* (London: Ebury, 1999)

Smith, Zadie, *On Beauty* (London: Hamish Hamilton, 2005)

Stoppard, Tom, *Rock 'n' Roll* (London: Faber and Faber, 2006)

Strieber, Whitley, *Communion: A True Story* (1987; New York: Avon, 1995)

Swift, Jonathan, *Gulliver's Travels* (1726; Oxford: OUP, 2005)

Tevis, Walter, *The Man Who Fell To Earth* (1963; New York: Ballantine, 1999)

Thompson, Dave, *Alternative Rock* (San Francisco: Miller Freeman, 2000)

Truss, Lynne, *Eats, Shoots & Leaves* (London: Profile, 2003)

Unterberger, Richie, *Unknown Legends Of Rock 'n' Roll* (San Francisco: Miller Freeman, 1998)

Also back issues of: *Alternative Press, Arena, Blender, Careless Talk Costs Lives, Daily Telegraph, GQ, The Guardian, Guitar Player, The Independent, Melody Maker, Mojo, NME, New York Times, New Yorker, The Observer, Q, Raygun, Rolling Stone, Select, Spin, Uncut, The Wire, Wired, The Word.*

Films

Apocalypse Now (Dir: Francis Coppola, 1979)

Being There (Dir: Hal Ashby, 1979)

Blade Runner (Dir: Ridley Scott, 1982)

Bodysong (Dir: Simon Pummell, 2003)

Brazil (Dir: Terry Gilliam, 1985)

Crash (Dir: David Cronenberg, 1996)

Dancer In The Dark (Dir: Lars von Trier, 2000)

The Day The Earth Stood Still (Dir: Robert Wise, 1951)

Falling Down (Dir: Joel Schumacher, 1993)

Fearless (Dir: Peter Weir, 1993)

The Fisher King (Dir: Terry Gilliam, 1991)

The Hitchhiker's Guide To The Galaxy (Dir: Garth Jennings, 2005)

It's A Wonderful Life (Dir: Frank Capra, 1946)

The Man Who Fell To Earth (Dir: Nicolas Roeg, 1976)

Psycho (Dir: Alfred Hitchcock, 1960)

Slacker (Dir: Richard Linklater, 1991)

Snakes On A Plane (Dir: David R Ellis, 2006)

Taxi Driver (Dir: Martin Scorsese, 1976)

Index

Index